Woman,

Body, Desire in

Post-colonial India

JYOTI PURI

Woman,

Body, Desire in

Post-colonial India

Narratives of Gender

and Sexuality

Published in 1999 by
Routledge
29 West 35th Street
New York, NY 10001

Published in Great Britain by
Routledge
11 New Fetter Lane
London EC4P 4EE

Copyright © 1999 by Routledge
Text Design by Debora Hilu

Printed in the United States of America on acid-free paper.

10 9 8 7 6 5 4 3 2 1

Library of Congress Cataloging-in-Publication Data

Puri, Jyoti.
     Woman, body, desire in post-colonial India :   narratives of gender and sexuality / Jyoti Puri.
          p.   cm.
     Includes bibliographical references and index.
     ISBN 0-415-92127-9 (hb: alk. paper). — ISBN 0-415-92128-7 (pb : alk. paper)
     1. Sex role—India.   2. Gender identity—India.   3. Man-woman relationships—India.   4. Women—India—Social conditions.
     I. Title.
HQ1075.5,I4P87   1999   99-23522
305.3'0954—dc21   CIP

To
Pritam Devi
Manorama Puri
Taranee Mohan-Puri

Contents

Isn't it curious how constructs that provoke criticism can also evoke visceral sentimentality? On August 15, 1997, India celebrated 50 years of independence and sovereignty. Listening to an excerpt of Jawaharlal Nehru's speech, the first prime minister of independent India, on the public radio channel in Boston, I was taken aback by the depth of emotions that this historic nationalist narrative triggered in me. But, on second thought, why would *not* Nehru's account of the awakening of the independent Indian nation while the world slept bring a lump into my throat? After all, I am part of the generation of middle-class women who came of age amid tensions of post-colonial Indian nationalism and whose bodies and identities are infused with its contradictions. Inasmuch as these experiences of middle-class womanhood over the last three decades have inspired this book, its roots are widespread and deeply personal.

I grew up in a Punjabi family in the suburbs of what was then called Bombay, where I attended an ethnically diverse convent school as a day scholar, and later college as a young woman. When I think of myself and my schoolmates then, what I am struck by is how alongside our ethnic differences and the influence of Christianity, our quotidian experiences of girlhood and womanhood were marked by the complexities of nationalism. These complexities were perhaps most pronounced in the putative notions of tradition and modernity. Although I will later argue that notions of tradition and modernity provide inadequate analytical tools for understanding how bodies, desire, and womanhood are shaped and regulated, I believe that these notions constituted the parameters of middle-class womanhood in our lives.

If I were to describe the experiences of my cohort with a broad brush stroke, I would say that we were expected to embody a "modern" India without jeopardizing our "traditional" roles as good mothers, wives, and daughters-in-law. At home and in school we were encouraged to perform well, to compete, and indeed, to excel. Our education prepared us to take on challenging professional careers and groomed us for upward mobility through marriage. Within this middle-class, urban context, a convent education and the ability to converse in English are virtual prerequisites for marrying well. At times, however, when the putative distinctions between tradition and modernity got blurred, the ambiguities reinforced what was socially expected. In the numerous discussions in school on issues such as dating, marriage, and parenthood, marriage was cast in modernity terms—as a partnership based on love. However, we were advised to plan our first pregnancies roughly two years after the wedding in order to prevent the fading of the first flush of marriage while rechannelling the relationship into the maturity of parenthood.

Yet, the differences between tradition and modernity would also become obvious in other instances. While it was important that we not be too traditional by embodying what were considered retrograde traditions—such as marrying too early or lacking self-ambition altogether—it was equally important that we become neither too modern nor too westernized. At home and in school, in myriad ways, the importance of being feminine, of protecting our reputations and our chastities was consistently emphasized. Some of us grew up in homes where strict codes governed our mixing with boys or attending mixed social events in the evenings; others grew up in families where parents were comparatively lenient on these issues, and still others were given occasional leeway. Nonetheless, the importance placed on managing external threats to our bodies and sexualities, as well as on containing our sexual impulses, remained consistent across this spectrum. Our femininity and sexual respectability were not negotiable and were linked to a national cultural tradition countering the pitfalls of modernity and westernization. Our bodies, sexualities, and gender identities were not immune to the influences of the complex, uneven configurations of modernity and national cultural tradition.

One strategy to negotiate these complexities of middle-class womanhood in our lives was to avow the liberal discourses of humanism. We firmly believed the promises of modernity—progress, development, and meritocracy—to be the routes to upward social mobility and consumerism. As middle-class girls and young women we were less reflexive about our role in perpetuating class-based distinctions, but we believed that modernity would provide ways out of the daily grind of poverty that we could see around us. At some level, we believed that we should not think of ourselves as women because we were not disadvantaged. If women's achievements were indeed unbounded—for a while our prime minister was a woman—then our individual merit and personhood were far more important than our status as women. Yet, each time we encountered forms of sexual aggression and the constraints of what it meant to be feminine, the limits of these liberal discourses became obvious.

Our beliefs in the liberal promises of progress and development as the means to bring about social justice were also tempered by a profound cynicism and hopelessness regarding our nation's political leadership.

Given these limits and tensions of liberal discourses to negotiate middle-class womanhood, as we emerged into adulthood we had to find more politically effective strategies. It seems to me that confronting the limits of middle-class womanhood meant identifying and challenging the broader intersections of social class, gender, nationalisms, tradition, modernity, sexuality, and ethnicity. For some of us who moved to countries such as the United States, it has also meant addressing the inequities of race. While race and racism remain attenuated in Indianness and Hinduness within India, they are highlighted in our lives as women of color in countries such as the United States. Confronting the challenges of middle-class womanhood, then, calls for strategies more reflexive than liberalism. It means identifying the inclusions and exclusions inherent in liberal discourses; it means recognizing the limits of respectable middle-class womanhood but also the responsibility of middle-class women in sustaining the exclusions of women of marginalized social classes, ethnicities, and sexualities.

For me, teaching and intellectual work open up crucial possiblities to this purpose. If education can be a source of upward mobility and political complacency, then, I believe, it can also be an important strategy of political dissent and social justice. Growing up in a supportive and nurturant family with its roots in civil service, I had to find ways of expressing my political activism. The works of Paulo Friere, Antonio Gramsci, Stuart Hall, and later, bell hooks, Chandra Talpade Mohanty, among other femininists, were important sources of inspiration. The writing of this book became the medium though which the meaning of my own personal experiences and critical scholarship could take shape.

Despite the personal and cohort-based experiences of middle-class womanhood in post-colonial India that I bring to my work, this book is not about me or a narrowly defined peer group. Specifically, it is about the 54 middle- and upper-class women who took the time to speak with me about various aspects of their lives. More broadly, this book delves into the tensions of female bodies, desire, womanhood, and social class, and the kinds of hegemonic codes that regulate these aspects of the 54 women's lives. This book is about understanding these categories of experience and self-definition from the viewpoint of women's reality. Finally, this book is about identifying and challenging the constraints of middle-class womanhood in contemporary India in ways that avoid reinforcing the privileges of social class and heterosexuality or essentializing notions of womanhood and Indianness. I hope that this book will be of use to an audience interested in issues of womanhood in contemporary India but also to an audience interested in grappling with the tensions of gender and sexuality across diverse social settings.

Acknowledgments

This book has been possible with the support of many people. Most significantly, I am indebted to the 54 annonymous women who so generously gave me their time and entrusted me with their narratives. I thank each for her willingness to share her life history with me, and if a gap exists between these women's words and my interpretation, I thank them for their understanding. Rajshree Kampani helped me immeasurably in organizing the interviews and by providing important insights. Many thanks also to Sangeet K. Malhotra, Vanita Seth, Nargis Mhatre, Kiran Gehani, Sanjeev, Manju, and Padma Prakash for their help in getting the project off the ground.

Manorama Puri and Rajinder Puri, each in a different way, have been sources of inspiration and strength to me. As parents they instilled in me a desire for fairness and justice, and I value their contribution to my personal and intellectual life. Pritam Devi, my grandmother, taught me that intelligence, wisdom, and maturity do not necessarily come with learning the three r's. I miss her presence. I am indebted to an extended family, especially Deepak Puri, for unfailing love and generosity, and to Gautam, Manu, and Monica for helping to provide a home away from home. Most of all, I am deeply grateful to Rohin Mhatre for his nurturance, creativity, and sense of humor. I cherish his role in my life, especially over the last 10 years. Thank you.

Various people helped me put this project together along the way. Since this project began as a dissertation, I wish to express my appreciation to Debra Kaufman, Christine Gailey, and Lynn Stephen, members of my dissertation committee, who helped shape my intellectual development in crucial ways. I am grateful for their guidance and nurturance. Herman Gray mentored me early on in my graduate career in the United States, and I continue to value his support and friendship. Charlie Derber and Tom Shapiro graciously provided helpful advice and support when I needed it. Claudia Mora has been a supportive colleague and friend. I owe a debt to Uma Chakravarti and Meera Kosambi for their feedback on this project and to Sudhir Kakar for calling my attention to the role of spoken English in talking about sexuality. I also want to thank Arvind Kumar for graciously sharing his reflections on Trikone with me.

My colleagues here at Simmons College have provided additional help in all kinds of ways. I owe many thanks to Becky Thompson for her encouragement and assistance at numerous stages of the project and to Diane Raymond for reading and thoughtfully commenting on pieces of the writing. Carole Biewener, Patricia Rieker, Stephen London, and Ellen Borges have been unfailingly supportive in their turn. I enjoyed the numerous conversations with Evi Hagipavlu and thank her for her insightful remarks on the Introduction. I also wish to acknowledge the administrative help that I received from the college, in the form of a course release and additional funds, without which this book would have been further delayed.

Lastly, my gratitude to the reviewers, especially to Kamala Visweswaran, who helped strengthen this book in its various stages. I wish to acknowledge the invaluable feedback that I received from Jackie Southern and David McInerney on the writing, and the consistent support from the editorial staff at Routledge, especially my editor, Ilene Kalish. Many thanks.

Chapter One

Fictions

of

Identity

L istening to the interview tapes is like visiting old acquaintances. But in fact, I met Seema—the subject of the first of 54 interviews with women of similar social backgrounds—only once. Comfortably seated in her office in Mumbai (formerly known as Bombay) on a midsummer afternoon, Seema, 21 years old, attractive and articulate, tells me about her life. She holds an administrative position at a nursing home and expects to marry sometime in the not-too-distant future. She describes herself as a little immature but passionate, and speaks at length about herself and her life. Frequently, especially when she is concentrating on her thoughts, Seema runs her fingers through her layered, loosely worn hair. She speaks about what matters to her, what it means to be a woman, her recollections about getting her first menstrual period, encounters with male sexual aggression, her sexual desires and practices, and her expectations related to marriage and motherhood.

As I sift through taped accounts of Seema's story and others that followed, it is clear that to do justice to these women's narratives, I must go against the prevailing wisdom of much of the literature that deals with aspects of gender and sexuality in contemporary, post-colonial India.[1] My first concern is that by not questioning the premises of Indian culture, this literature helps reinforce stereotypes about Indian national cultural identity related to womanhood, gender, and sexuality. My second, interrelated concern is that this literature implicitly reinforces categories of womanhood, gender, and sexuality. From a feminist, postcolonial lens I argue that the narratives included in this book not only tell us much about contemporary aspects of womanhood and sexuality but help question these categories as well. When considered against

the grain of the nation-state, these narratives challenge putative characterizations of the narrators as Indian women.

Broadly described, this book uses personal narratives of gender and sexuality in contemporary, post-colonial India to explore the ways in which middle-
and upper-class women's bodies, sexualities, and gender identities are regulated. These narratives highlight how social control is routinely enforced
through definitions of what is normal and natural. But to consider how aspects
of gender identities and sexuality are controlled through notions of normality
is to throw into question the categories of womanhood and (hetero)sexuality.
In effect, not only do these narratives provide important clues to social mandates on womanhood and female (hetero)sexuality, but they also suggest how
the categories of gender and sexuality are made to appear natural and coherent in our lives.

Given the daunting breadth of the constructs of gender and sexuality, for the
purpose of the interviews I emphasize aspects that are considered culturally
normal in the life cycle of these middle- and upper-class women. The onset of
menarche and early menstruation, and the realms of sexuality, marriage, and
motherhood provide the focal points for these life history interviews. Of these
aspects, the onset of menarche, early menstruation, and sexual aggression especially help realize the perception and experience of the female body. If menarche marks a burgeoning but chaste heterosexuality, then it is widely believed
that women should express their sexualities within marriage. Thus, social
expectations of heterosexuality and sexual respectability are sustained both
before and after marriage. Furthermore, marriage and motherhood represent
the more definitive markers of gender identity for women. But, as women's narratives indicate, these seemingly commonplace aspects of their life cycles are
also sources of normalizing and disciplinary strategies.

In this book, I focus on the narratives of middle- and upper-class urban
women because their bodies, sexualities, and gender identities are sites where
cultural notions of normality and, indeed, social respectability are contested.
By highlighting their gender and social class affiliations, I do not suggest that
such differences as ethnicity and religion are unimportant. The gross resur-
gence of Hindu nationalism and its articulation of Hindu women's identities
and roles are an alarming reminder of the significance of ethnic and religious
differences among women. Rather, I argue that strategies of social control cut
across ethnic and religious affiliations in the narratives that follow, and these
strategies are not only produced and reinforced within contemporary India,
but were also part of its transfomation into an independent nation-state.[2]
Collectively and individually, middle- and upper-class women are expected
to embody national cultural identity. If their bodies and identities are used to

articulate discourses of modernity and development in post-colonial India, then these are also the sites where fears of loss of national tradition are expressed. Cultural beliefs that middle- and upper-class women embody a changing, modernizing national cultural identity are frequently offset by concerns that these women are being corrupted by the influences of modernization, and especially, "westernization." Viewed in this way, at the very least, these women's narratives on gender and sexuality are hyphenated—neither one nor the other; at most, they challenge what means to be "Indian."

I argue that it is necessary to identify and challenge the role of the post-colonial Indian nation-state in generating discourses that shape and constrain middle- and upper-class women's narratives on aspects of gender and heterosexuality. More specifically, I highlight the kinds of hegemonic codes of gender and sexuality produced within the post-colonial nation-state that mark women's narratives. But if it is necessary to identify these discourses, then it is equally important to consider the effects of transnational cultural codes in normalizing and regulating women's narratives. An exploration of the effects of transnational, globalizing cultural discourses shows that these class- and gender-based forms of social regulation and normalization may not be unique to the Indian nation-state. Nationalist and transnational hegemonic codes unevenly crisscross women's narratives, and the narratives help illustrate these complex and pernicious processes of regulation. Thus, the narratives problematize larger questions of how fictions of their gender, sexual, and national identities are shaped and normalized. At the same time, these narratives provide important insights into how women contend with and undermine these normalizing and disciplinary effects in their lives.

I analyze accounts on the onset of menarche, sexual aggression, erotic sexuality, marriage, and motherhood to isolate the effects of normalizing discourses and disciplinary strategies. Once these discourses and strategies are made explicit, I explore how the interviewees' lives are shaped and regulated through daily experiences of their bodies, selves, and sexualities. Sometimes the women articulate the connections in their accounts, and at other times I attempt to highlight and analyze the more tacit aspects of the links between middle- and upper-class women's narratives and the hegemonic codes of the post-colonial nation-state. In some instances, women recast social mandates—for example, sexual respectability—in ways that draw upon more transnational cultural discourses, and destabilize putative notions of chastity. Furthermore, women's narratives are complex on at least one other account: As their narratives evince normalizing discourses and disciplinary strategies, they also reveal how the women internalize, reproduce, and challenge these strategies of social control.

On the one hand, women's narratives foreground how strategies of control are somewhat effective precisely because they are reproduced and reinforced in the narratives on the body, on womanhood, and sexuality. What is also incontrovertible is how their narratives are shaped by forms of social privilege. As members of the middle and upper classes, the women who are the focus of this study are privileged. Moreover, as women speaking about normative aspects of sexuality and marriage, they are able to draw upon the privileges of a social system that mandates heterosexual relations. Therefore, to look for the ways in which these women are socially regulated is also to raise questions about their entanglements in that process. On the other hand, partly reflecting their discomfort with the nature of social regulation that attends privilege, these women also suggest how they undermine and challenge these constraints in their lives.

What became clear, after the completion of the interviews, was the importance of not limiting this study to explorations of normality through middle- and upper-class women's narratives, but also through examining narratives from the margins, namely, from gays, lesbians, bisexuals and transgendered peoples. Clearly, these narratives evince the impact of the post-colonial nation-state—both in terms of nationhood and transnational cultural effects. The last chapter of this book considers queer narratives that speak to the post-colonial nation-state, nationalisms, and transnational cultural codes. What is perhaps most compelling about these narratives that are self-consciously produced from the social margins is how they recast notions of national identity and attempt to forge transnational alliances as political strategies. To that extent, these queer narratives launch, in comparison with middle- and upper-class women's accounts, a fuller and more illustrative critique of the construct and legacies of the post-colonial state and nationalisms.

Conceptualizing the Constructs

Sex and Gender

Over the last few years, putative definitions of sex and gender have been challenged by feminist and queer theory.[3] Standard sociological textbooks define sex as the raw material upon which culture operates in the form of gender attributes.[4] Within this framework, sex is the pre-social, biological body, and gender is the cultural script that socializes the body and thereby produces women, men, and, where applicable, additional genders, in a given sociocultural context. If "sex" is male and female, then "gender" is femininity and masculinity, and the categories of woman and man fuse dominant perceptions of femaleness with femininity and maleness with masculinity. Such understandings of sex and gender are also pervasive in introductory texts used in courses in women's studies and in the exploding field of gender studies.[5]

The problems with these understandings are manifold. To derive gender as the cultural overlay upon sex suggests that biology precedes or lies outside the domain of culture and history. Critical theorizing on sex or the sexed body belies such interpretations.[6] What this theorizing has persuasively demonstrated is that seemingly raw biological sex and the body are no more outside the purview of cultural context and history than gender is. But it is not enough to merely revise sociological understandings by saying that sex, like gender, is constructed. For one, it makes the constructs of sex and gender redundant—instead of two constructs, only one is necessary. As Judith Butler astutely notes in her book *Gender Trouble*, if sex is gender, then it makes little sense to argue that gender is the cultural interpretation of sex.[7] Furthermore, to argue that gender (and sex) are the product of social construction runs the risk of conceptualizing the body as a passive instrument of culture; instead of biology, culture becomes destiny of the body, according to Butler.[8]

Sociological understandings of sex and gender miss the crucial point that these constructs may be the effect of regulating, normative mechanisms of power.[9] Indeed, it becomes necessary to uncover how and to what purposes the construct of sex operates to sustain the fictions that sex is biological, dual (male and female, and heterosexual), that there are two sexes for the reproduction of the species, or that gender is about women and men.[10] Seen in this way, the slide from sex to gender to heterosexuality becomes disputable, and the attempt to privilege sex as the founding premise of gender, and implicitly, heterosexuality, becomes untenable. As Rosalind Morris succinctly notes in her review of the relation between sex and gender, contrary to sociological understandings of sex as the premise of gender, the reverse is true: Gender is the founding premise of sex.[11]

There is at least one additional problem with putative sociological conceptualizations of sex and gender related to the category of "woman." Within this framework, sex and gender are imbricated in the category of woman, and this category provides theoretical, methodological, and political stability to forms of feminist criticism and analyses. But, clearly, woman as a category cannot be privileged within feminist discourse to the exclusion of categories of race, sexuality, ethnicity, nationality, color, class, and caste, among others. African-American, Asian-American, Chicana, Jewish, Latina, and "Third World" feminist theorizing has been at the forefront of complicating unitary notions of women as the basis for feminism; thereby, the category of woman occupies a much more fragmented space within feminism.[12] Nonetheless, a persistent concern is that the category of "woman," when taken as the common ground of feminist analysis, not only obscures ways of being that are anormative but implicitly requires that one identify as a woman.[13]

While these insights are more widely germane to theories of sex, gender, body, and sexuality within sociology and women's studies, they are directly relevant to the project of this book. Drawing upon feminist insights into the strategies of power that produce the fiction of coherent sexualities and identities, I understand gender as an effect of disciplinary practices and regulating mechanisms of power.[14] If the normative effects of gender in part sustain the appearance of natural links between sex, gender, and sexuality, then it is helpful, as Butler suggests, to see gender as performativity—"as the process through which difference and identity are constructed in and through discourses."[15] In Butler's words, gender is not an essence but a set of repeated acts that only appear to be substantive.[16] This conceptualization of gender identity necessitates understanding how gender is made to appear coherent through the category "woman" (or "man"), but also how it is produced and possibly sustained and disrupted through mundane repetitive acts. In the following chapters, I seek to unravel how the fictions of normative gender identity are sustained and disrupted through narratives on matters of menstruation, sexual aggression, marriage, and motherhood.

Conceptualizing gender in this respect, then, also casts serious doubts on ascribing the narratives to "women." If gender is indeed a process of normative repetition that is occasionally repudiated, then not only do prevailing notions of womanhood and femininity become suspect, but using the category of "woman" is fraught with contradictions. Attributing the narratives to "women" paradoxically reinforces the requirement to identify as a woman even as the process of how the fiction of womanhood is sustained is questioned and challenged in the following chapters. At the same time, to cast doubts on the viability of the category of "woman" invariably throws into crisis the political ground of feminism. These tensions are frequently caricatured in feminist debates within the United States as the theoretical and political differences between postmodernism and identity politics.[17] Thus, the category of "woman" appears to be at a theoretical and political impasse.

In the following chapters I use multiple strategies to negotiate this impasse. First, I understand the category of woman to be inextricable from history, culture, colonialism, nationalism, race, class, sexuality, postcoloniality, and transnational processes. Second, I focus analytically on the *narratives* of womanhood and heterosexuality. I take the approach that these narratives tell us much about the process through which the mundaneness of gender is repeated, sustained, and sometimes disrupted as identity. By focusing on marked aspects of gender identity—marriage and motherhood but also menstruation and sexual aggression—it is possible to see how the appearance of a stable identity of womanhood is reproduced and repudiated in the narratives. It would be naïve to suggest that women are not socially and culturally positioned as "women" but it is worthwhile not to outright reinforce the sociocultural requirements of identifying within a gender category.[18] Third, I explore queer narratives which, by challenging the norms of heterosexuality, also unsettle normative notions of gender identity—"women" and "men."

Drawing upon feminist theory, I understand sex, like gender, to be an effect of regulating and normative mechanisms of power. But sex is not the same as gender because sex acts to mark and signify the body in terms of sexual difference and heterosexuality. Sex serves to constitute a newborn child as this or that sex and to specify expectations of sex-appropriate development. The seeming reality of physical differences, encapsulated in what we understand as "genital," makes it possible to assign the newborn infant a sex, and the process of "normal" sexual and gender development begins. This originary sexing of the body is the product of two interrelated, epistemological frameworks: the medical framework, that organizes our perceptions of the reality of sex; and the social framework that organizes perceptions of sex based on cultural concepts of gender. Despite claims of the medical establishment to pre-social, objective facts, sex is the product of this dual framework that both produces obstacles in the development of knowledge and provides conditions for definitions of normality. Put differently, sex enables the mechanisms of power upon the body that make it impossible to view a body outside of the limitations of sex and to engender the compliance and consent of the individual to expectations of "normal" sexual and gender development.

Therefore, I take the approach that sex is the deeply rooted medicalized, binary construct that shapes the narratives that follow especially on matters of menstruation and sexual aggression. Sex shapes the nature of biological differences that appear self-evident at the birth of a child and at various sensitive conjunctures thereafter in order to determine sex-appropiate biological and social sexual development—for example, in menstruating. Whether manifest in accounts of menstrual pain or the trauma of sexual aggression, narratives on the body cannot be separated from sociocultural notions of sex that make it possible to have or experience the body. Furthermore, sex and gender are intertwined in terms of a heterosexist normalizing structure where "appearance" seems to correspond to "reality" and the concept of deviation or pathology serves to fill the gaps where there is a possibility of dissonance between appearance and reality, between sex and gender, or between sex and heterosexuality.

Sexuality

Finally, I analyze women's narratives on sexuality apart, but not disconnected, from the narratives on the sexed body and aspects related to gender identity. Within feminist and queer theorizing in the United States, Gayle Rubin's essay "Thinking Sex" is considered to be the analytic turning point of challenging the conflation between sexuality, gender, and theories of women's oppression.[19] Although not uncontroversial, this article seems to have triggered caution within feminist theorizing as to conflating sexuality with gender, while also insisting that sexuality cannot be isolated from the effects of gender.[20] Not only gender but sexuality is thoroughly suffused by the social effects of race, nationality, class, age, and religion, among others. Broadly put, separating sexuality without isolating it, especially from the effects of gender, helps implicate social mandates of heterosexuality and elaborate the ways in which these mandates are both reproduced and disrupted in our daily lives.

In Chapter Five I analyze how women negotiate, reproduce, and repudiate aspects of heterosexuality in their narratives. It is imperative not to assume that the narratives highlighted in the ensuing chapters can be ascribed to heterosexual women. In the interviews, I did not ask and none of the women voluntarily identified as heterosexual, nor as homosexual or lesbian. But what their narratives offer is a substantive site for the analysis of the links between sex and gender identities and heterosexuality. All of the 32 women who are married and the 22 women who are single speak to matters of normative social expectations of heterosexuality. While the narratives on sexuality, explored in Chapter Five, do not confirm that these are heterosexual women, they do help understand how sociocultural notions of gender reinforce the mandate of heterosexuality in contemporary, post-colonial India. The task is to separate the constructs of sex, gender, and sexuality as well as investigate how sexuality is shaped by a heteronormative lens.[21]

In Chapter Seven, I seek to disrupt the social mandates of heterosexuality in at least one additional way—by turning to queer narratives. Where women's narratives on sexuality speak to particular aspects of heteronormativity, I argue that it is equally important to consider the meaning and ramifications of narratives on sexuality that wittingly or unwittingly disrupt social assumptions of heterosexuality. In this chapter my aim is to highlight and explore narratives on sexuality that are more consciously produced from the social margins. I argue that as these narratives contest the politics of dominant discourses on (hetero)sexuality, they are also profoundly shaped by these politics. In effect, queer narratives repudiate the politics of heterosexuality even as they are normalized in other significant ways.

Clearly, this concern with the reiteration and repudiation of normality across the narratives of women and queer narratives in order to decode the relation between sexuality and power implicitly challenges the notion of sexual repression as the sole or primary discourse of sexuality in contemporary India. Drawing upon Foucaultian insights, I question the prevalence of the "Repressive Hypothesis" as the primary mechanism through which sexuality is regulated in the lives of these middle- and upper-class women.[22] Belief that the middle class, especially, is profoundly uncomfortable with sexuality as a result of sexual repressiveness is widely held. Especially during the first few interviews with middle- and upper-class women, I approached issues of sexuality with some trepidation. My concern with women's level of comfort or outright reluctance to discuss matters of sexuality with a stranger was shaped by prevailing notions of repression and the refusal to speak. Yet only one woman declined to answer a specific question about her first experience with sexual intercourse. Instead, these middle- and upper-class women chose to speak about issues of sexuality by strategically selecting appropriate language and indicating meaning through verbal and nonverbal language. Sifting through these narratives from a Foucaultian position helps direct attention to the ways in which sexuality is regulated through normalization and the elaboration of pleasure instead of repressions and taboos. To that end, women's narratives on sexuality—its sensations, pleasures, feelings, and acts—become the necessary focus of unraveling the relation between heterosexuality and power. And queer narratives foreground the ways in which alternative sexual identities can paradoxically be disruptive and normalized at the intersection of the relationship between discourses of sexuality and power related to contemporary India.

I also go against the wisdom of studies on (hetero)sexuality in contemporary India by questioning, from this Foucaultian perspective, whether kinship is the most relevant context in which to understand sexuality. Foucault argues that since the seventeenth century in Western societies the deployment of sexuality occurs through multiple incitements and stimulations that penetrate into and regulate the most minute and intimate aspects of our lives.[23] Instead of the sexual taboos and constraints that characterize kinship, the sources of the deployment of sexuality are the state and population control, pedagogy, medicine, and legal institutions, among others, according to Foucault. In

Chapter Two, I question the relation between the state and pedagogy by analyzing state-sponsored sex education materials. My point is that this Foucaultian approach helps attenuate the role of kinship as the primary focus for the control and regulation of sexuality toward a more complex understanding in which the contemporary family plays a significant but ultimately instrumental role.

But if this Foucaultian approach to understanding sexuality as well as gender and sex in the foregoing discussion is productive, then from the perspectives of the narratives considered in the following chapters, this approach is also beset by limitations. As a dense transfer point of power, sexuality is intersected by the vectors of class, gender, the state, race, and nationality, among others. Foucault's Eurocentric theories on sexuality are remarkably quiet on race and nationality thereby raising crucial questions for women's narratives. Yet such matters as race and nationality cannot simply be added to the construct of sexuality, or to considerations of sex or gender, while leaving Foucault's theories intact.[24] To bring constructs of gender and sexuality within the same analytical field as constructs of race, nationality, and class leads to a paradox. On the one hand, it raises questions about how constructs such as race, nationality, and class are inextricable from the constructs of gender and sexuality. Middle- and upper-class women's narratives provide a specific starting point to explore and analyze these intersections. On the other hand, it also raises questions about the extent to which constructs of nationalisms, race, and class provide sufficient insights into narratives on gender and sexuality.

Looking at narratives of gender and sexuality through the lens of nationality, class, and race, then, highlights three interrelated points. First, what is inarguable is the importance of understanding the specific, culturally unique nature of women's narratives on gender and sexuality. As Chandra Talpade Mohanty succinctly notes in her introduction to *Third World Women and the Politics of Feminism*, black, white, and other Third World women have very different histories with respect to post-fifteenth-century Euro-American hegemony, and therefore, I suggest, would tell culturally specific narratives of femaleness, body, womanhood, or sexuality.[25] Second, that these narratives on body, heterosexual desire, and womanhood need to be analyzed against the grain of constructs such as nationality, race, and class is also incontrovertible. In the collection *Scattered Hegemonies*, the editors, Inderpal Grewal and Caren Kaplan, rightly argue that feminist theorizing that posits a critique of modernity devoid of modernist constructs such as nationalisms is incomplete and inadequate.[26] The editors suggest that such critiques of modernity are unable to address the concerns of many women across the world, including the place of women in the nation-state, the resistance to revivals of "tradition," and the relationship between gender, the nation-state, and transnational capital. Analogously, studies of gender and sexuality in contemporary India that rely on uncomplicated notions of national cultural identity or the West provide limited and inadequate insights. Third, foregrounding issues of nationalisms, race, and class in women's narratives of gender and sexuality raise the possibility that constructs such as nationality, race, or class may provide only partial insights. The narratives may be both culturally specific but also more general in ways that make the constructs of nationality, race, or class inherently unstable. Put differently, women's narratives on gender and sexuality need to be explored against the lens of India, Indianness, and class, but also against the effects of transnational cultural discourses.

Nation-State and Nationalisms

Feminist theorizing on nations and states has emphasized the importance of not conflating the constructs of nation and state. As editors Nira Yuval-Davis and Floya Anthias suggest in *Woman-Nation-State*, it is crucial not to conflate nation with state as the impact of nationalisms and state policies are not always the same; as an apparatus of control and enforcement, the state can be either more delimited than the nation or extend beyond the boundaries of the nation.[27] But if Benedict Anderson's reworking of the nation as an "imagined community" and nationalisms as cultural artifacts has helped challenge the nation as natural and as an essence, then the state cannot be seen as a unitary and coherent apparatus of control either.[28] The contemporary, post-colonial Indian nation-state may be bounded territorially but is characterized by multiple policies, institutions, and discourses. The Indian nation-state is shaped by the legacies of hegemonic nationalisms and their contemporary representations but not synonymous with them.

What I am especially interested in are the kinds of discourses on gender and sexuality generated by the Indian nation-state, invested with nationalisms, and the ways in which these discourses shape and constrain middle-class women's narratives on the sexed body, desire, and womanhood. To this purpose I draw on strands of feminist theorizing on the ideological and normalizing effects of nation-states and nationalisms with respect to women, gender, and sexuality. These links have been identified primarily in two ways: by noting the centrality of women of various class, ethnic, and racial groups to contemporary states and articulations of nationalisms; and by analyzing the emergence of modern nation-states and nationalisms as gendered, sexualized, and racialized formations.

In the first case, if feminist theorizing has been useful in indicting the links between nation-states and women, and has emphasized the role of women in reproducing and resisting dominant ideologies, then it has not sufficiently challenged categories of womanhood or nation-states. This scholarship is best captured in collections such as *Woman-Nation-State, Feminism and Nationalism in the Third World*, and *Women, Islam and the State.*[29] In *Woman-Nation-State*, and more recently, in *Racialized Boundaries: Race, Nation, Gender, Colour and Class and the Anti-Racist Struggle*, Yuval-Davis and Anthias suggest that women are linked to the politics of the nation-state in five overlapping ways: as biological reproducers of members of ethnic collectivities; as reproducers of the boundaries of ethnic/national groups; as participators in the ideological reproduction of the collectivity and the transmitters of culture; as signifiers of ethnic/national groups; and as participants in national, economic, political, and military struggles.[30] While the editors do not adequately problematize the category "woman" in their arguments, they nonetheless take a necessary step to redress the absence of categories of woman, gender, and sexuality in theories of nationalism.

In its second contribution—nations and nationalisms as gendered, racialized, and sexualized formations—feminist theorizing has not only elaborated and challenged these links but also made them more complicated by calling these modernist categories into question. This second strand of theorizing is perhaps best exemplified in the collection *Nationalisms and Sexualities.*[31] In this collection the editors draw on Benedict Anderson's *Imagined Communities: Reflections on the Origin and Spread of Nationalism* to recast nationalism as a much more ambivalent, cultural artifact of modernity. Juxtaposed with feminist and Foucaultian theories on gender and sexuality, this collection attempts to challenge the normalizing links between nationalisms, sexualities, and genders by simultaneously destabilizing these categories. What this collection does not sufficiently address is the role of nation-states and their links to nationalisms.

In the following chapters, my aim is threefold. First, I seek to examine the kinds of normative discourses of gender and sexuality generated within the contemporary Indian nation-state that not only shape and constrain women's narratives but also maintain intertwined, class-based notions of womanhood, heterosexuality, and national identity. In Chapter Two, I show how contemporary state-sponsored sex education texts define and regulate categories of gender and sexuality while attempting to alleviate anxieties of sexual development among teenagers and young adults. In Chapters Three, Four, Five, and Six I examine how these hegemonic discourses shape women's narratives on the sexed body, heterosexuality, marriage, and motherhood. In Chapters Five and Seven I also focus on the effects of nationalisms in women's narratives on heterosexuality, and queer narratives on marginalized sexual identities. Second, I challenge how these normalizing and disciplinary strategies are reflected and repudiated in the women's narratives. By looking at these strategies through the lens of women's narratives and then queer narratives, I also show how disciplinary and normalizing strategies are not always effective.

Finally, I consider to what extent the normalizing and regulating discourses of gender and sexuality can be ascribed to "India" and "Indianness" by emphasizing the effects of transnational hegemonic forms. These transnational hegemonic effects on gender and sexuality are part of the dramatic social, economic, and cultural shifts that seem to destabilize the boundaries of the state, rewrite nationalist scripts, and call into question whether nation-states are adequate as units of analysis for understanding the lives of women in various parts of the world. As Mohanty notes, with the proliferation of transnational economic structures and massive migrations of ex-colonial populations leading to multiethnic and multiracial social contexts, the nation-state for many purposes is no longer an adequate unit of analysis.[32] That the post-colonial Indian nation-state is still relevant for understanding women's narratives on gender and sexuality is inarguable. However, whether the nation-state is sufficient to understand what kinds of putative notions of the sexed body, identities of womanhood, and heterosexuality are produced is the pertinent question. What is especially striking is the uneven and sometimes contradictory presence of these transnational cultural discourses in women's and queer narratives.

The Transnational

The conceptualization of the term "transnational" has been partially informed by theorists of the world-systems approach, perhaps most typically associated with Wallerstein. Proponents of this approach have compellingly challenged the historical, unequal conditions under which nation-states, international economic structures, and a global world system were created and are sustained. Although significant differences exist among of theorists such as Wallerstein, Frank, and Amin, their general approach is partially useful in its attempt to theorize how international inequalities (developed/underdeveloped nations, First World/Third World, center/periphery, global/local) were set in motion by the insertion of national economies into a transnational capitalist world market by the colonial and neocolonial nation-states. This approach has rightly been faulted for its lack of attention to culture. As a result, theorists such as Wallerstein, Hannerz, and Robertson have paid special attention to the concept of culture in the reproduction of inequalities and as resistance reflected in social movements.[33] Yet, as Janet Wolff notes, rather than a discursive, differentiated understanding of culture, it is granted an essential existence in these analyses.[34] Moreover, issues of gender and sexuality remain conspicuously absent.

More usefully, postcolonial scholarship has ventured beyond the political economy of the world systems approach to disassemble putative categories such as Europe, West, Third World, race, nationality, and more recently, categories of gender and sexuality that emerged amid transnational discourses of imperialism, colonialism, and modernity. This scholarship has promoted an understanding and intellectual skepticism of not only the transnational economic but also the cultural and social forces that have shaped the received categories of nationalisms, race, gender, and sexuality in the late twentieth century. The recent collection *Tensions of Empire* represents a vital step in theorizing the emergence of bourgeois cultures, of recognizable categories of national differences, race, gender, sexuality, class, ethnicities, and tradition against the projects of building empires.[35] Where this collection is most innovative is in its attempt to bring colonies and metropoles into the same analytical field, thereby highlighting how strategies for generating and managing notions of racial, national, gender, and sexual differences in the colonies were related and parallel to what was occurring within the metropole at the same time. This scholarship helps highlight the importance of considering imbrications of nations, gender, race, and sexuality within a transnational context of empire building. For contemporary studies of gender and sexuality, this approach necessitates the recognition of the connections and parallels in discourses of gender and sexuality that cut across national boundaries.

Analogously, in another useful elaboration of considering the impact of transnational cultural and social discourses, the editors of the collection *Scattered Hegemonies* call into question transnational cultural flows that materially structure women's lives in diverse social locations.[36] Grewal and Kaplan emphasize the importance of unraveling the transnational and material conditions of postmodernity that affect and constrain women's lives in diverse and contradictory ways. In this sense, it becomes vital to identify the parallel and related ways in which women's lives are shaped and constrained across national, ethnic, and racial boundaries. To map the transnational connections and tensions between hegemonic discourses of gender and sexuality is equally necessary in challenging their effects in women's lives; as Grewal and Kaplan suggest, such links help marshal effective oppositions to economic and cultural hegemonies that are taking transnational, global forms. Similarly, in *Feminist Genealogies, Colonial Legacies, Democratic Futures*, M. Jacqui Alexander and Chandra Talpade Mohanty emphasize the importance of transnational social and cultural forces to think about women facing related issues in different geographic locations and to rethink democratic feminism as forging transnational alliances.[37]

Drawing upon this feminist scholarship, I explore the effects of transnational discourses on narratives of gender and sexuality for two reasons. First, I argue that in order to sustain a critical perspective toward middle- and upper-class women's narratives on gender and sexuality which does not abide by putative notions of Indianness, it is necessary to identify the transnational, globalizing cultural codes in women's narratives. In so doing, I implicitly raise the tensions between how culturally unique these narratives about womanhood and sexuality may be but also their similarities to parallel narratives produced in other social contexts. Second, I wish to highlight the discernible effects of transnational cultural discourses on women's narratives of gender and sexuality. Specifically, I refer to the prevalence of scientific paradigms, medical discourses, the use of (Indian) English, the fusion of romantic love and heterosexuality, and heterosexual ideals of marriage and marital relations—discourses that inform but are not fully explained by implicating the politics of nationalisms and state policies.

Thus far, I have suggested two reasons for including a chapter that focuses on queer narratives within India and of Indian affiliations elsewhere: to explore the ways in which queer narratives destabilize links between gender identities and sexualities and to explore how these narratives undermine heteronormative frameworks. But, there is a third and most compelling reason to extend the focus from middle- and upper-class women's narratives to queer narratives. I argue that queer narratives are no more immune from the constraints of normalizing strategies associated within nationalisms and transnational codes. To that extent, queer narratives are not outside the purview of this political arena. But, what is most instructive about these narratives are the ways in which they negotiate and challenge the normalizing and regulating strategies by forging transnational alliances that destabilize putative notions of sexual and national identities.

Specifying the Context of the Narratives

This sociological study is considered from a postcolonial, feminist perspective. I use the term "post-colonial" in two noninterchangeable ways. In its hyphenated form, the term *post-colonial* connotes the emergence of an independent nation-state after the end of colonization in 1947.[38] But, the term *post-colonial* offers a wide-ranging feminist critique, challenging the intersecting histories of modernity, colonialism, capitalism, and nationalism. A postcolonial, feminist orientation calls for a thoroughgoing critique of the construct of nation-state but also of hegemonic discourses and inequalities that cut across national societies.

I place narratives of middle-class women and queer narratives at the heart of this feminist critique of normative aspects of gender and sexuality. In so doing, I rely on sociological methodology instead of on abstract literary texts built on real-life material, and there lies its strength. Gayle Rubin correctly notes in an interview with Butler, that while literary analysis or film criticism contribute important insights, this scholarship cannot adequately "generate descriptions of living populations or explanations of their behaviors."[39] Thus, these narratives provide crucial insights into perspectives on womanhood, sexed bodies, and heterosexuality. Furthermore, this ethnographic approach is useful in highlighting the oppositional practices encoded in the narratives that frame this book—especially in their transnational possibilities. But, equally, this approach cautions against the romanticization of middle- and upper-class women's narratives and queer narratives. After all, some narratives are produced only as others are suppressed.

The interviews herein were conducted in the summer of 1994 in Mumbai and New Delhi. All the women are urban. Most of the 22 single women are what would be considered of marriageable age. I use the distinctions between married and single women less to endorse the cultural mandate of marriage than to suggest the cultural importance of marriage as the turning point in a woman's life cycle. What is more striking is that in the interviews all of the currently single women suggest that they expect to get married at some time. Thirty-two of the women in this study have been married. Of these, one woman is currently divorced. Among the 31 currently married, 23 have at least one child, but none has more than two children.

The women in this study are between the ages of 15 and 38, spanning a period of approximately 25 years. A few of the married women in the upper end of the age group have children who are as old as the youngest women in this study. But these age groupings do not conveniently overlap with marital status. A number of currently single women are in their late 20s, and one woman is 31 years old. On the other hand, a number of currently married women are in their early 20s and have already been married for a few years. What is clear, then, aside from the loose categorizations of these women as belonging to similar social class backgrounds, is that they are a diverse group that is not easily slotted into categories. These women can be collectively described only through a broad brush stroke.

All 54 women are self-identified as middle- or upper-class, with a prepon-derance of middle-class women. This subjective self-definition is especially meaningful since social class is a shared, but inexact, social construct. Although there are putative cultural notions of middle and upper class, they are not easily pinned down. As it turns out, income is a rather inefficient indicator of social class. For example, one woman who reports a monthly family income of Rs. 8,000 (Rs. 32 = $1), identifies herself as upper-middle-class. Another woman identifies herself as middle-class but reports a monthly family income of Rs. 15, 000. Nonetheless, social class is a material reality in contemporary India. Especially in a context where there are an overwhelming number of people and families below the poverty line, these incomes signify a life of privilege. On the basis of the returned questionnaires that I left with women at the end of the interview to gather demographic data, the lowest reported income is Rs. 6,000. Moreover, most of the women are working toward a college degree, are college graduates or have completed equivalent education—for example, a three-year degree in commercial arts or hotel management. For the purpose of this study, a number of cultural factors together describe the meaning of social class, including, but not reducible to, income, occupation, patterns of consumption, access to formal education, ritual or caste status, and historically specific relationships with the contemporary nation-state. Therefore, I use the term "middle class" from here on to loosely describe this group of women who self-identify as middle- or upper-class. I am interested in what their self-definitions of social class say about how they may act as individuals who conduct themselves respectably and as representatives of Indianness.

With regard to their ethnicity, these women self-identify in overlapping categories and classifications. Three women identify as Catholic, two as Parsi, one as Jain, one as Muslim, one as Sikh, and one as part Muslim and part Sikh. The other 45 women can be broadly identified with categories that are loosely included under the category of Hindu but include important cultural and ethnic differences associated with geography and language. Of these 45 women, three identify only as Hindu, and two do not identify as Hindu but only in terms of their ethnicity—Sindhi. The remaining 40 who identify as Hindu as well as a specific ethnic category, can be described as follows: 15 Sindhi, 14 Punjabi, four Rajasthani Rajput, two Marwari, two Saraswat Brahmins, one Baniya, one Telugu Brahmin, and one Tamil Brahmin. Through these classifications, the 54 women in this study indicate a complex overlap and interplay of religious, ethnic, and caste categories. Religious categories overlap and are offset by caste and ethnic categories in curious ways. For example, one woman who identifies herself as Roman Catholic also locates herself as a Goan Brahmin in response to a question on caste. Yet, putatively, "Catholic Brahmin" is a contradiction in terms. In other cases,

Hindu women identify what may be considered their ethnicity, such as Sindhi, as their caste status. From the perspective of this class position, these women note the cultural shifts in the categories of caste, ethnicity, and religion in late twentieth-century India.

What is incontrovertible, underlying the range of ethnic and religious differences, is that these 54 women are socially privileged and live in an urban setting. However, given the differences between them and the unique stories they tell, it is equally clear that one woman's story cannot substitute for another. Through the next few chapters, I interweave women's accounts with my analyses. In so doing, I highlight some narratives not because they are somehow typical of other women's stories but because the narratives capture the underlying themes that thread through most or all of the accounts. Where appropriate, I note exceptions to the various themes that are explored in each of the chapters. In some instances, I focus on women's words to highlight how they recount experiences of aspects of gender and sexuality in their lives. At other times, I turn to their narratives to trace the links between middle-class women's narratives on these issues and hegemonic codes of gender and sexuality.

Listening to these women was a stimulating part of this project for me. As a sociologist, I was fascinated by these middle-class women's stories and the complexities of seemingly mundane lives. What was perhaps most intriguing was how broad social themes and patterns intersected the more personal and individual aspects in each of the interviews. Aside from the introductions, brief questions, and requests for clarification, I was mostly quiet through the interviews. The stories were easy to listen to, and for the most part, the women seemed to enjoy speaking about their lives, about growing up as girls. But, for some women, speaking about particular aspects of their experiences—such as sexual aggression or the problems encountered in conjugal families after marriage—was upsetting. It was also upsetting to listen to. At these times, we paused momentarily or shifted focus. But such moments were rare. Instead, it appeared that the interviewees edited and shaped their accounts in ways that enabled them to narrate the various aspects of their lives, including those that were sources of pain and discomfort.

I also recognize that these women were willing to speak with me and, as the following chapters will indicate, were quite forthcoming and thorough about the details of their lives only because we shared gender, social class, and a national cultural background. Even though, when setting up the interviews, I told the women that I was doing work for a doctoral project and was affiliated with a university in the United States, at the time of the interviews only some women seemed conscious of my educational background. Others

seemed altogether unconcerned with my reasons for conducting the interviews. But what they were all able to identify from my presence was my social
class background. As feminist researchers have reminded us, these shared
aspects between the researcher and women who participate in studies are crucial for establishing a sense of rapport or trust. In my case, the affiliation to
higher education in the United States also provided an additional measure of
self-confidence in conducting interviews with women in their upper-class
homes, where I would have been otherwise intimidated because of class differences between us. At the same time, these commonalities and differences
do not altogether erase the power differences that emerge between the
researcher and women who are being interviewed. In this respect, I hope that
I have been able to capture the spirit of and do justice to women's words,
especially when I do not share their viewpoint.

I was able to gain access to these middle- and upper-class women through
personal networks. This snowball method of sampling was most suitable to
my purposes because I was less interested in characterizing a typical middle-
class Indian woman or typical answers to questions related to gender and sexuality. On the contrary, I was more interested in unraveling the discourses
that shape these women's narratives on sex, gender, and heterosexuality.
Friends and relatives helped me to get in touch with a number of these
women, who often recommended friends or acquaintances. This created
small clusters of women in the sample who were friends, relatives, or acquaintances. Since the largest such cluster consists of five women, this group of 54
women is relatively more diverse than a typical snowball sample may have
been. While this was by no means a random sample of women from an age
and social class range, I did not turn down the opportunity to interview any
woman. This method had the merit of including women I did not know and
would perhaps have not met otherwise, but it also had the limitation of not
including an overall more diverse range of women—more Muslim, Catholic,
or Parsi women.

The interviews occurred at the women's choice of sites. Most frequently,
we met at their homes. A few women preferred to come over to where I was
staying, while others chose a more neutral location, such as a quiet corner in
a public garden. Five of the 54 women expressed their discomfort with the
conversation being tape-recorded. Instead, I took copious notes. With the
exception of two interviews, where we had to meet twice because of time limitations, the women's narratives are based on single interviews, typically lasting between two and three hours. For the most part the interviews were conducted in the culturally specific form of English spoken among the urban
middle and upper classes. In this form, English is the primary language of

communication but liberally interspersed with colloquial and Hindi phrases. Some women relied more heavily on English to express themselves whereas others constantly switched between English and Hindi. Four women spoke primarily in Hindi through the interviews but also employed English phrases to express their thoughts. Since their language is a crucial aspect of the interviews and the analysis, I try to cite their words as accurately as I can, making changes in parentheses only for purposes of clarity for a wide audience.

Sifting through the interviews, for the purpose of analysis, I take the approach that these are narratives of women about their lives, about growing up as women, about what matters to them, and about aspects of gender and sexuality. I believe that interviews, the staple of sociological methods, are partially limited because they are arranged, manipulated conversations—both by the researcher and the person interviewed. But, the limitation is also the strength of the interview format. It provides the opportunity for people to generate accounts of their lives or their selves that they consider appropriate to the circumstances. This is how I approach these interviews and the narratives generated therein: The narratives are what women choose to represent as experience in the context of the interview.

But given the problem that our experiences are not simply static events of the past that are easily accessed through memory, what women express through the interviews are not mere recollections of past experiences. Instead, they are ever-changing accounts of the past that are told through the lens of the present. In effect, I understand women's interviews as stories of experiences that are told through the present. This is not to argue that these middle-class women's narratives are suspect or less than real in their lives. On the contrary, their narratives reveal crucial insights about what matters to them, what they recall as experience, and most importantly, what these experiences mean to them. To put it differently, the issue is not whether women are telling the truth about their lives or remembering their past experiences accurately. The more pressing issue is that through the interviews—their narratives—women provide important clues about deeper, more fundamental systems of meaning that continually shape their perceptions of experiences. Over and above all else, I am interested in the language women use to describe aspects of their lives and their life experiences, and I attempt to decipher what this language tells us about hegemonic discourses that shape and regulate women's perceptions of their gender, bodies, and sexualities.

Taken collectively, middle-class women's narratives are not without contradictions, either within each interview or across all interviews. Sometimes, women will contradict themselves over the span of the interview. More frequently, they will give different accounts about various aspects of their lives.

To that extent, there is no singular, overarching narrative of body, gender, and sexuality that emerges from the interviews. Instead, these narratives shed crucial light on the tensions and contradictions of womanhood and female sexuality that shape and constrain these middle-class women in the context of the post-colonial nation-state. Underneath the differences among the narratives, the more fundamental themes that shape women's language on matters of gender and sexuality provide important indications about the impact of the post-colonial nation-state and transnational processes in their day-to-day lives.

Conclusion

My specific task in this book is to explore how middle-class women in post-colonial India are being regulated and constrained through normative definitions of their sexed bodies, sexualities, and gender identities. I analize these women's narratives of what it was like to grow up as women, to get their first periods, to experience sexual aggression, or of what (hetero)sexuality, marriage, and motherhood mean in their lives, in order to trace the ways in which womanhood and sexuality constrain and discipline them. On the basis of these narratives, I challenge the uneven, multiple hegemonic codes that shape what these women recount as experience.

By looking at the role of the contemporary Indian nation-state and transnational cultural discourses in producing and sustaining normative categories of womanhood and sexuality, I hope to show how gender, sexual, and national identities emerge as complex, unstable processes that are sustained and disrupted through the mundane, intricate acts of everyday lives. These women's narratives can help us understand how the hegemonic codes of identity and disciplinary strategies that affect our lives in complex and uneven ways are only obscured by concepts of "modernity," "westernization," or "tradition." By identifying the role of the contemporary nation-state and transnational cultural processes in producing discourses of gender and sexuality, study highlights the importance of neither essentializing these as Indian women nor lapsing into broad, overarching generalizations of womanhood across diverse social locations.

I rely on sociological methods to generate women's narratives on aspects of sex, gender, and sexuality. I avoid essentializing the narratives as women's experiences and, instead, delve deeper into the discourses that shape women's accounts of the sexed body, heterosexuality, and prescriptions of womanhood. Thus, sociological methods provide a crucial means to fill the gaps between feminist concerns with aspects of gender and sexuality and a preponderance of abstracted literary and textual analyses. At the same time, feminist theories foreground the importance of challenging fictions of womanhood and normative sexuality and raise broader questions about how these categories are made to appear natural in our day-to-day lives. To that extent, I draw upon critical feminist theories to vitalize a fundamental sociological concern at the heart of this study—the relationship between the self and social setting—by complicating the conceptualizations of self and society.

In the next chapter, I identify hegemonic codes of gender and sexuality that are produced and sustained within the contemporary nation-state, focusing on contemporary educational literature developed by state-funded agencies to normalize adolescents' sexual development. In exploring the limitations of these sex education literatures, I analyze the ways in which normative discourses of sexed bodies, heterosexualities, and gender identities are sustained in these texts. I also argue that although these discourses are bolstered through notions of national cultural identity, they also incorporate the effects of transnational processes in defining and reinforcing gender and sexual norms.

The next four chapters are more explicitly focused on the narratives of women who participated in this study. In Chapters Three and Four, I explore middle-class women's narratives on the onset of menarche and menstruation, and sexual aggression directed against them. What I am especially interested in is how sexed bodies are produced at the intersections of gender, class, and sexuality. I am equally interested in the strategies through which these sexed bodies are regulated but made to appear normal.

Chapter Five focuses on matters of erotic sexuality to decipher women's narratives on nonmarital chastity and its circumvention, marital sexuality and meaning of sexual satisfaction, initial marital sexual experiences, the role of pornography, and the association between sex and marital intimacy. Throughout Chapters Four and Five, I place special focus on the tensions of gender- and class-based norms of "sexual respectability" to identify the hegemonic codes of sexuality that are reflected in women's narratives on sexual aggression and erotic sexuality.

The purpose of Chapter Six is to explore the meaning of marriage and motherhood to middle-class women in contemporary India. The narratives included address pervasive social expectations but also provide clues to how the women negotiate these social norms in their roles as wives and mothers.

In Chapter Seven, I shift to narratives of gay/lesbian/bisexual identities within India and among people of South Asian origin in countries such as the United States. Rather than base my findings on interviews, I approach key texts—such as collections, magazines produced by queer organizations—as the sites where narratives of identity are produced. I argue that these narratives that are consciously produced from social margins have much to tell us about the deleterious effects of the post-colonial nation-state shaped by transnational processes on matters of gender and sexuality. But, what these narratives also exemplify are the kinds of transnational alliances that might be not only politically strategic but will extend the more narrowly conceived politics based on identity.

Finally, in the Conclusion, I reexamine the threads that run throughout the book and consider a recent film written and directed by Deepa Mehta, *Fire*, as an example of how the politics of gender and sexuality in post-colonial India may be challenged from the viewpoint of middle-class women. What is especially intriguing about *Fire* is that its oppositional politics are not easily categorized as feminist or lesbian and thereby not easily co-opted.

Chapter Two

Sex, Sexuality, and the Nation-State

There are numerous possible ways to probe how the contemporary nation-state articulates and reinforces hegemonic and normalizing scripts of gender and sexuality. In this chapter I focus on one such aspect, namely, state-sponsored sex education materials. I am interested in how these materials reveal the state's ability to articulate hegemonic, normalizing, and regulating codes of gender and sexuality. These hegemonic narratives not only provide clues about the ways in which the correlates of gender and sexuality—in the form of female bodies, heterosexuality, and social expectations of marriage and motherhood for women—are normalized; they also subsume strategies of enforcement. Here they provide a foil against which to consider the accounts of middle-class women. In their accounts, these women invoke, reinforce, and sometimes repudiate the discourses that organize the sex education materials.

In the last decade, feminist theorizing has drawn attention to the role of the nation-state in producing hegemonic narratives on gender and sexuality. But the nation-state cannot be conceptualized as a unitary, coherent source of social enforcement. On the contrary, the territorial state is characterized by a much more uneven set of discourses, apparatuses, and institutions that serve to regulate and reinforce. Looking at legal discourses, discourses of development, or state-affiliated media may reveal multiple and contradictory scripts of gender and sexuality.[1] Indeed, as Louisa Schein argues about post-Mao China, the state may tolerate, if not support, the proliferation of unruly differences in hegemonic discourses of gender and sexuality.[2] What is necessary, then, is to problematize and interrogate the state instead of reinscribing or reifying it as an immutable force. From this perspective, state-sponsored sex education materials provide a slant into dominant scripts of gender and sexuality but also call for a more complex and nuanced analysis of the links between nation-state, womanhood, and sexuality.

Furthermore, the links between the uneven discourses of nation-state, gender, and sexuality are deeply intertwined and not unidirectional; capturing their dynamics is not exhausted by describing the regulating effects of the nation-state on discourses of gender and sexuality. On the contrary, for example, feminist historiographies of colonial India address the overlaps between nation, gender, and sexuality. These historiographies explore how changing scripts of gender and sexual identities for middle-class, mostly Hindu women articulated an official, masculinist, anticolonial nationalism and how, in turn, this form of nationalism, in its struggle against colonialism, was expressed in terms of gender and sexual characteristics.[3] Viewed from this perspective, state-sponsored sex education materials do not simply raise questions about the role of the nation-state in producing and reinforcing hegemonic discourses on gender and sexuality—on sexed bodies, on mandating heterosexuality, aspects of womanhood, and normative gender identity. These texts also raise larger questions about the imbrication of discourses of nation-state, gender, and sexuality in contemporary, post-colonial India.

While not synonymous with the contemporary state, notions of national cultural identity shape and reinforce hegemonic codes of gender and sexuality in the texts that are considered below. That there is a generally accepted and unique national culture is both an assumption and an outcome of these texts. On the one hand, these sex education literatures are implicitly, and sometimes explicitly, premised on a putative and definable Indian cultural identity. On the other hand, by juxtaposing aspects of gender and sexuality with assumptions of an "Indianness," these texts also reinforce notions of an essential and unique national cultural identity. Furthermore, the premise of cultural identity is sustained by opposing the modernist constructs of India and the West. But to simply critique these normalizing codes on gender and sexuality against the disputable narratives on India and Indian culture would be to ignore the contradictory ways in which the premises of nationalisms and nation-state are sustained.

What becomes clear in these state-sponsored sex education literatures is that assumptions of nationalisms and nation-state are not only sustained through oppositions of modernity but also intermingle with selective transnational cultural discourses. In these texts, to challenge the premise of national cultural identity only from the point of the underlying oppositions (India vs. Western culture) is not sufficient. It is equally necessary to identify those transnational cultural discourses that help sustain the hegemonic narratives of gender and sexuality. Arguably, these discourses on gender and sexuality express assumptions of nationalisms but also the mutating contradictions of official nationalisms intersecting with transnational cultural discourses. In other words, these texts rely on the premise of an Indian national culture and transnational cultural discourses to produce and reinforce hegemonic narratives on gender and sexuality.

As noted above, there is surely more than one way to analyze intersecting discourses of gender, sexuality, nationalisms, nation-state, and transnational cultural processes. For example, recent feminist theorizing on right-wing movements and the role of women in these movements in India would be one way to intervene.[4] But I focus on texts aimed at providing sex education for two primary reasons. First, these texts provide a more specific and convenient way to analyze how the nation-state can produce and reinforce discourses of gender and sexuality. These texts are specifically aimed at alleviating anxieties associated with sexual development and lessening the trauma that may result from the transition from childhood to adolescence to adulthood. This avowed attempt at making issues of sexual and gender development "normal" and "natural" is precisely what makes these texts intriguing and useful—to highlight how definitions of normality encode social prescriptions riven with inequalities of gender, sexuality, and class. Second, I focus on these texts because these texts not only provide clues about how, for example, the gender and sexual identities of young women are produced and normalized but also about the strategies that are integral to the process.

From the perspective of the 54 middle-class women, these texts reveal the intricate ways in which the female body, (hetero)sexuality, and gender identities are produced and sustained through commonplace discussions on sexual development and physical, emotional maturation. What these texts also reveal are the kinds of strategies of regulation that complement the prescriptions of sexed bodies, heterosexuality, and aspects of gender identity. Highlighting the detailed, mundane strategies of controlling bodies, Foucault argues that since the eighteenth century power appropriates the body as an object.[5] What is perhaps most historically unique about these ways of controlling bodies is the reliance on access to the individuals themselves, to their bodies, their gestures, and their daily actions.[6] Indeed there is no need for arms, or physical violence. According to Foucault, only an inspecting gaze is necessary, a gaze through which each individual exercises a surveillance over, and against, himself.[7] I explore the extent to which these regulating strategies are inextricable from the attempt to define normality in sexual and gender development in the sex education literatures.

What is especially noteworthy is that there is a history to the use of educational and didactic materials to shape notions of womanhood and female sexuality sustained by disciplinary mechanisms. Feminist historiographies of colonial India persuasively demonstrate the ways in which discourses of liberal reform and education disguised how middle-class women's gendered bodies, sexualities, and gender roles were realigned to the purpose of an emergent anticolonial, elitist nationalism. Reform became interchangeable with regulation. More specifically, analyses of the use of didactic literatures and instruction manuals suggest how changing narratives of womanhood and sexuality were essential to regulating middle-class, upper-caste, mostly Hindu women.[8] In the context of colonial state and anticolonial, hegemonic nationalisms, education had to serve a dual role—to elaborate and specify changing, politically charged definitions of womanhood and sexuality as well as make them appear normal and natural to the audience. It is this dual-edged role of sex education literatures in contemporary India that I am especially interested in.

Viewed in this way, state-sponsored sex education literatures call into question the role of liberal education literature in mandating issues of gender and sexuality, especially for middle-class young women. Although these texts are not exclusively targeted toward them, their class and gender status make them a central audience. More specifically, these texts call into question the underlying tensions of didactic texts; they take the liberal viewpoint that factual information can normalize sexual development for teenagers, but end up prescribing gender and sexual norms and regurgitating pervasive social inequities in a new guise. Produced by state-funded agencies, such texts reflect putative notions of national cultural identity and what is socially acceptable on matters of gender and sexuality. From the viewpoint of middle-class women, then, the texts provide a glimpse into normalizing discourse and disciplinary strategies of gender and sexuality produced and supported by the state. These texts necessitate a close examination not only of the impact of cultural nationalism, but also patterns of transnational cultural homogenization in the definitions of what is appropriate and normal on matters of sexed bodies, gender, and sexualities.

Nationalisms, the State, and Sex Education Literature

Nowhere are limits of liberal discourses of gender and sexuality more evident than in the sex education materials published by the Family Planning Association of India (FPAI) and its Sex Education, Counseling, Research Training/Therapy (SECRT) division. Under the aegis of family planning,

FPAI and SECRT put out a series of texts to promote knowledge about family planning, raise the status of women, prepare men and women for "responsible family living," and promote responsible sexual behavior, especially among the youth.[9] FPAI is a nongovernmental organization at the national level that nonetheless works closely with the state in multiple ways. Since as early as 1953, FPAI has been closely affiliated with state policies on family planning and population control. Over the years FPAI has worked with the state to coordinate issues of family planning and population policies.[10] Furthermore, as the largest and most well-established nongovernmental organization on matters of family planning and population policies, FPAI acts as the dual link between the state and smaller nongovernmental organizations: on the one hand, distributing governmental grants to these agencies, and on the other, articulating the needs of the people to the state through the work of the smaller agencies. FPAI's relation with the state is further concretized through a heavy dependence on state funding.[11] As an institutionalized voluntary organization dependent on state resources, the family planning association complements, supplements, and articulates state policies. As one FPAI official said, "It works in tandem with the government."[12]

SECRT was formed in 1978 to dispel misconceptions related to human sexuality and contraception. SECRT aims to combat the growing incidence of marital discord, divorce and separation, out-of-wedlock pregnancies, abortions, sexually transmitted diseases, drug and alcohol use, and other problems. In its mission statement, SECRT espouses a humane and liberal approach to human sexuality. "Sexuality has a deep and significant human value during the life cycle, no matter what age, gender, sexual disposition, economic status, state of health, nationality or religion,"[13] an agency pamphlet states. Men and women need to be educated to behave in sexually responsible ways, and children need to be given honest answers to their questions and need to develop the self-confidence that comes with understanding their bodies and their feelings. What is notable is that this pamphlet also indicts societal double standards on sexuality, the distorted view of sexuality promoted in pornography, and sexual abuse of children. But even in these statements on the meaning and relevance of sex education, the pamphlet is unable to avoid tensions inherent to liberal strategies of education. Although as an organization SECRT clearly takes a wider and relatively critical view of sex education, it is unable to avoid generating and regurgitating the deeper inequalities that mark the making of sexed bodies, heterosexuality, and gender identities. In this respect, SECRT may not be unique but it surely plays a role in this process. The numerous texts produced by SECRT and FPAI related to matters of sex education are riven with these contradictions.

Texts related to matters of gender and sexuality, produced and distributed by the FPAI and SECRT, can be grouped into four categories. In the first category are booklets such as *Growing Up . . . Facts and Feelings, Problems of Adolescent Sexuality*, and *Teenagers Ask, The Doctor Answers*. These booklets attempt to provide education on matters of general sexual development to both adolescent girls and boys. Of these, some booklets such as *Parivartan Ka Swagat: Kishoriyon Ke Liye Margdarshika*, or its English version, *Bloom and Blossom: A Girl's Guide to Growing Up*, are more exclusively aimed at girls. The second category of educational literatures aim to promote awareness, and thereby prevention, of sexually transmitted diseases, including HIV/AIDS. Written in a number of different languages, such as Hindi, Marathi, and other regional languages, as well as English, the title translates as *Teenagers Ask, The Doctor Answers: STDs and AIDS*. Other titles include *Youth, STDs and AIDS* (translated from Marathi) and *What You Should Know About STDs and AIDS*. The third category includes a range of issues more relevant to young adults and others preparing for events such as marriage and motherhood. *Safe Motherhood, Preparing for Marriage, Child Growth, and Family Planning: Your Questions Answered* are some of the texts that fall into this category. The group includes texts that are targeted at educators in the field, such as *Education in Human Sexuality: A Sourcebook for Educators* and *Youth Sexuality: A Study of Knowledge, Attitudes, Beliefs and Practices Among Urban Educated Indian Youth 1993–94*.

Sex Education, Gender, Sexuality, and Nationalisms

That these texts are rooted in the premise of a national social unit but shaded by constructs such as society, cultural heritage, and modernity, is clearly visible. Perhaps these assumptions are most strikingly evident in a pamphlet titled *Sex Education: What Why How & Who*, put out jointly by FPAI and SECRT. Response to the question, "What is sex education?," reveals the overarching philosophical premise of these organizations:

> Sexuality implies psychological reactions associated with "maleness and femaleness" and determines behavioral responses. These sex-related behavioral responses are further conditioned by cultural heritage and social norms. Cultural heritage is the sum total of religious precepts and traditional concepts. Social norms are the product of compromise between bio-emotional needs of the individual and existing socio-cultural patterns in the society. Hence sexuality is a much broader term than sex which denotes only gender. [14]

Framed as a matter of a singular cultural heritage, including religious precepts and tradition, the quote leaves little doubt about the bearing of official national society and culture. But secured on the parameters of the national, the quote also foregrounds inherent political tensions: between the psychological and the social, between the individual and the social, between behavior and its societal context. Thereby, not only are societal/national norms pitted against the individual, but the role of education in regulating such tensions is masked under the guise of education as information and improvement.

Specific texts, such as *Problems of Adolescent Sexuality*, are based on the assumptions that a unitary, traditional cultural system—characterized by a 5,000-year-old paternalistic family system—is undergoing rapid transformation under the effects of industrialization, urbanization, and development. Where this assumption takes a more explicit nationalist flavor is in the discussion on the nature of "Indian society." In this discussion, the national cultural past is described as a closed society with uniform standards, powerful religious sanctions, and a family unit where elders held positions of unquestionable authority, men had superior standing, women were accepted as wives and mothers, and children were obedient. If this representation of the past reaffirms the belief of a unitary national culture, then it is only further reinforced through the suggestion that beneath the changes and upheavals the national cultural core is relatively unchanged and definable. Sometimes foregrounded, and at other times part of the backdrop, national culture and society make up the edifice of these educational materials across the various categories.

Making, Sexing, Heterosexualizing, and Regulating Bodies

Through discussions of aspects of sexual development, what is notable is how notions of the dual-sex system that is the basis for gender identity and heterosexuality are produced and normalized in these texts. Nowhere are the intricate overlaps between sex, gender, and heterosexuality more evident than in the first category of texts that address aspects of sexual development—changing bodies, psychologies, and emotions associated with puberty and adolescence. The text *Growing Up . . . Facts and Feelings* maps physical, sexual, and emotional changes associated with adolescence and the transition from childhood to adulthood. What is curious is that in the explanations provided for the changing pubertal female and male bodies, physical changes in girls are primarily marked by the onset of menstruation, but for boys the changes are marked by the onset of sexuality. For girls, menstruation is described as a normal sign of maturation and ability to "produce a baby," whereas erections, "nocturnal emissions," masturbation, and ejaculations mark the signs of normal development for boys.

In this example, despite the claim that girlhood is based on the female body's natural ability to menstruate, the sexed body is derived from notions of gender—or what it means to be a girl or a boy. Explanations that address issues of the female body through menstruation and baby-making, on the one hand, and erections, ejaculations, and masturbations for the male body, on the other hand, are the result of assumptions of girlhood and boyhood. Similarly, booklets targeted exclusively at girls, for example, *Bloom and Blossom: A Girl's Guide to Growing Up*, focus almost entirely on matters such as menstruation, development of breasts, and emotional changes. In its 20 pages, the topic of sexuality is limited to two sentences on the possibility of attraction to boys.[15]

Unquestionably, these texts produce explanations of sexed bodies that are rooted in the hierarchies of male/female, active sexuality/passive sexuality, sexual/restrained. If these explanations of changing and maturing adolescent bodies are grounded in the dual-sex system, then they also implicitly reinforce the wider assumptions of inherent, evolutionary heterosexuality. Although aimed at alleviating anxieties about growing up, these texts produce and reinforce deeply embedded and unequal notions of female and male bodies, heterosexuality, girlhood, and boyhood. They become instrumental to producing passive female bodies and heterosexuality while promoting them as normal. Moreover, sexuality is conflated virtually without exception with heterosexual relations.

For example, on the matter of premarital sex, *Problems of Adolescent Sexuality* states,

> Boys are eager for physical sex; they look on performance as proof of virility; sometimes the relationship develops out of bravado. Unfortunately many male adolescents are unaware of, or unconcerned about, the consequences of such a relationship to the girl.
>
> Girls who are brought up more strictly tend to be cautious. A very small section of Indian girls indulge in pre-marital sex because of the sexual urge. Some seek to assert their freedom; others for a lark or "out of sheer defiance." The majority of those who indulge in pre-marital sex do so because they have been persuaded by their boyfriends to "prove their love," or because they fear that their boyfriends might leave them.[16]

Whether the author is challenging or implicitly reinforcing the sexual double standard for boys and girls is less clear. More troubling is the way that boys are constituted as actively needing "physical sex" as proof of virility. But, related to matters of upbringing as Indian girls, girls appear to have a more passive relationship to premarital sex. They act less on "sexual urge" than comply to premarital sex in service of their heterosexual relationships. It is through these intricacies of changing bodies, sexual maturation, and "sexual urges" that the coherence of binary gender identities are maintained.

These texts reveal the significance of the sexed body in eliciting the consent of the individual to the normalizing expectations of heterosexuality, gender role, and gender identities. Despite the seeming naturalness of the sexed body, critical readings of these texts belie the possibility of objective or unmediated representations of ostensibly natural phenomena such as the sexed boby. As suggested above, the explanations of the dual-sexed body are colored by underlying social and gender belief systems. At the same time, the underlying medical discourse reinforces the premise of the biological, natural sexed body. Within this paradoxical framework, the sexed body is instrumental to the numerous instances that make social events such as menarche, mestruation, sexual aggression, abortion, and pregnancy, among others, appear natural. These social events constitute opportunities for the individual woman to grasp what is happening to her and consent to the normalizing expectations related to these newly discovered aspects of her body.

That the sexed body as an instrument of social regulation is bolstered by mechanisms of individual self-surveillance and self-regulation is reflected in the premise of generating texts of these kinds. Arguably, when information that seeks to normalize gender and sexual development is rooted in structural social inequalities, it is suspect for its content. But, texts of this kind are equally suspect for the mechanisms through which normality of gender and sexuality are enforced. Helping individual girls and boys manage their adolescence and transition into adulthood also serves to ensure that they will assume responsibility for regulating their bodies by internalizing what is normal for their bodies and sexualities according to prevailing social norms. This is not to suggest that these are the intended effects of these texts or that they are entirely successful. But, insofar as these texts aim to normalize gender and sexual development, they also incorporate ways of producing what Foucault calls "docile bodies"—bodies that rely on individual self-surveillance and monitoring.

In some instances, these mechanisms of social regulation through individual self-surveillance become vividly clear. For example, the text *Teenagers Ask, The Doctor Answers* responds to the following question in this manner:

> *Question:* Should girls and boys mix freely?
> *Answer:* In most parts of India, both society and parents feel it unwise to allow too much freedom between boys and girls. Except in certain groups or co-educational institutions in cities like Bombay, New Delhi and other metropolitan towns, segregation of the sexes is common. Due to the prevailing social mores, boys and girls who mix too freely are often censured by the elders. Often a bad reputation is attached to the young person and this makes marriage difficult in a country where arranged marriages are still the norm.

> If you belong to the more westernized type of modern society, and your parents do not object to your having friends of the opposite sex, it is very much your responsibility to ensure that whatever you and your friend do together must be well thought out in the light of what has been written above.[17]

This question and answer present putative notions about the difference between traditional and westernized society in India, and the differences in the kinds of social control that might be appropriate to each. If bad reputations and the difficulty in arranged marriage ensure the taboos against "free mixing" in most parts of India, then social interaction between the sexes in the "more westernized" society is marked by personal responsibility and self-monitoring. Parents and social norms are not entirely redundant in these cases but coexist with the internalized forms of social regulation.

Defining Respectable Sex/Normal Sex

In these texts, discussions of sexual behaviors and practices encode notions of "normal sex," but also of "sexual respectability." If discourses of normal sex appear to undergird texts in the first and second categories, then they are bolstered by notions of what is sexually acceptable within the parameters of the national culture—in other words, sexual respectability. Discussions of sexually transmitted diseases are implicitly shaped by notions of normal sex and sexual respectability. While providing information about sexually transmitted diseases, despite a liberal framework about individual behavior and choices, these texts address issues related to sexually transmitted diseases—defining and explaining the diseases, at-risk sexual practices, safe sex practices—but implicitly suggest both what is socially acceptable and what is normal. In this framework, heterosexual, marital, and monogamous sexual relationships provide the edifice for interchangeable definitions of normal and respectable sexuality. Notably, the problems of sexually transmitted diseases, including HIV/AIDS, are framed as matters of sexual deviance from societal and legal standards. If these diseases are related to forms of sexual deviance, then the discussions are also about meanings of normal sex.

In response to the first question on what kinds of diseases are defined as STDs, the Marathi and Hindi versions of *Teenagers Ask, The Doctor Answers: STDs and AIDS* emphatically state that STDs are not the result of sexual relations between husbands and wives. Although the next question/answer concedes that if one of the spouses is infected, then the disease can be transmitted to the other, elsewhere marital monogamy is urged. Therefore, by implication, "normal sex" occurs between noninfected, monogamous husbands and wives.

Curiously, the English-language booklet *What You Should Know About STDs and AIDS* more inclusively recommends safe sex between partners, rather than spouses, mutual masturbation, caressing, and monogamy, but offsets the advice with a cartoon of a penis wearing a condom and a sketch of a man and a woman. The texts are to be recommended for their care in dismissing misconceptions related to STDs, especially AIDS, but the problem is that they are unable to address these matters without privileging heterosexual, marital, and monogamous sexual relationships.

Such codes of normal sex are not limited to booklets on sexually transmitted diseases and are intertwined with notions of "sexual respectability." For example, another question/answer in the booklet *Teenagers Ask, The Doctor Answers* provides a particularly useful instance of how notions of normal and respectable sex coincide to shape and organize hegemonic discourses of sexuality generated in these texts. What is notable is that, compared to the booklets on sexually transmitted diseases, *Teenagers Ask, The Doctor Answers* has a much wider scope and, possibly, a much wider audience. This booklet attempts to educate adolescents on matters of sexuality in keeping with, in the words of the author, "our customs and traditions." It also seeks to provide useful information to parents to answer questions that growing children or teenagers may ask. Purposively written in an accessible question/answer format, the text addresses a wide range of issues including the meaning of and advice on puberty, virginity, menstruation, premarital sex, masturbation, drugs, sexually transmitted diseases, contraception, acne, sexual development, circumcision, rape, homosexuality, conception, and abortion. *Teenagers Ask, The Doctor Answers* appears to be an especially popular booklet. First published in October 1975, it is now in its sixth edition (last updated in December 1990) and is regularly updated and reprinted in languages such as English, Hindi, Marathi, Gujarati, Gurumukhi, and Braille.

On the matter of premarital sexual intercourse:

> *Question:* Am I old-fashioned because I think differently from my friends who think it is all right to have sexual intercourse before marriage?
>
> *Answer:* Generally every person has a right to his own opinions in personal matters. Believing in sexual intercourse after marriage does not make you old-fashioned at all. In fact, in the context of Indian morality (which does not approve of the "free sex" attitude of the West), you are perfectly right.
>
> Every girl indulging in free sex runs the risk of having an unwanted baby and becoming unmarried mothers. Every year in this country such avoidable tragedies are increasing. Pre-marital sex being furtive and snatched in dark corners causes tension due to the fear of being found out. Also both the boy and girl can develop venereal disease and AIDS, which can have serious effects on their lives.

> Finally, except in rare instances sex outside marriage often means the loss
> of love, warmth, kindness and understanding, that are so essential in sus-
> taining a meaningful relationship between the two people involved.[18]

What is immediately notable in this specific quote is that this discussion frames (hetero)sexual intercourse as a matter of national cultural traditions, past and present. With a brief qualification that (hetero)sexuality is essential-ly a personal, individual matter, the response quickly goes on to endorse that the belief that (hetero)sexual intercourse should occur within marriage is still relevant and appropriate to Indian culture. In one broad stroke, the ques-tion/answer unequivocally reinforces the certitude of "Indian morality" and links it to premarital celibacy in opposition to the "free sex" attitude of the "West." Two aspects of the juxtaposition of (hetero)sexuality and nation-alisms are particularly noteworthy: that premarital (hetero)sexual intercourse is situated on a scale that favorably measures Indian culture and its morality against the self-styled West; that the discourse of sexuality is reasoned as a matter of national cultural tradition. It is perfectly conceivable to evaluate Indian morality in other ways but, as elsewhere, the West is the obvious back-drop. The construct of Western culture is used to offset Indian cultural iden-tity. Within this questionable context of meanings that treat sex as a matter of national morality, it appears reasonable to suggest that consigning sexual intercourse to marriage is to comply with national customs and traditions. In one fell swoop, "sexual respectability" is the domain of the nation-state.

That inequities of gender are imbricated in discourses of sexuality and sex-ual respectability is also clear. The text recognizes but does not challenge gender differences between teenagers with respect to premarital (hetero)sex-ual intercourse. Shifting to what are considered the avoidable and tragic con-sequences of premarital intercourse, the next paragraph also shifts from the masculine or neutral subject ("person has a right to his opinions") to girls indulging in "free sex." The tragedy of pregnancy remains a problem of girls indulging in free sex, contrary to the morality of the national culture. The discussion also maintains the premise of sexual respectability by conflating sexuality with heterosexuality. Precisely because the question of homosexu-ality is separated into one question and answer elsewhere in the booklet, it is effectively contained; in all other question/answers, sexual respectability is implicitly authenticated as a matter of heterosexuality.

Also, on closer inspection, the question/answer implicitly specifies the meaning of normal sexual intercourse, not premarital sex. The question/answer addresses the issue of premarital sexual intercourse but indirectly defines what it considers to be normal, heterosexual sex. Sexual intercourse and marriage are linked together through desirable qualities—love, understanding, and kindness—and favored over premarital sex, which is associated with furtive encounters and sexually transmitted diseases. This language of sex is noteworthy. In its manner of casting what sexual intercourse really is or ought to be, this question/answer on premarital sex also discloses the broader, transnational context of the meaning of sexuality. Not only does it suggest the interface between women, (hetero)sexuality, and national cultural identity, but also transnational cultural processes. The fusion of marriage, love, and understanding is not unique to post-colonial India.[19] This is not to suggest that there is something inherently wrong with these characteristics of sex, but my concern is with how this language is creating a normative, interpretive framework of sexual intercourse, one that seems to extend beyond the boundaries of the nation-state but is appropriated to bolster notions of sexual respectability and national cultural identity. In effect, with rare exceptions, anything outside of marital sexual intercourse characterized by love and understanding is placed outside the domain of "normal/respectable sex."

In the context of global culture, this language of "normal sex" hearkens prevailing systems of sexual meanings in countries such as the United States and England. While the differences in the language of sex between India and societies such as England or the United States are pervasive in popular imaginations in each of the contexts (such as loveless, sexually unhappy, arranged marriages in India versus romantic, sexual, but unstable marriages in England and the United States), the transnational cultural similarities are also worth noting. If through this process of normalization of sexuality across national societies sex is made to appear natural and transhistorical, then other possible meanings are suppressed. Thus, not only is it enough to identify the role of nationalisms in defining meanings but to also challenge the larger, globalizing cultural context that designates and denies meanings of sexuality.[20]

Good Marriages, Good Mothers, and Womanhood

The third category of texts that address gender roles such as marriage and motherhood are aimed at young adults preparing for these life changes and provide glimpses into prevailing social conceptions. Though the pamphlet addressing marriage, *Preparing for Marriage*, does not suggest that marriage is preordained for women, it does reinforce the transhistorical mystique of marriage and heterosexuality. The opening sentences are: "Thousands of years of human history have failed to resolve the mystery of sexual attraction. The struggle and delight of sustaining the intimate relationship in a marriage still baffles men and women."[21]

Nonetheless, the pamphlet is useful in advocating marriage as a partnership based on gender equality. With regard to the marital relationship, the text recommends an egalitarian and companionate model of marriage, based on mutual love, respect, care, sacrifice, and the participation of wives in decision-making. Sex as a shared experience and equal participation in lovemaking are also encouraged. The "4 T's," trust, time, touch, and talk, are presented as the cornerstones of an emotional and sexual relationship. To that extent, this text reflects the effects of transnational cultural discourses of marriage and intimacy.

What makes this text inadequate is its assumption that marriage and marital relationships are limited to a psychological framework. On the one hand, selection of marriage partners and what are the primary criteria of marital relationships are framed as matters of personal choice. Married women and men are encouraged to plan their parenthood instead of succumbing to social pressure or having children out of accidental pregnancies. Contrary to the complex nature of the social institution, not only is marriage posed as a matter of concern between a man and a woman, but careful screening and selection of a marital partner is suggested. Against the web of complicated social relationships that shape the decisions of marital partners and govern the rules of premarital social interaction, personality characteristics are highlighted as appropriate criteria and the period of courtship is said to be best spent exploring each other's personalities.

Analogously, the pamphlet *Safe Motherhood* is useful but limited to its emphasis on ensuring that pregnancies for women are not too early, frequent, or the result of social pressure. There is little ambiguity in the text's emphasis on motherhood and marriage as voluntary choices made by individuals. But by emphasizing the role of the individual and her choices in matters of marriage and motherhood, the individual also assumes the attendant responsibilities. Within this individualized and psychologized framework, marriage and motherhood are not mandated for women; however, avoidance of marriage and motherhood are not presented as options. More disputably, if marriage and motherhood are reinforced as normal aspects of our lives, then the only uncertainty is to what extent individual women (and men) can ensure their personal happiness by making all the right choices—in the selection of partners, the intimacy of the relationship, correctly timing the birth of children, and so on.

Medical Discourse, Science, and the Role of Experts

Since the fourth category of texts is grounded upon the assumption that the nature of sex education and human sexuality is such that it should be imparted only through appropriate social institutions based in the knowledge of experts—trained educators, doctors, scientists—it is aimed at educators. Social problems cited as creating a need for sex education—problems brought on by urbanization, industrialization, rapid social change, the erosion of "traditional" social structures, confusing and conflicting values, dearth of information on sex as a natural part of human behavior— are also seen to make the task of sex educators challenging. Amid these social problems and uncertainties, it is believed that trained educators and experts should provide sex education that is grounded in medical facts and scientific knowledge. But as the explorations of the texts above suggest, experts who can impart knowledge on sex education and human sexuality—such as the teacher, the scientist, and the doctor—are not only the mediators of knowledge but, in fact, the certifiers of knowledge.[22]

By now it should be clear that one of the central mechanisms upon which these sex education texts and the role of experts in imparting sex education are based upon is the medical discourse. This medical discourse not only generates and reinforces notions of dual-sexed, biological bodies upon which cultural scripts of girlhood and boyhood may be written, but also legitimizes them. By emphasizing reproductive sexualities as biological and pre-social, this medical discourse helps generate and reiterate cultural notions of sexed bodies, heterosexualities, and binary gender identities as natural. This medical discourse is bolstered through the lens of science and the beliefs that objective and factual knowledge can be socially beneficial. But, feminist and postcolonial critiques of science and the medical discourse argue persuasively that there is little objectivity to science or the facts that undergird medical discourse.[23] The same is true of these sex education texts. Despite the attempts to present facts and alleviate anxieties about issues such as sexual development, sexualities, diseases, marriage, and motherhood, these texts encode hegemonic discourses of gender and sexuality.

Considering Alternatives

Before the close of this chapter I would like to briefly explore an alternative text that seeks to inform women on matters of their bodies and gender identities in ways that are markedly different from the state-sponsored sex education literatures considered above. This text, titled *Sharir Ki Jankari* (Knowledge About the Body), addresses issues of the female body, menarche, menstruation, menopause, heterosexual intercourse, and male bodies, from a perspective shaped by a critique of gender inequality.[24] Strikingly different from the institutional texts considered above, this text provides a useful counter-instance of how knowledge can be used as a form of social critique for women, rather than a source of social control.

Sharir Ki Jankari is different in several ways. First, it seemingly targets rural working women, which separates it from the materials generated by FPAI and SECRT. Although in the latter case, many of the texts are written in Hindi by women, *Sharir Ki Jankari* is collectively written by a health initiative in conjunction with women from nearby villages. Instead of relying on the role of experts, science, and the medical discourse, *Sharir Ki Jankari* is based on women's experiences of bodies, sexualities, and most clearly, gender inequality. This accounts for its radically different perspective and content.

The preface establishes the purposes and the premises of the text: to explore the nature of societal perceptions toward women and women's status in society; and to explore aspects of the body connected to what is presented as reproductive power. By not separating the issue of women's bodies and reproductive roles from a societal perspective, the text raises a series of thought-provoking questions from women's perspectives at the outset: Why are there so many restrictions on me? Why am I beaten repeatedly? Am I dirty? Is menstrual blood dirty? Why was I deserted when children were not born? Is the birth of girls my fault? Why do I have to suppress my desires? Written on the premise of women's collective experiences, questions, issues, problems, and struggles, the text seeks to not only provide information but also to move the readers to plan strategies for social change. The preface concludes with the phrase, "is sangharsh ko age badhayen" (let's move the struggle forward).

Interspersed with drawings and figures with little flaps that invite the curious reader to explore women's and men's genitalia, the text begins by raising the context of girlhood from a personal but critical perspective—issues of the greater social burden on women without adequate opportunities, nourishment, and nurturance. Only then is the issue of menarche introduced as a matter of bodily changes alongside emergence into youth and maturity. Thus, the capacity to give birth is presented as having attendant social constraints and restrictions, and these are called into question. What is most compelling about the text is that it describes menstruation as the result of the maturing of the ovum without separating this description from the importance of charting the menstrual cycle, conducting self-examination of breasts, and promoting health through good nutrition. At the same time, discussions of changing female bodies are juxtaposed with issues of rape within marriage, violence toward women, and the essentialization of women to their reproductive capacities. To that extent, *Sharir Ki Jankari*, compared to similar FPAI/SECRT booklets, unsettles essentializations of womanhood to the sexed body and its ability to reproduce. In contrast to *Teenagers Ask, The Doctor Answers*, a question/answer format is used to inform and provoke social criticism.

More than anything else, *Sharir Ki Jankari* illustrates how knowledge for and by women about their bodies, genders, and sexualities can be used to effect rather than quell social change. Instead of becoming an instrument of social control and discipline of women's bodies, this text exemplifies the possibilities of subverting and disrupting normative discourses of sexed bodies, womanhood, and to a lesser extent, heterosexuality.

Conclusion

This chapter was aimed at tracing the hegemonic codes of gender and sexuality that are produced within the contemporary Indian nation-state. While the following chapters will examine how and to what effects these discourses shape and are reflected in middle-class women's narratives and queer narratives, in this chapter the focus was on the nature of hegemonic codes in state-sponsored sex education literatures. Though texts produced by FPAI and SECRT are relatively liberal, they mask inequalities of gender and sexuality that are perhaps inherent to these liberal discourses and strategies. This indicates the importance of unraveling the post-colonial nation-state as a more uneven, contradictory, multiplicitous source of power and regulation.

Considering the four categories of texts produced by FPAI and SECRT helps understand the ways in which hegemonic discourses on gender and sexuality are normalized and made to appear transparent. These texts also provide ample evidence for how discourses of gender and sexuality supported by the state are imbricated with notions of national cultural identity. Sexed bodies, normal and respectable sex—heterosexual and adhering to national cultural parameters—and aspects of gender identities are all generated and reinforced within this framework. Juxtaposing these materials against a text like *Sharir Ki Jankari* helps highlight the limitations of liberal codes and reveals strategies of social regulation and enforcement that organize these state-sponsored sex education literatures.

The texts produced by SECRT and FPAI also show how transnational discourses help shape and reinforce the ways sexed bodies, sexualities, and gender are normalized and regulated. More broadly, I refer to medical discourses and science, and more specifically, to the links between sexual intercourse and intimacy, and the psychologized and individualized prescriptions of marriage and motherhood. In the following chapters I consider the role and effects of these transnational discourses on women's narratives and queer narratives more carefully. Identifying and analyzing the effects of transnational cultural discourses not only helps establish the broader context for narratives on gender and sexuality, but also raises questions about possibilities of cultural homogenization. Put differently, exploring the effects of transnational discourses across these texts, women's narratives and queer narratives suggest that aspects of gender and sexuality and strategies of regulation may not be fully grasped by an analytic emphasis on the nation-state. Transnational cultural discourses necessitate the importance of considering globalizing cultural discourses and how they are reproduced in women's and queer narratives.

Chapter Three

Docile and Disruptive: Narratives on Menarche and Menstruation

I n her award-winning novel *Phaniyamma*, M. K. Indira narrates a woman's fate as *madi* (widow), and more compellingly, her ability to survive against cultural odds.[1] Spanning the period from the mid-nineteenth to the mid-twentieth century, the story documents not only how Phaniyamma is forced to embody tradition but also moved to question it. Although her child-husband dies within two months of their marriage when she is nine years old, what triggers the final passage into the life of a widow is the onset of menarche. Thereafter, Phaniyamma lives a celibate and frugal life; she is forced to shave her head to make herself unattractive, be restricted to one meal a day, and relentlessly serve members of her family. Eventually, Phaniyamma raises her voice against these oppressive "traditions" to intercede on behalf of another young and more defiant widow. Quietly, yet evocatively, Phaniyamma questions:

> Why should I say anything? I never even saw my husband's face. And this poor girl lived with her man for two years. Our times were different. Everything's changed now. Those who live in the city and are old enough to have grandchildren don't even feel the need to shave their heads. So what if a women has hair on her head? Does all the impurity rest there? What punishment do you want for a child who has just begun to open her eyes?[2]

Phaniyamma's story calls into question the tragic consequences of how the female body is used to demarcate and remove into the margins anything other than what counts as tradition. Since the conflation of categories of gender, sexuality, and cultural tradition is contested in the narrative, her story also defies making the female body the passive repository of discursive traditions. *Phaniyamma* explores the historically and politically charged nature of the female body and raises questions about how the body is produced and sustained.

Much of the literature of contemporary India analyzes the female body through categories of tradition, modernization, patriarchy, and male dominance. This is especially true of the feminist literature on menarche and menstruation. Rituals, taboos, and changing cultural beliefs under the onslaught of industrialization and modernization give form to the analyses of menarche and menstruation. But, these analyses do not reveal how the sexed or female body is produced and regulated, and how this shapes what women recount as experience. To that extent, this literature does not address the nature of discourses on the female body and womanhood. As a point of departure, in this chapter I focus on women's narratives on menarche and early menstruation in an attempt to understand how the female body is reinforced as reality and deployed as an instrument for the regulation of womanhood. Menarche and mestruation represent especially sensitive points at which sex serves to elicit the consent of women to their social regulation. In their narratives I am especially interested in the framework through which women recount experiences of menarche and menstruation and what this framework suggests about the ways in which female bodies and womanhood are normalized and regulated. Therefore, I also highlight a central tension underlying the class- and gender-based regulation of the body: the contradictions between the social significance of middle-class women's bodies and the premise of the body as a private, personal domain of experience.

Nowhere are the contradictions of the private, individual nature of the female body more evident than at the onset of menstruation in the life of a young girl. In any cultural context, a "natural" event such as monthly bleeding has a particular significance and is coded to include and exclude a range of meanings. In contemporary India, menarche and menstruation signify the emergent gender and sexual status of the hitherto presexual and prepubertal girl. Culturally, menarche represents a turning point in the life of the young girl; Leela Dube argues that menarche introduces dramatic changes.[3] So thoroughly is the perception of menstruation shaped by cultural knowledges and practices that it is impossible to argue menstruation is a "natural" event. This is not to suggest that at its core menstruation is merely a "natural" event with varying cultural overlays across time and space. Rather, I take the approach that menstruation is the effect of prevailing discourses; menstruation, like "the female body," is not prediscursive. On the contrary, where menstruation is presented as a personalized and individualized domain of experience, it calls for a healthy dose of feminist skepticism.

Ironically, in middle-class women's narratives on the onset and continuation of menstruation, what is immediately notable is the individual nature of the experiences. Instead of descriptions of rituals and social events that should mark menarche, considering its social significance, more specific accounts dominate the narratives of the middle-class women in this study.[4] The emphasis is on the particulars of when it first happened, what it has been like since, and what it means in their lives. At the same time, the women describe increased familial concern toward them since menarche. The seeming chasm between the individualized nature of the experience recounted by women and the social significance of menarche and menstruation calls into question strategies of regulating female bodies in contemporary post-colonial India. These strategies not only prescribe class-based notions of womanhood and female sexuality but heighten middle-class women's recounted experiences of menarche and menstruation.

These attempts to regulate female bodies are incorporated into everyday bodily practices and experiences—what Susan Bordo calls the "direct grip" of culture on the body.[5] Bordo suggests that the bodily lessons we learn through routine and habitual activity are far more effective politically than explicit instructions on appropriate behavior. The emphasis on the mundane also calls into question the strategies of self-surveillance and self-monitoring that are acutely necessary to this "direct grip" on the female body. Viewed as part of the everyday strategies of power in making docile bodies—subjecting, using, transforming, and improving bodies,[6] narratives of menstruation problematize precisely what it means to be a normal young girl in the cultural context and women's complicity in their normalization/regulation.

What is defined as normal marks the predicates for knowing and experiencing the body so that middle-class women in this study are both the objects and subjects of knowledges of their bodies, of menarche and menstruation. As Foucault suggests, power produces effects at the level of knowledge; rather than preventing it, power produces knowledge. Power makes a physiological, organic knowledge of the body possible, according to Foucault; whether pleasurable or painful, no bodily experience is exempt from the strategies of power. In effect, as Bordo succinctly captures it, "Viewed historically, the discipline and normalization of the female body—perhaps the only gender oppression that exercises itself, although to different degrees and in different forms, across age, race, class, and sexual orientation—has to be acknowledged as an amazingly durable and flexible strategy of social control."[7]

Whether prevailing strategies of social control are entirely successful is to be determined. More clear is how particular forms of knowledge are one means through which such control is exercised. In response to the traumatic experiences that are reported of young girls starting to menstruate, scientific explanations are presented as the alternatives to alleviate anxieties and provide adequate information. But the scientific perspective can potentially normalize girls' experiences of the onset of menstruation only by providing a framework within which to define experience. As Emily Martin compellingly suggests in *The Woman in the Body*, the facts in medical science accounts of menstruation may only be cultural metaphors grounded in social hierarchies of gender, class, and race.[8] Therefore, menarche and menstruation emerge as central mechanisms for regulating female bodies through definitions of normality while obscuring underlying social inequities and mechanisms of social control.

But, the narratives on menarche and menstruation reveal the fault lines of power/knowledge. If menarche and menstruation indeed write culturally significant scripts of body, gender, and sexuality for women, then the question is how do women negotiate these meanings and events. Middle-class women may learn important lessons about normative aspects of gender and sexuality with the onset of menstruation but that does not mean that they do not contest these received meanings. Not only do women internalize and resist prevailing discourses of menarche and menstruation that shape the seeming reality of the female body, they also disrupt them.

Middle-class women's narratives on menarche and menstruation are richly textured and illuminating. Women speak colorfully, painfully, and at length about their memories of their first blood. They describe related life changes and the role that menstruation has played in their lives since. By listening to the narratives on their experiences and responses to the first sight of blood, it is possible to understand how sexed bodies are shaped and regulated through these seemingly commonplace events in women's lives. Contrary to available feminist literature, these women's narratives on menarche and menstruation tell us much about the meaning of the declining discourse of pollution and menstrual taboos. The narratives help understand not only the trauma and extensive discomfort that is consistently recounted but also the larger framework that shapes their language and experiences. Middle-class women's language on menstruation redirects attention to how transnational cultural and economic codes affect the regulation of female bodies through the processes of normalization and commoditization. Thus, it demystifies putative notions of "Indian" or "Third World" women and their bodies to highlight the heightened significance of class and gender in a transnational context.

The Onset of Menarche and Paradoxes of Embodiment

Middle-class women vividly narrate their experiences of the onset of menarche. What is most striking in their accounts is the sense of shock and anxiety at the first sight of menstrual blood.[9] Through their descriptions, women invoke troubling images of young girls encountering their first blood. In terms of stunned horror and fear, they describe their reactions when they first see blood on their panties, realize that they have stained their clothes, or see bloodstains on a school bench. So, in the words of Chandni, a 24-year-old married woman,

> I just screamed one thing, "My *Masi* [mother's sister] will scold me, my *Masi* will scold me." I didn't know anything about it. The thing was that the first 2–3 days I bled very heavily. I was at my grandmother's, my cousins had come down, my Mom was here at our home and I was at Peddar Road. I didn't have the guts to tell my Masi. I was very scared, I was wondering whether I had got hurt somewhere. Although my mother had told me, it didn't strike me. Then I started getting terrible pain in my stomach. I didn't keep any padding or anything. I don't know how I managed to pass [those days]. On the third day I told my Masi as I was getting terrible stomach pains. She guessed immediately, I don't know how. Then she took me inside the room and showed me how to use a sanitary pad. The next day she sent me home with a note. After that my Mummy took over. It was not very traumatic except for the first two days.

Twenty-two-year-old Sheila's words also resonate with this sense of fear but are spoken more matter-of-factly. She says,

> My mother had gone out somewhere. I was at my granny's house, and I was very scared what's happening to me. I didn't know about that. I got very scared that something is wrong with me. The first month I didn't tell her. The second month I told her let's go consult the doctor. I told her this is happening. I thought it was a real headache. I was very happy that I didn't get it when I was expecting [her daughter]. Big headache every month. First two days there is a lot of pain and giddiness.

Similar descriptions of trauma or anxiety prevail across the narratives. In some cases, menarche triggered a kind of paralysis. For example, Babita, who is 38 years old, says that she stayed in bed for three days. In another case, Seema, a lively 21-year-old, says that over the few months after her first menses, she quietened down considerably. But to the extent that there cannot be any inherent responses to first menses, not shock, or for that matter, delight, there is nothing self-evident about menstrual blood; these responses require explanation. Analyzing theories of menstrual symbolism, Thomas Buckley and Alma Gottlieb emphasize the specificity of menstrual blood—that unlike other forms of bloodshed, menstrual blood is unique for it does not issue randomly or accidentally, and it flows uncontrollably from a single source.[10] Needless to say, middle-class women's disturbing descriptions of menarche not only call into question assumptions that there is indeed anything natural about these events, but also the conditions under which shock and fear are women's predominant responses at menarche.[11]

In their narratives on the onset of menarche, women seem to "instinctively" react to the social significance of first menstrual blood. There appears little doubt that menarche represents a critical marker of the female body. Anthropological feminist literature documents the social significance of menarche as a girl's social transition into emergent womanhood and sexual maturity. Veena Das argues that the menarche heralds a radical change in the orientation to the female body and, based on her fieldwork among Punjabis in Northern India, she notes that menarche represents a shift from a pre-pubertal, ambiguous gender status to a stage where gender socialization is both unambiguous and central.[12] Das and Dube both note how the onset of menstruation heralds a changing gender status for girls and their emergent sexuality that prepares them for motherhood. In their narratives these middle-class women describe what may be visceral reactions to the broader social significance of their bodies, and to imminent changes in terms of their sexualities and gendered identities.

A marked tension between women's narratives on menarche and the anthropological literature appears in the role of rituals. With the exception of Das's fieldwork among urban Punjabis, anthropological literature has consistently emphasized the presence and meaning of ritual ceremonies associated with menarche. These rituals that announce the changing gender and sexual status of girls appear to serve two functions: to protect the young girl but also to contain the threat posed by her sexual maturity. For example, Das argues that in the cases of groups such as the Coorgs, the Nayars, the Newars, and the Brahmins of Tamil Nadu, the rituals acknowledge the woman as a concrete sexual being.[13] In her work Catherine Thompson supports the argument that ritual elaborations of menarche are likely to occur where the status of the physically mature, unmarried girl presents a threat to the caste and line.[14] On the contrary, women's narratives do not suggest the prevalence of ritual ceremonies of menarche neither as means of announcing and celebrating the changing gender and sexual status, nor as means of controlling the threat of the sexually mature young girl. Women's narratives, as evident above, emphasize the trauma and anxiety of menarche.

Only Radhika, of the 52 women asked about menarche and menstruation, says that her first menses was ritually announced. She describes,

> Mummy had not told me anything. I knew through my friends. The day I got it I was so scared. My panty was full of blood. It was early in the morning when I went to the bathroom. I shouted from there. I showed it to my elder sister, and then my Mummy came. The first day was horrible, I could not walk properly. We make sweet pohas and distribute them on that day, it's a celebration. Everybody comes to know, it's embarrassing. Everyone smiles and says, "Oh, you've become a big girl." They start treating you differently.

As the exception to the others, Radhika's narrative raises questions about the links between the absence of rituals and the trauma and discomfort of menarche. As Das notes for the cases where menarche is not ritually announced, there is no acknowledgment at the level of the collective group. Instead, maintaining the practices associated with menstruation and learning new and appropriate rules of behavior are the responsibility of the individual woman, according to Das. Put bluntly, then, not only is first blood laden with cultural meanings and limitations of womanhood and deeply ambivalent notions of female sexuality, but in the narratives of these women the transition to maturity is the responsibility of the individual woman and not the collective. It is this disjuncture between the socially marked but individually experienced female body that shapes women's narratives of shock and trauma.

In the narratives of these middle-class women, the emphasis is on the realm of the individual, not on ritual or the collective. Knowledge of the event of menarche is limited to the parents, sisters, friends, and a few immediate relatives—such as the *Masi* in Chandni's case. More noticeably, the women seem self-aware of the social ramifications of the onset of menarche. In her interview, Seema makes the connection between a crystallizing consciousness of her girlhood and the onset of menstruation. She says that there was an indescribable feeling associated with menarche that made her realize that she was changing into a woman. Although Seema says that this realization left her feeling confused, Rati suggests that getting her period made her feel not only self-conscious but, as a result of the more visible bodily changes, quite beautiful. Other women elaborate on the more negative connotations of this connection. Despite the fact that she does not describe unusual menstrual discomfort, Neha, a 22-year-old who has been married between two and three years, says in no uncertain terms that "getting your chums" is one of the negative aspects of being a woman. Equally telling is the women's emphasis on the specifics, the personal, the more intricate details of feelings, relationships, restrictions, emotions, and physical changes as they describe the onset of menstruation. Not only are individual women at the center of their scripts on menarche but they appear to assume the responsibility for the burden of the event.

Within its sociocultural connotations, menarche is located by the middle-class women as a matter of the individual and the personal. Menarche may well be the sociocultural turning point in the life cycles of women, but through it these middle-class women quickly assume responsibility for their bodies. Menarche augurs deeply conflicted notions of womanhood and sexuality. In their narratives, menarche heralds possibilities but also limitations. It triggers shifting mechanisms of social control in the lives of young girls that rely on fear, anxiety, and self-discipline. Put differently, these women narrate menarche at the intersection of a series of deep-seated cultural contradictions. Menarche marks a social transition into culturally prescribed notions of womanhood and female sexuality, yet women respond in a profoundly individualized capacity. Arguably, the trauma, the fear, and the anxiety at the onset of menarche are generated out of these contradictions. They assume that they have somehow brought this affliction upon themselves. It becomes their problem.

Where an event like menarche is socially significant but individually centered, feelings of guilt and self-blame compound the fear and anxiety at the first sight of blood. Speaking to this contradiction, Bella, a 27-year-old woman, says in Hindi,

> I felt strange, really bad. I felt that I had done something wrong, that if I told my mother she would scold me. I thought that I had hurt myself. I didn't know anything. I was about 13 or 14 years old. I felt really bad, and I just went off to school. When I returned and the menses were still happening, I told her with trepidation. She said that all girls get them. It felt like an illness, I did not understand. It was as if there should be a cure for this, and I should be able to get rid of it.

Seeing their first menstrual blood, they appear certain that they are responsible for the affliction; somehow they did something wrong or in some way hurt themselves. Sujata, a 29-year-old Sindhi woman, says her mother had not told her anything about menarche. And even though representatives of Carefree products had visited her school a few days earlier, she did not quite understand the concept. So when Sujata first encountered the sight of blood in the bathroom, she screamed, "I've got hurt, I've got hurt," and despite her mother's attempts to calm her, she cried inconsolably. In the case of other women, this sense of personal guilt or wrongdoing often makes women reluctant to tell others, including mothers.

Recall Chandni's reluctance to tell her *Masi* or Sheila's attempt to conceal what happened to her until she thinks it is an illness that needs medical attention. Nargis, a 30-year-old divorced woman, says that she was in the care of some family friends when she got her period. She reports not feeling good, having cramps and general discomfort. She says,

> I had some mixed feelings. I got my period when my parents were not there. I was not aware what was to be done next. Mummy told someone to look after me while they were out. I didn't feel like telling her because I did not know what to tell her, and I was literally scared and waiting for my parents to return. The number of underwears I washed must have been five or six because nobody was prepared that I would get it there.

In her narrative, Nargis describes the grip of silence on two accounts: of fear and of not being able to characterize or describe the experience. Girls bide their time in hopes that the problem will go away. When it does not, it becomes unbearable, or it recurs, and they are likely to break their silence and confide the event.

Though lack of knowledge and preparation for the onset of menarche aggravated these women's anxieties as girls, according to their narratives, prior information does not necessarily forestall these responses. As many as 25 (48 percent) of the 52 women did not know about menarche ahead of time. They were caught unawares and clearly this made menarche more traumatic for them. More frequently, information is inadequate. Eleven (21 percent) women were told by their mothers, and in one case both parents were involved, whereas others had some information through sisters, friends, cousins, or through school; having some information still did not prevent the trauma and anxiety. Of these, only four (8 percent) women suggest that menarche was relatively uneventful. As Nargis says, she knew about it vaguely but not what to do when she got her period. In the case of Kavita, a 35-year-old Punjabi woman, her cousin had talked to her about menarche a few months before but that only made her more anxious. She continually checked to see if there was any blood. The slightest sense of stickiness would make her worry, and she was somewhat relieved that it happened early one morning when she was preparing to go to school. Clearly, there is a chasm between knowledge and experience.

In the narratives, after the initial shock of menarche, what is striking is how embarrassment mars women's experiences of menarche and early menstruation as young girls. Their emphasis on embarrassment suggests that menarche caused them to be self-conscious and distressed. The discomfort of unfamiliar bodily fluid, the reported messiness, and kin members becoming aware of the event, make it an embarrassing and unpleasant experience in the narratives of women in the study. As Prakiti, a 27-year-old, said, "Everything about it is embarrassing." Seema describes how the initial discomfort of menarche was worsened by her father knowing about it.

> My mom did not explain anything to me. My sister told me. She told my mother that she had. The day I got it I felt "yuck," "Oh God, what's happening." Someone explaining is different from it actually happening. When I got it she [sister] showed me everything. To get back at me she told my father. I felt like drowning. Today it's OK my father knows I am not well, but that day it was different. He just smiled. I could not face him for a few hours. I was so embarrassed. My Mom told me he knows. Indian families saying something like that is a very big deal, so it was very embarrassing for me. Now it's cool.

The embarrassment is triggered by others, such as fathers, brothers, uncles, and aunts knowing about the event. It appears to be related less to the uncontrollable flow of menstrual blood than what might have been a private event being brought to light. Therefore, Radhika is first horrified at the sight of blood and then mortified when the event is announced within her kin group. Piya, a 28-year-old, describes being so embarrassed to tell her older sister about her first menses that she expressed it in a note and sent it to her sister in the adjoining room. Erica, a Catholic woman of the same age, describes her profound sense of embarrassment when her mother gave her a brown paper bag filled with pads saying "You may need them" as she dropped her off at the boarding school.

Erica is also one of the women who described getting their first menses relatively early. Those women who suggest that they were the first among their peers to experience menarche describe feeling like the odd ones or feeling embarrassed among the peer group. As a result of getting her first menses rather early, Erica felt alienated from her friends and was teased by them. In her case, the embarrassment and alienation were compounded by the development of her breasts. She suggests that she was "enormous" at the time. For Mitali, an attractive and intense woman of 22 years, the alienation was alleviated only when she realized that she was not the only one to experience menarche and menstruation. Until then, she suggests that the experience was difficult and isolating.

> I got it very early, around ten and a half. The doctor said that because it was early it would last even eight or nine days. I felt I was guilty of doing something at school. It was very difficult. I would take a holiday and sit at home. But then I realized that I was not the only one. In the sixth standard [grade] we had a sex education class where everybody got close, and I realized other girls were getting them also. I got over the guilt.

In other cases, women who start their first menses relatively early sometimes also attempt to gain leverage among their peers. Venita describes not only being discomfited by her first menses at the age of nine and a half but then quickly using it to assert her grown-up status in school. In the accounts of women who narrate getting their first period relatively later than their peers, the discomfort may be mixed with a sense of relief. So, even as Piya says that she was too embarrassed to "face her sister," she was also relieved because she was among the last of her peers to start menstruating. She says that she feared otherwise becoming a *hijra* [hermaphrodite]. Jennifer, a 29-year-old, also describes her sense of relief that finally she was growing up but it was offset by the teasing from her brother and the feeling of being left out by the boys she used to play with. In the narratives, feelings of embarrassment, self-consciousness, relief, and isolation are inextricably intertwined.

Such descriptions of menarche and early menstruation are further characterized by a persistent fear of staining clothes or leaving telltale signs of menses. When transgressions do occur, they are described in terms such as "very embarrassing," "highly embarrassing," or "horrible." In her account, Piya describes several such experiences.

> I was in a co-ed school. We sat on a bench of two—one boy and one girl. It was very embarrassing. Sometimes I would get up and even the bench would be stained. So I couldn't get up until the recess period when the boys were out and I could do something about it. Teachers are not very understanding. You can be begging to go to the loo [bathroom] when you need to change, and if they are strict, they won't let you. You are in a bad shape, and you can't change. You are not open with the teacher or others that you can say that you want to change, at least not in India. I don't know about places outside. I feel when teachers are female they can sense these things. They should be more understanding, and they should let you go.

For Jaya, that she got her first menses was less the issue than the fact that she got it when she was in class. At the end of her class, her teacher brought it to her attention. In Sheetal's case, even though she says she knew about it, menarche was a traumatic event. Due to the relatively recent death of a sibling, at first sight she feared that it was cancer. Yet, in her narrative she both emphasizes and reiterates the embarrassing aspect of attending a coeducational school and being in a constant state of anxiety that she would stain her uniform.

Challenging Liberal Discourses

Is it not profoundly unsettling that an event that may be described as so "natural" and socially significant is effecting such havoc in women's narratives? Not only are these narratives invoking the contradiction of socially significant bodily changes that are the responsibility of individual women, but they are doubly vitiated. Just as these middle-class women appear to accept inexorability of menarche as a marker of the female body, it is clear that menarche is also a matter of the personal and individualized body. But, precisely as they assume its responsibility, menarche threatens to spill beyond the individualized boundaries of the female body. Women describe feeling more self-conscious and embarrassed as the event of menarche comes to the attention of others. Any sense of individual control is easily undermined. That fathers, brothers, sisters, friends, and other relatives know about the event serves to contradict the notion of menstruation as private or entirely personal. Women also express great anxiety about staining their clothes or somehow bringing their menses to the attention of others. In their narratives, they indicate the manner in which they learn to vigilantly manage and control the flow of menstrual blood so that it remains within the realm of the private, individual body. In effect, their narratives express the centrality of self-regulation and self-discipline to experiences of menarche and early menses. As reflected in their narratives, these women learn important lessons about bearing the responsibility for bodies that are not quite their own.

Against the grain of these narratives, "educating" women about menarche and menstruation at best seems inadequate, and at worst compounds the problem. For example, the author of the text *Problems of Adolescent Sexuality* expresses the importance of guiding girls encountering puberty. She concurs that the first sight of menstrual bleeding creates fear, even among girls who are prepared for it. The ignorance, lack of guidance, superstitious talk, and fear of incurable diseases cause the anxiety and fear, according to the author. She emphasizes that girls from "orthodox homes" that observe menstrual seclusion suffer from shame and embarrassment. Instead, she recommends,

> Menstrual hygiene, calm assurance, simple scientific explanations linking the event to the joy of growing up into womanhood, would counteract the needless suffering of thousands of girls who grow up in an environment of ignorance and superstition in regard to this normal process of development.[15]

On the one hand, the promise of hygiene, calm assurance, and simple scientific explanations is inadequate given the pervasiveness of the anxiety and embarrassment. On the other hand, considering the more profound structural contradictions visible in women's narratives, it does not help to suggest that the resolution lies in scientific knowledge. It is not clear how "simple scientific explanations" will alleviate the dramatic changes in the lives of women. Surely they cannot address the threats that burgeoning female sexuality might pose to its cultural environment. Such measures are probably not only relatively ineffective but will reinforce the structural contradictions by refusing to challenge them.

Similarly, in the text *Teenagers Ask, The Doctor Answers*, a detailed "medical" explanation of menstruation is expected to move the reader from ignorance to knowledge. The question/answer reads as follows:

> What is menstruation?
>
> Menstruation occurs monthly in a girl or woman in the child-bearing age. It is also referred to as having "periods." About two weeks before a girl menstruates, an egg cell matures inside her in one of the ovaries. The egg travels through an internal tube (fallopian tube) to the womb or uterus. Under the influence of special sex hormones, the internal lining of the uterus becomes velvety in appearance due to increase in blood vessels and tissue.
>
> If the woman has had intercourse and the ovum or egg has been fertilized in the tube by the male sperm, the fertilized egg moves into the tube where it is nourished by the rich tissues of the uterus. If not, the lining of the uterus is not needed and is gradually released during menstruation which lasts from four to six days.
>
> During this period some girls feel low, unstable and moody. This is due to changes in body chemistry. With the onset of the menstrual flow, the tension wears off. Menstruation is proof that you are perfectly normal and healthy.[16]

But, as Martin astutely notes, there is nothing innocent about the medicalization of menstruation.[17] She suggests that medical accounts reflect and reinforce the cultural fragmentation of female bodies. According to Martin, by writing scripts of menstruation that signal hierarchy, failure of the authority structure of the body, failed production, deterioration, and breakdown, medical understandings cannot connote knowledge over ignorance. The above account normalizes menstruation but posits it as a failure of fertilization. Within this medical-scientific framework a new discourse of menstruation is created; fertilization of the egg as a result of intercourse is normalized. Put differently, biology *is* rendered destiny. If this medical discourse of menstruation may be ineffective in alleviating women's anxieties about menstruation, what is equally perturbing is how it displaces discourses of menstruation pollution and menstrual taboos and shapes the narratives of these middle-class urban women in other ways.

Displacing the Discourse of Menstrual Pollution and Menstrual Taboos

Besides the emphasis on ritual announcements of menarche, anthropological literature in various cultural contexts has emphasized the significance of menstrual pollution and the prevalence of taboos. This literature is inadequate at best and misleading at worst. Available literature on menstruation confirms prevalent beliefs of menstrual pollution in India as well. Scholars appear to concur that, underlying the range of menstrual practices and taboos, menstruation is seen as a source of a pollution, and the menstruating woman is seen as being in a state of pollution. Das suggests that in communities which practice initiation rituals, the onset of menstruation marks an oscillation between states of pollution and purity throughout the reproductive life of a woman. On the basis on her fieldwork in a village in south-central India, Vanaja Dhruvarajan elaborates on the beliefs that females are more susceptible to pollution particularly through the menstrual period.[18] Thompson suggests that women in the Malwa village in Central India, when in a state of pollution, are perceived to be in danger but also a source of danger to others and, therefore, a source of threat.

Anthropological descriptions document and establish the range of menstrual restrictions and taboos that are linked to notions of menstrual and female pollution. Menstrual restrictions and taboos ranging from ritual seclusion, restriction of daily activities such as cooking and cleaning, playing, jumping, and sexual activity to personal taboos such as not bathing and washing one's hair, are consistently described and emphasized in the literature. It is also suggested that women may be prevented from entering certain spaces such as the kitchen or the place of worship. Furthermore, Thompson suggests that menstruating women are required to curtail their contact with men and to a lesser extent with other women, particularly premenstrual girls. In their cross-cultural study of 14 sociocultural groups across 10 countries, Robert Snowden and Barbara Christian note that Hindu women in India are far more likely than women in other research sites and countries, even those who see menstruation as polluting, to follow related menstrual restrictions—such as water collection, washing the family clothes, and cooking.[19] But, when considered against the narratives of middle-class women, it is less clear what the relative absence of these taboos and manifestations of pollution possibly mean.

Though the widespread prevalence of menstrual taboos is unambiguously established in anthropological literature, the meanings of these restrictions are much debated. In the literature, these taboos are viewed variously, as expressing perceptions of menstrual pollution, containment of women's power, and female inferiority. In her analysis of the meaning of menstrual taboos among Hindu castes, Jocelyn Krygier theorizes that these ritual restrictions express and secure gender inequality.[20] Dhruvarajan further supports the analysis that ritual menstrual restrictions such as seclusion reinforce the premise of female inferiority. Although Thompson reads the association of women with pollution more ambiguously, she concurs that in traditional Hindu village societies, prevalent belief systems of female pollution encourage women to subordinate their interests to male interests. Any threat posed by women's power to pollute and potentially disrupt the status quo is contained by menstrual taboos, according to Thompson. If in the context of deep-seated inequalities of gender, caste, and class, the social restrictions of menstruation may be correctly seen as expressing the subordination of women, then the ramifications of the lack of such restrictions in middle-class women's lives are unclear. Put differently, what does the absence of ritual expressions of menstrual pollution and taboos in middle-class women's narratives mean, and what does this say about gender, class, and caste parities?

Nowhere does this perplexing problem become more obvious than in the theoretical framework developed by the well-known anthropologist Mary Douglas, which is central to the above anthropological interpretations of menstrual taboos. In her well-cited work *Purity and Danger*, Douglas argues that menstrual taboos based on the concept of pollution exist because of the perception of pollutants as anomalous to the social order, an analysis that Buckley and Gottlieb suggest is far too idealistic and simplistic.[21] Critical of her fundamental assumptions, they also counter that neither are anomalies culturally universal nor are women the passive recipients of male-created cultures. Perhaps the more intriguing aspect of Douglas's argument is that the most elaborate theories of pollution exist where there are ambiguities and contradictions in social systems. In social systems characterized by directly enforced male dominance, theories of sex pollution are redundant; where it is contradicted by the rights of women, such as protection by virtue of being the "weaker sex," then the concept of sex pollution will flourish, according to Douglas. Citing Yalman's work on the Malabar castes in southern India, Douglas suggests that women's purity is both gateway of entry to caste status and proof of caste membership. Women's sexual purity is power and threat. Therefore, Douglas suggests, elaborate notions of pollution are necessitated.

For the middle-class women in this study, is the social system of male dominance so sufficiently elaborated that the prevalence of menstrual taboos are the exception rather than the rule? Probably not. At best, menstrual restrictions appear to be relatively insignificant. Only four women describe any experience with ritual menstrual restrictions. From the perspective of these women, anthropological theories on ritual beliefs of menstrual pollution and taboos are inadequate. This literature assumes the collective as the enforcer and mediator of female bodies. Although Das does not support these assumptions, she does not address the meanings of these shifts in control of women's bodies from the collective to within the family. I argue that the "direct grip" is enforced through individual women and not through the collective. This form of control and discipline does not rely on notions of female inferiority; rather, it resorts to notions of female difference.

The descriptions of the four women who have experience with ritual taboos are illuminating for their infrequency and peculiarities. Meenakshi, who is Marwari by ethnicity, says she had to observe menstrual taboos like sleeping and eating separately with the onset of menarche. Since her wedding, with the exception of entering the kitchen, none of the taboos apply. Indeed, she says dismissively in Hindi, "Nobody comes to know." Ketaki, who is also Marwari, elaborates on the difficulty of maintaining these ritual taboos and also how she negotiates them.

> In this house there were restrictions for three years. My mom's house, no restrictions. You can have restrictions when someone else is living with you to do the work. After marriage, I was not allowed to enter the kitchen, I had to sit in my room. I was not allowed to touch the vessels, my mother-in-law used to give me food in my room. Gradually it started changing. After my sister-in-law moved, I started going into the kitchen. Today is my first day [period], but who will do [the work] now? My mother-in-law is not fond of cooking. For her sake maybe she has allowed me to go. I used to feel very ashamed and shy; everyone would know what was wrong. I think it is wrong, these restrictions. I used to feel so ashamed, shy. I feel like I am lowering myself. Then, I started feeling it's normal: Their wives are also having this problem. We have to do puja [ritual prayer] every day, and now I don't do puja. I tell my father-in-law, "I can't do [the puja.] You do [it]."

To Ketaki and others who have some experience with menstrual restrictions, the restrictions do not appear to be seen as ways of minimizing their workload or providing some kind of respite from routine household responsibilities. On the contrary, Ketaki suggests that menstrual restrictions are impractical and invasive. They represent a breach of privacy. Clearly, it took Ketaki a while to come to terms with the ramifications of not being able to do puja in her conjugal family. Moreover, because Ketaki resists the idea that menstrual taboos represent her pollutedness, she is not unwilling to cast the daily responsibilities of ritual worship through the menstrual cycle.

The narratives of the other three women who have experience with menstrual restrictions also take exception to them. Two of the women say that they adhered to menstrual restrictions but only in the past. For Nargis, who is Parsi, and Nipun, a 30-year-old Tamilian Iyengar woman, the restrictions do not apply anymore. Nargis was exposed to these restrictions for the nine months that she was married. Heatedly, she challenges both the restrictions and her mother-in-law's role in enforcing them. She says,

> The worst was if I got my periods, they believed in all that. "Don't touch this, don't touch that, don't touch the gas [burner]." I mean it was like too much! My mother-in-law said, "Don't touch your cupboard, if you want something, I will remove it for you." If I want a panty, or a pad, or anything, how could I tell my mother-in-law to remove it? It is something personal, I wouldn't like anybody to do that.

Nipun says after menarche she was forced by her grandmother to sleep and eat separately the duration of her period. But she rebelled quickly, and eventually they compromised on Nipun not participating in religious worship or festivals. She also clearly establishes that she does not follow these restrictions anymore.

This is not to suggest that the women in this study do not link menstruation with "pollution." They recurrently use words such as dirty, unclean, and messy, and in a few cases use them when citing menstruation as reasons for not participating in religious worship. Of the 52 middle-class women asked, seven observe the sole taboo of abstaining from ritual worship. Bindu, an expressive 23-year-old, stresses that her mother is "really strict" about this taboo and since she feels unclean at that time, she does not mind adhering to this restriction. Three women, who ethnically identify as Sindhis, also skeptically describe restrictions such as not wearing the color red, and not watering the *Tulsi* plant. Only one Punjabi woman mentioned being told not to consume milk and milk products. She was not sure of the reasons and did not follow this rule.

These narratives on the infrequency of menstrual taboos and ritual notions of menstrual pollution redirect attention to the more individualized mechanisms through which the female body is marked and strategies of control that rely on self-surveillance. On the other hand, studies that document declining menstrual taboos and restrictions but explain the changes through constructs of westernization and urbanization are equally misleading as the anthropological literature noted above. For example, in a 1947 study of 50 Western-educated elite Hindu women between the ages of 20 and 25, Rama Mehta reports that none of them observed menstrual restrictions in their own homes with the exception of not entering the kitchen or the room for worship.[22] However, Mehta imputes the erosion of menstrual taboos to the influences of westernization. In their cross-cultural analysis of menstruation, Snowden and Christian suggest that we account for the decline of the so-called traditional beliefs around menstruation due to factors of urbanization and education.

But these discourses of urbanization, westernization, or education are inadequate to explain the changes in menstrual practices. Indeed, it would be misleading to view the changes described by middle-class women as erosions of "traditional" menstrual taboos. Instead, the menstrual narratives of women in this study have been shaped by a qualitatively different perception of menstruation. The menstrual taboos are not about ritual forms of purity and pollution. Menstruation is construed as an individualized, privatized domain of experience and concern. Since menstruation is specific to women, notions of female inferiority are redundant. Menstruation's concomitant sequelae—discomfort, perceptions of dirtiness, messiness—are not residuals of ritual pollution or overt indexes of female inferiority and potential threat. Rather, they are aspects of a fundamentally different, transnational discourse.

The Language of Menarche and Menstruation: Clean but Painful Bodies

Read closely, the language these middle-class women use in their narratives links menstruation with personal rather than ritual impurity, with individual rather than social pollution. The emphasis is on what the perceived dirtiness and messiness of menstrual blood does to their experiences of their bodies. Menstrual blood flow is described as something that is happening to them, an alien phenomenon, rather than an organic part of their bodily experience. Yet, precisely because menstrual blood represents an uncontrollable function of the body, especially in their narratives on early menses, they struggle to gain control over it.

Perhaps more than anything else, the importance of concealing and containing menarche and early menstruation marks women's attempts at gaining control over the experience. Chandni indicates how her discomfort with early menstruation eased only after she learned to manage it or, put differently, control it. She clearly articulates the process,

> I had to condition my mind to be comfortable with it. I was very uncomfortable the first three years, very uncomfortable. I had this phobia that I would stain my dress. First three years were terrible, every time that I would get them I would start crying, "I don't want them, I don't want them." But then I learned, I took it upon myself to have proper care, poise. If I was too uncomfortable, I would change my napkin very often, carry a spare, and slowly and gradually I realized that people are not looking at me. When I get my period now nobody in the house comes to know also.

Not only is the fear of revealing traces of menstruation striking in Chandni's narrative, but so is the significance of taking "proper care" and having "poise." This language connotes the concept of self-management. Elaborating on it, Meenakshi emphasizes the importance of "managing" herself so that her brothers would not know but also suggests the treacherous nature of this self-control; she adds that "there was never any mental security." The anxiety related to early menses is managed in various ways, but it can only be temporarily contained, never erased. It drives the constant surveillance of themselves and their menstruating bodies.

Overlapping the language of control and concealment is the emphasis on personal hygiene. In their narratives, women appear preoccupied with observing rules of personal cleanliness and making sure that they manage the menstrual blood and not stain their clothes or other items. What is striking is the way consumer products, not coincidentally labeled *sanitary* products, become central in maintaining personal hygiene. Sanitary products, such as tampons and pads, are not only integral to managing menstrual blood but also consistently held to be improvements over the past—represented by cloth and cotton. The social class of the women in this study, and their consequent ability to purchase these relatively expensive commodities, is entirely relevant. Bindu is able to qualify her narrative about women being unclean and in a weakened state while menstruating with the notion that "Now we are dealing with it in a cleaner way—earlier they were using the cloth." Babita's horror at the heavy flow of menstrual blood through early menstruation was reinforced by having to use "dirty cloth." Elaborating on the importance of sanitary products to personal hygiene, Jennifer says that menstruating was "horrible" until she stated using tampons. In her account she suggests that it is because of its messiness that she dislikes having sexual intercourse while menstruating. Indira, a 34-year-old woman, also agrees that sanitary products help alleviate the anxiety of using cotton. Arguably, notions of personal hygiene enabled through the consumption of sanitary products are ways to protect the boundaries of menstruating bodies.

Thus a personalized language of dirtiness, messiness, and embarrassment offset by emphasis on concealment, control, and hygiene characterizes the discourse of menstruation from the viewpoint of middle-class women in this study. This discourse is markedly different from that of ritual pollution and menstrual taboos. Both discourses may signify attempts at social regulation of female bodies, but in profoundly different ways. Unlike the discourse of ritual pollution and menstrual taboos, the discourse of personal pollution and cleanliness relies heavily on middle-class, urban women's internalization of the responsibility for menarche and menstruation, on self-regulation and self-surveillance. The state of ritual uncleanliness is qualitatively different from the state of personal uncleanliness; arguably, it is supported by a symbolic order that is decreed in religious texts and practiced customarily. Far more insidious, the individualization of menstruation not only infuses women's narratives, but it is legitimated on the premises of science and medicine. Ironically, these nuances of menstruation are captured in a question/answer of the same text that seeks to better inform women about menstruation, to dispel the myths of menstruation.

In *Teenagers Ask, The Doctor Answers* the question/answer reads,

> *Question:* My elderly aunt tells me not to take a bath during my periods and to abstain from all house-work. What hygiene do you recommend?
>
> *Answer:* For all ages, in almost all communities in India, custom decreed the woman to be "unclean" during the time of her menstrual period. The origin of the custom was probably due to the belief that during menstruation the person was unwell and discharge might contaminate food. Therefore, women were relegated to a separate corner of the house and not permitted to participate in household activities. In rural areas, this custom enabled women to take rest and freed them from the heavy work in the fields. Sexual intercourse during this period was and is considered to be unhygienic.
>
> Nowadays, with the development of medical science, a more rational and healthy attitude prevails.
>
> Women are not barred from carrying on their normal activities nor can working women afford to take days off from work.
>
> It is perfectly hygienic for women to have a daily bath. Some women, during menstruation, exude a certain odor, they need to use a deodorant or perfume to counteract this. The best protection is a sanitary pad, worn externally, or a rolled-up specially made small cotton pad, highly absorbent, known as a "tampon" which is worn internally.[23]

In order to present menstruation through a scientific, medical, and nationalist lens, the question/answer has to resurrect past images of ritual pollution. The seemingly ordinary discussions about menstruation cannot be invoked without the discourses of nationhood based upon tradition and modernity. In this framework, the juxtaposition of science and ignorance makes sense because women's liberation from superstition serves as a sign for the historical breach between past and present. Furthermore, the scientific discourse is paradoxically unable to coexist with (or exist without) oppositional forms of knowledge— those that science defines itself against and dismisses as ignorance, insanity, and irrationality. Therefore, juxtaposing "for all ages" against "nowadays," the question/answer places value on the contemporary prevalence of a more scientific, and therefore more rational and healthier attitude toward menstruation.

However, in this binary framework, rational and healthy attitudes cannot be isolated from strategies of control and containment. Curiously, the concept of personal hygiene displaces ritual impurity. Deodorants, perfumes, sanitary napkins, and tampons counter ritual states of impurity. From a state of ritual impurity and a potential social threat, the female body is reconstituted as a nonhygienic, odorous body that can be aestheticized with the use of cosmetics and disposable, rather than reusable, collectors for menstrual discharge. The physical and symbolic segregation of women, which is essential to the practice of ritual menstrual pollution, does not require the practice of personal hygiene, nor is this possible, according to the pamphlet.

Not only is the menstrual experience reasserted as an essentially private and personal bodily experience, but the disciplining of female bodies is clearly revealed. In a Foucaultian sense, the discipline of female bodies is enacted not through denial but through knowledge. Through the framework of science, menstruation is normalized as a matter of personal hygiene, easily corrected through the consumption of products. Shaped by liberal principles that more objective information will automatically alleviate the trauma of menarche and early menstruation, the language of the text suppresses other knowledges. Such explanations of menstrual hygiene at first glance appear not only quite reasonable but natural. On closer inspection, however, these explanations appear to reassert the social regulation of bodies precisely through the claim to knowledge about menstruation. Stressing the importance of work and mundane productive activity for women is part of that same impulse to discipline through knowledge and notions of what is normal.

Where individual women's bodies are central to both social norms and social regulation, it is not surprising that women's narratives of menarche and menstruation are aggravated and magnified. As reflected in the last few pages, women in this study tell their experiences of menstruation through this lens colored by a heightened awareness of bodily peripheries. This bodily awareness is marked by a preoccupation to conceal the visible transgressions of the menstruating female body but also to express them; for example, the reiteration of pain, discomfort, heavy bleeding, and an inability to function in the narratives is important to consider. The menstrual experience, contained in certain ways, is also expressed through other means. Mediated through the discourse of scientific normality and rationality, bodily control and bodily affliction are two effects of the same phenomenon.

Language of Pain and Discomfort

In their study, Snowden and Christian suggest that, in general, high-status urban women appear more anxious to control menstrual odor and to conceal the fact that they are menstruating.[24] Moreover, these women tend to report greater levels of physical discomfort and mood fluctuations than low-status rural women and are more likely to decrease physical activity and assume a sick role during menstruation, according to Snowden and Christian. Similarly, parallel and pervasive accounts of physical pain and discomfort are told by women in this study as well.

Where women's narratives are clearly focused on maintaining the integrity of the individual body, physical pain and emotional unevenness are likely to be expressed frequently. The narratives are often marred by descriptions of severe and, in some cases, debilitating menstrual pains. Venita vividly describes the effect of menstrual pains in her life and her dependence on painkillers.

> I have very, very painful periods. I have low b.p. [blood pressure]. I feel weak and nauseous a week in advance. I feel totally drained. If I have to work, I have to pop regular painkillers. I find it a disadvantage. It's very painful. Sometimes, I can't get out of bed. I wish I didn't have to. You can control things that are mental, but you can't control this. You have to go through this ridiculous thing that is supposed to make you fertile. I wish it would happen only when you want to have children and then get out of the way.

Nipun, who experienced menstrual taboos prior to marriage, describes the effect of physical discomfort that has since attenuated. Reflecting the excruciating pain in her tone, she describes,

> I hated it because of very bad cramps. I couldn't eat, I would vomit and collapse. It went off after my son was born. The mild irritation is there but no severe pain. After marriage I would go and sleep until the pains had passed. It would take my body four to five hours and be pale and tired for the day. In this house I was not embarrassed because they [in-laws] are okay. There [natal home] it was a problem because my movements were restricted.

Although Snowden and Christian attribute the greater likelihood of higher-status women expressing physical discomfort to changes such as a decrease in physical exercise, related to industrialization, I believe that these sequelae of menstruation are more closely related to women's heightened and individualized experiences of body and menstruation. It is not merely possible changes in physical activity related to industrialization that account for women's discomfort. On the contrary, heightened perceptions of individual bodies, of bodily integrity, help explain the nature of women's narratives on menstruation and its attendant discomfort. Where this link is clearly evident is in the ways that physical discomfort is fused with the individual/social discomfort of menstruation. For example, Nipun fuses the discomfort of debilitating physical pain with the social restrictions imposed on her. Sujata vividly recounts her physical discomfort through her early menses within the context of the trauma of menarche; she had to tie belts around her stomach to ease the pain. Seema describes hormonally triggered irritation and depression alongside her anxieties over when she is going to get her next menses—"When will I get it? Will I be carrying anything at the time?" Mehernaz, a 29-year-old, describes the bodily discomfort of menstruation by linking words such as "painful," "upsetting," "dreadful," "pain," and "inconvenience." It would be a mistake to isolate the language of physical pain, emotional and social discomfort from the regulation and disciplining of female bodies.

Summarized briefly, the contradictions of the socially significant but individually regulated bodies shape middle-class women's narratives on menarche and early menstruation. Although these are ostensibly natural events, the underlying social contradictions of containing menarche and menstruation within the realm of the individual are reflected in the narratives. Women tell their stories through a language of personal impurity and personal hygiene, concealment, surveillance, and control. The stories are also riddled with accounts of menstrual pain and discomfort. Ironically, institutional impulses to inform and assuage experiences of menarche and menstruation only end up rewriting the strategies of social control that are reflected in women's narratives.

Sexual Regulation and Sexual Respectability: Narrating and Subverting

Perhaps the most visible means of regulating young menstruating women is reflected in the social/sexual restrictions imposed thereafter. Describing the regional similarities in the perceptions of puberty in girls, Dube emphasizes that with puberty the girl enters the most critical stage of her life when her body has acquired the capacity to reproduce but has no authority to do so.[25] Since a young woman is held to be at her most vulnerable between puberty and marriage, restrictions on movements, interactions with males, and special safeguards characterize this period, according to Dube. Reflecting the social and familial preoccupation with their sexual propriety, women's narratives emphasize the nature of the social control and the roles of mothers and parents in enforcing the controls. And though menarche and menstruation thus far seem dominated by disciplining and regulation, accounts of social/sexual regulations are even more contentious.

In account after account, women describe social/sexual restrictions imposed after the onset of menarche. Restrictions on clothing, on interactions with males, and on staying out late or attending parties were some of the most frequently mentioned changes. These restrictions coincide with the more visible changes in girls' bodies such as the development of breasts and hips. As young girls grow up and seek more time with their peers and more autonomy, the restrictions may be somewhat relaxed or intensified. Culturally, menarche fixes the gender status of a young girl through her biological capacity to reproduce. But it also signals her sexuality, which is perceived as a source of danger to her and, contingent upon her actions, a possible danger to her family. Thus, a range of restrictions is seen as a means to contain the sexual threat posed by the postpubertal girl. Unlike ritual taboos that regulate the precarious nature of female sexual purity, these impositions and monitoring lie within the purview of the family and elicit the cooperation of women, but not without opposition.

What is noteworthy is the role of mothers in disciplining and regulating the bodies of their daughters. In middle-class women's narratives, mothers mediate not only their experiences about menarche and menstruation but also enforce the social restrictions in their daughters' lives. Mothers shape women's experiences by not adequately preparing their daughters for the onset of menstruation. Twenty-year-old Preeta says that her mother failed to inform her about menses, and it was the housemaid who told her to use cotton. What is equally important are mothers' immediate reactions when their daughters inform them about their first menses. Frequently, women say that their mothers were shocked. For a development that is so certain for its "naturalness," the suggestion that mothers are caught completely off-guard is especially curious. Hansa says that her mother cried, and Meenakshi says that her mother cursed her outright.

Sheila, who is 22 years old and has been married two years, wryly describes the restrictions her family tried to impose:

> Before marriage—no late night, can't go out, no male friends. Till today. I was talking to guy friends and my father said, "Go and sit there with your mother." I went to college only for two years. He [father] would leave me and pick me up. I was not an extrovert, so it was not a problem. My mother wanted me to wear Western dresses only because, she said, "You look big [older] when you wear [salwaar] suits."

Sheila suggests that such restrictions may not completely abate after marriage. Interactions with unrelated males remain suspect. To keep her looking like a young girl, her mother insists that she should wear Western dresses rather than salwaar suits. But, if salwaar suits signal the adultlike status of a postpubertal girl, they also cover her body in a way that is not possible with Western skirts and dresses.

Thirty-five-year-old Kavita, who like Sheila is ethnically Punjabi, reverses the link between Western clothes and bodily regulation to describe attempts at prolonging childhood. She says evenly but forcefully,

> Initially I was not happy [about menarche], the bother was too much, although it was never painful. It has never interfered in my work. I was not happy about getting them, I was 12 and a half. I thought 14 was the right age. It has too many hassles. You are expected to do so many things all of a sudden. You had to be well behaved, you had to be conscious of yourself. In my time you had to have your legs covered. Immediately. I couldn't wear skirts. I really felt very rebellious. You switch over to salwaar suits. You start feeling so clumsy, those clothes don't go with you. My mother made me wear those tight vests so that my breasts won't show. What notions they had! Really tight cotton vests so that my breasts won't show.

Kavita's description is atypical, probably because this practice is associated with Punjabis and not pervasive anymore. Yet, it does reveal the centrality of clothes in containing the gender and sexual status of postpubertal girls. More frequently, women describe not being allowed to wear clothes without sleeves, what are seen as short skirts, short tops, or clothes that reveal or unduly accentuate their bodies. For this group, with the exception of a few cases in which wearing Western clothes such as dresses, skirts, and trousers may not be permitted, for the most part, the emphasis is on the construct of modesty through clothes—"Western" and "traditional."

This concern with maintaining the sexual modesty and respectability of postpubertal girls is most clearly evident in the restrictions regarding interactions with boys their age. In some narratives, girls are not encouraged to interact with boys prior to the onset of menarche. But, postpubertally, such restrictions clearly intensify in most cases. Anshu, a 23-year-old who on the day of the interview was dressed in shorts and a T-shirt in the privacy of her home, angrily describes how her grandmother would not let her wear shorts or visit the home of a friend who had a brother. Anjali also 23, describes not being permitted to write to two male friends away at school, despite the fact that they were younger than her. Although she is currently financially independent (and living with her parents until her marriage), Anjali says she is still not allowed to socialize with male colleagues outside of work—she can't go out for dinner or to the movies with them, nor even talk on the phone.

Nineteen-year-old Puja describes a more permissive upbringing compared to Anjali but also notes changes in parental attitudes over the last few years. Not only are they more cautious about her relationships with her male friends but frequently discourage them. Firmly asserting that gender is secondary to friendship, she describes how her male friendships and 1 a.m. curfew have recently become significant points of conflict with her mother. In her narrative,

Sujata says she was not discouraged from talking to boys, but was forbidden by her mother to go out to parties in mixed company. Women describe the restrictions through phrases such as "keeping tabs on me," "more protective," "I was not allowed," among others. Across the narratives the intensity of the restrictions regarding male friends and parties varies, but what does remain consistent is the concern with monitoring and containing the gendered and sexual implications of puberty. If such restrictions appear pervasive in women's accounts, then it also calls into question the underlying reasons for such concerns.

What is striking in women's narratives is the reflection of parental fears about women's sexualities. When asked why parents and other family members clamp various controls on their lives, the women suggest two interrelated factors: to protect women from dangers triggered by their burgeoning sexualities, and to monitor their behaviors. The limitations reinforce and heighten the paradoxical links between female bodies and sexualities. In women's narratives, puberty is indeed culturally coded in sexual terms. In this framework, women's seemingly passive sexualities might nonetheless trigger male passion and result in their being led to inappropriate sexual behavior. Put differently: Without regulation, middle-class women are easily made sexually impure.

In their narratives, the women are quite articulate about familial motivations for imposing restrictions upon them. Anjali says that her parents worry about her safety when she returns home late at night. Thirty-one-year-old Sadhana unequivocally elaborates on the fears underlying women's safety: "Virginity. That's the only damage they can apprehend. The basic worry is that somebody might try to molest her."

Kanika suggests that so concerned were her parents for her safety, since she is considered to be beautiful within her ethnic community, that she did not once travel alone before marriage. Even when she worked as a vice principal in school, her father dropped her off and picked her up from school without fail. With a slight smile on her face, Kanika says that she was brought up "behind seven curtains," so to speak. Fathers can be protectors but, as Vani suggests in her narrative, not exempt from the changing rules that govern women's sexualities. She says,

> In our families, [we] are taught that when girls grow up, you are supposed to maintain a distance even from fathers, brothers. Dad is very close to us, he would come hug and kiss us. My granny told him. They are aware in our family, and they teach us how we are supposed to handle ourselves and how to sit when the men are there.

As the above narratives suggest external threats to a postpubertal girl as a result of her sexuality, women also express how, from the perspectives of their families, they are implicated in these threats. Puja explains her parents' fears:

> I guess they trust me but don't want me to get too close to a person so that
> I will get carried away and do something that I will regret. But, I am pretty
> sure of myself that I won't get carried away. But, that's what they worry
> about. I guess they didn't worry before because I was too young.

That the fear is expressed in terms of the daughter getting carried away suggests that, at one level, women concur that theirs is a more passive form of
sexuality. None of the narratives suggests that they might initiate sexual
encounters; rather, in this framework, women can only acquiesce. Radhika
elaborates on the fear and the consequences of losing control from the perspective of her parents. According to her, her parents think it is acceptable to
interact with male friends as long as she is not by herself, which they consider unsafe. Her loss of control and possible pregnancy are their overriding
fears, according to Radhika. She reiterates their emphasis on her knowing the
social consequences of these possibilities.

Whether parental injunctions regarding sexual behavior are entirely effective
will be discussed in Chapter Five. But, what is clear from the narratives on menarche, menstruation, and postpubertal physical changes, is that the impositions
and restrictions reinforce a negative perception of womanhood. Coupled with
prevailing negative perceptions of menarche and menstruation, familial restrictions through puberty and early adulthood make the changing female body
ambiguous. Though a woman may take some pride in the physical changes of
gender and sexual development, the strong link between postpubertal female
bodies and social regulations may prompt ambivalence about womanhood. For
example, Anita, 25, describes the capacity to give birth as the advantage of being
a woman. On the other hand, she cites as its disadvantages the double standards
that prevail in women's lives. Sujata also cites the restrictions that women are
subjected to as the biggest disadvantage to being a woman.

The social/sexual restrictions shape women's ideas of what it means to be
a "respectable woman." For them, women's clothes, sexual behaviors, and self-
presentations do signal propriety or lack of it. For example, according to
Seema, there is no question but that women call attention to themselves
when they wear short skirts. Twenty-nine-year-old Monica says that it is outright foolish for women to go into the more conservative suburbs of Mumbai
dressed in revealing clothes. She says she does not support the premise of
women's propriety, but must acknowledge the reality within which women
live. Distancing herself from women who dress in what she considers to be
inappropriate ways—low necklines, and short skirts—Bindu says that she is
disquieted enough to not be friends with them.

These middle-class women reflect not only prevailing perceptions and concerns with their sexual purities, but, in their narratives, the concerns are articulated in the immediacy of their relationships with their mothers or with both parents. Not only are concerns with their sexual purities pervasive, but they are monitored within the family, rather than the community or the collective. In their narratives, the women document, negotiate, and internalize these perceptions of sexual purity—postpubertal virginity as well as day-to-day sexual respectability and propriety. Women's postpubertal virginity is protected against the external threat of sexual assault and the threat of personal impropriety, not without their cooperation, nor without their opposition.

Disrupting and Subverting

Though women ambivalently specify the meaning of their familial/social regulation, what is far more striking is how they constantly subvert such controls within their narratives. Challenging such restrictions, refusing to restrict their daughters similarly, and, in a few instances, disrupting the disciplining of their bodies, are some of the ways in which women tell subversive narratives. Just as women use language that clearly implicates them in their regulation and disciplining through notions of normal body development (menarche and menstruation), they simultaneously undermine this strategy of control. Not one or the other, not one woman more than another, subversions of their gender and sexual prescriptions intensify through puberty and crisscross throughout the narratives.

What is immediately noticeable is how in their accounts women repeatedly question the range of restrictions related to menstruation that are imposed upon them by their families. On being restricted from ritual worship, 19-year-old Malini says ingeniously,

> First I was not happy. I said, "What a problem." I used to sit at home, I had so much pain. I couldn't go down to play, I used to feel very shy. Mom said, "Don't tell anyone." Now I feel it's good it comes—otherwise there are pains anyway. My mom says don't wear red. Earlier elders used to say don't go to the *mandir* [temple], and don't put water in Tulsi [an auspicious plant], it will die. I put water on that day and nothing happened. I wore red also, nothing happened. I don't know why. It's God-given, so it's no sin. He is the father of the world, then how can it be wrong?

Similarly, both Indira and Anu emphatically say that they question the legitimacy of such restrictions related to menstruation placed on them.

The social/sexual restrictions of menstruation catalyze concern and vehemence in the women's narratives. More than any other issue, women express their ire in this regard, which, as mentioned earlier, is a major source of contention with their mothers and/or fathers. Anita says that especially as she grew older she stopped being easily intimidated by her father's outrage at her staying out late in the night while at a party. She says somewhat matter-of-factly that since they would clash only once every four to five months, she became more immune to his silent treatments. In another instance, 15-year-old Nilima questions,

> After you get your period you are not supposed to mix up with guys that much. The common lecture you get, everyone gets it. I found it pretty awkward. What's wrong? What's wrong with me now that I can't mix up with guys?

Unconvinced of the role of these restrictions in her life, she says that, unknown to her parents, she has a steady boyfriend.

Both Hansa and Meeta emphasize that they will prepare and tell their daughters about the onset of menarche. Piya says that it is vital that she should have a relationship based on trust and friendship with her daughter. Kavita says she refuses to do to her daughter what was done to her. She says,

> According to me that [binding vests] will stilt the development, I would never do that to my daughter but that was what was done to me. That makes you more conscious of yourself in some way. You feel this must be wrong, that's why she is doing this.

In a few instances, in their narratives women recount more directly disruptive behavior related to menarche, menstruation, and the female body. Nipun, who was subjected to restrictions in her natal home, says that out of disregard for these constraints in her life, she did not tell anyone for as long as a year that she was menstruating. Concealing her menses meant that she was not bound by ritual restrictions. In her account she is able to disrupt these taboos until her aunt confronted her on whether she was pregnant. Since Nipun hid the signs of menstruation as a form of rebelliousness against the restrictions related to menstruation and not pregnancy, they compromised that thereafter she would abstain only from idol worship during her menstrual period. In 20-year-old Preeta's case, not only does she iterate that she will tell her daughter and help her deal with menarche, she says that she quickly made sure that her sisters knew about menstruation. In her account, Preeta feels that she went through unnecessary discomfort because she did not know about pads and also because her mother did not get her a bra as soon as she needed it. She showed her younger sisters how to use sanitary pads with belts and also bought them bras to ensure proper development of their bodies, according to her. Failed by her mother, Preeta attempts to ensure more positive experiences for her sisters.

Conclusion

Listening to middle-class women's narratives provides vital clues to the process of defining and normalizing the female body. Central to the process are strategies that heighten individual bodily peripheries and perceptions that the female body is personal and private. These strategies rely on women's self-surveillance and self-monitoring. Therefore, these women seem less inclined to question their implication in this process of social regulation. The role of parents, especially mothers, is instrumental to, but not the source of, social control. According to the women, parents attempt to enforce overt norms of social and sexual respectability. That these attempts are not always effective is equally clear in the narratives when women subvert and disrupt the constraints associated with menarche and menstruation, and less directly, with the making of the female body.

Read against the grain of hegemonic discourses of gender and sexuality produced and supported by the nation-state, the narratives clearly indicate that strategies of social control exercise a "direct grip" on women's bodies. This is most clearly revealed in texts such as *Problems of Adolescent Sexuality* and *Teenagers Ask, The Doctor Answers*, where questions of menarche and menstruation are explored as inextricable from notions of past and present national cultural traditions and practices. Therefore, if the past was characterized by myths, superstitions, and ignorance, in the present menarche and menstruation need to be interpreted through the "joy of growing up into womanhood" and scientific knowledge. Whether these discourses are accounts of menstruation and womanhood or nationhood only reflects their inextricable nature. As reflected in these texts, although menarche and menstruation are matters for individual women, they are unquestionably shaped by what is considered normal and socially consonant with national cultural identity.

However, it is debatable that the "direct grip" on middle-class women's bodies is solely the effect of hegemonic codes supported by the contemporary nation-state and putative notions of national cultural identity. Broadly put, the mechanisms of producing and regulating gendered bodies, as reflected in middle-class women's narratives on menarche and menstruation, raise imperative questions about their pervasiveness across national boundaries.[26] Examining women's narratives for the effects of transnational, globalizing cultural discourses makes clearer the class-based parallels in the shaping and regulation of sexed bodies, womanhood, and, implicitly, heterosexuality across national societies. This approach to understanding women's gendered bodies and sexualities would also greatly help demystify stereotypical and uninformed assumptions between the generic categories of Western and Third World or Indian women. The narratives included in this study are especially instructive on these issues.

These women's narratives on menarche also implicate the effects of transnational cultural discourses in multiple and specific ways. The scientific-medical lens through which menarche and menstruation are widely interpreted and reflected in women's narratives and the discourse on personal hygiene belie the possibility of a hegemonic discourse confined to an insular nation-state. The narratives show the effects of transnational cultural relations in the regulation and commoditization of women's sexed bodies—for example, "sanitary products." It is important not to ignore what these middle-class women's narratives suggest about the role of the nation-state and transnational cultural processes in shaping and sustaining hegemonic codes and strategies of regulation in their daily lives. What is equally useful in their narratives are the instances in which they subvert and disrupt these hegemonic codes.

Chapter Four

Tensions of Sexual Respectability: Accounts of Sexual Aggression

One aspect of growing up that uniformly stirs anxiety and anger in middle-class women is sexual aggression. In their narratives, these aggressions appear to leave indelible, but not uncomplicated, marks upon them. Women seem to have more trouble speaking about these experiences than recalling them. Hesitations, withdrawal of eye contact, outrage, demeaning characterizations of male aggressors, nervous gestures, and indignation mark the way these women tell the stories of sexual aggression that they have experienced.

The aggression begins in childhood, with invidious sexual violations by adult men. As adults, the women endure aggression in public spaces, euphemistically called "eve-teasing," which may include being whistled at, being subjected to catcalls, comments, lewd behavior or gestures, being touched or sexually assaulted. Routine events—returning home from school, walking down the street to a nearby store, and traveling by bus or trains—expose women to sexual harassment daily. Women also recount sexual aggression in the workplace, the home, even the family. Aggressors include strangers, familiar strangers such as a man running the grocery store, live-in house workers, uncles, cousins, coworkers, and friends. What delineates these experiences as sexual aggression is that women describe them as offensive, threatening, and, especially, in childhood, injurious.

In this chapter, women tell narratives about the ways in which experiences of sexual aggression help crystallize their consciousness of their bodies. These accounts, then, not only provide further insights into the making of sexed bodies but also highlight the specific tensions that mark women's narratives on sexual aggression. What these narratives show is how experiences of sexed bodies are thoroughly permeated by the tensions of gender, sexuality, as well as class. Contrary to prevailing discourses, these narratives also indicate that explanations rooted in male dominance are not adequate to understanding issues of sexual aggression. Such explanations obscure the interrelated effects of gender, sexuality, and class in shaping narratives on sexual aggression, and implicitly, on the female body. I focus on women's narratives to highlight the ways in which class- and gender-based hegemonic codes, such as sexual respectability, color what women delineate as experiences of sexual aggression and how they express those experiences.

These accounts of sexual aggression chronicle the transition from childhood into womanhood and from the inchoate sexuality of the girl child into the contradictions of adult female sexuality. As they come to terms with menarche, girls experience a level of sexual aggression that reinforces the realization of embodied womanhood in all of its complexity which is not to suggest that girls do not encounter sexual aggression before puberty; indeed, the women whose stories are given in this book recount troubling episodes of early sexual abuse within the presumed safety of their homes and neighborhoods. But, as the narratives attest, the social/sexual significance of puberty and the attendant changes in a girl's life expose her more widely to sexual aggression.

What is most unsettling is that as women speak about the day-to-day experiences of sexual aggression from childhood through the present, they evince the "direct grip" of the culture on their sexed bodies and, in effect, on their womanhood and sexualities. Arguably, sexual aggression is aberrant or unusual compared to the normality of menstruation; culturally, it is not represented as a requisite phase in the socialization and coming of age of women. Yet, precisely because sexual aggression toward women is only in the process of being culturally identified and managed as a problem (for example, only recently have newspaper articles referred to the importance of forewarning children about sexual aggression), it occupies a relatively ambiguous space within the culture. This makes the pervasiveness of sexual aggression more disturbing and the production of docile female bodies through these mundane, culturally unacknowledged experiences only more suspect.

Foucault's insights about the appropriation of the body enacted through self-surveillance are nowhere more useful than in application to these middle-class women's narratives on sexual aggression. When speaking of sexual aggression, they use language that reveals how these experiences crystallize the significance of the female body and internalize its responsibility and respectability. For example, when they recount the experiences of sexual aggression in their childhood years, these women suggest that they learn to fear the sexual threat posed by men. They also seem to perceive their vulnerability as children as the failure of parental protection. Yet when they describe experiences of sexual aggression through adolescence and early adulthood, these women internalize the burden of protecting their bodies against male sexual aggression. Thereafter, the female body is primarily their responsibility.

These narratives on persistent, mundane forms of sexual aggression, while revealing the ways in which women's bodies, genders, and sexualities are regulated and managed, also raise questions about the effects of such aggression. It may be that through experiences of sexual aggression these women learn lasting lessons of managing and protecting their sexual respectabilites, essential to their positions as middle-class women, but they are also taught how to relate to themselves, to their bodies. As John Berger suggests, women's bodies are cultural objects not only to men but also to themselves.[1] Mediated through the gaze of the culture, women learn to gaze at themselves; according to Berger, men watch women and women watch themselves be watched. Especially for these middle-class women, experiences of sexual aggression heighten not only the significance of the body, but also their self-consciousness of embodiment.

The narratives on sexual aggression directed against them highlight prescriptive notions about middle-class women's sexual respectability that are ensured through internalized forms of social/sexual controls. What do I mean by sexual respectability with respect to these narratives? Sexual respectability encodes expectations of what is socially and sexually appropriate for middle-class women. As a standard of acceptable social conduct, notions of sexual respectability prevail mainly in two dimensions: the threat of male sexual harm to women bodies, and the threat of women's transgressing the lines of acceptable social/sexual behavior. In its former meaning, sexual respectability shapes women's narratives on their experiences of sexual aggression. In its latter meaning, the premise of sexual respectability is more clearly evident in women's narratives on aspects of erotic sexuality in the following chapter. As a social norm, sexual respectability is indisputably gender- and class-based. But as the hegemonic codes explored in Chapter Two also manifest, sexual respectability is deeply riven by discourses of nationalism. Rooted in these tensions of nationalisms, gender, and social class, the discourse of sexual respectability shapes these middle-class women's narratives on sexual aggression and reveals how, when internalized by women, the notion of sexual respectability can become an instrument of social control over their gendered bodies and sexualities.

In the narratives, when women describe what happened, how it made them feel, and especially when they characterize the men involved, the politics of female bodies and sexual respectability are foregrounded. Where women bear the burden of their socially and politically charged bodies, it is likely that they will have much to say about incidents of sexual aggression and that these experiences will be recounted through the lens of trauma, anxiety, and outrage. Where the sexual significance of puberty does not indicate active, desiring female sexualities but views young girls and women as the objects or victims of male sexuality, women are more likely to describe themselves as negatively affected. Where class-based concerns of sexual respectability prevail, women are also more likely to describe themselves as dirtied or sullied. On the other hand, they are likely to characterize men, at the very least, as sexually aggressive, and as damaging their sexual respectability.

Feminist scholars and activists have been at the forefront of conceptualizing, challenging, and calling attention to issues of violence against women. Violence has been broadly conceived in feminist literature, and specific issues related to sexual violence have been at the frontlines of feminist campaigns in recent times.[2] Issues of domestic sexual violence, stranger rape, and custodial rape have been consistently addressed by feminist activists.[3] Other aspects of sexual aggression, including what is called "eve-teasing," sexual harassment at work, are routinely dealt with at crisis-intervention centers and by grassroots women's organizations.[4] But, what is less clear from available feminist scholarship is the meaning of aspects of sexual aggression from the viewpoint of women. It is this aspect that I seek to explore in this chapter. How middle-class women talk about sexual aggression implicates deep structural tensions of gender, class, and sexuality that shape hegemonic discourses within contemporary India.

In general, there is little social research on issues such as eve-teasing, sexual harassment at work, sexual abuse, or incest, especially from the perspective of women, and what research exists seems to be beset by significant limitations. For example, two related research articles, *Attitudes Toward Sexual Harassment of Women in India*, and *Sex-Related Differences in Perceptions of Sexual Harassment of Women in India* address the issue of sexual harassment.[5] In each case, a hypothetical incident was presented to undergraduate students at the University of Bombay to measure attitudinal differences between women and men regarding sexual harassment at work. The studies confirm that, based on their samples, men are more likely to "blame the victim." Each of the studies also attributes the more endemic and blatant problem of sexual harassment in India to the "very low status of women and the high dominance of men in our country and the relative lack of free interaction between the sexes" compared to "Western countries."[6] But such comparisons are based on some deeply flawed assumptions about cultural and gender differences between "India" and "Western countries."

By contrast, popular magazines and newspaper are replete with discussions on various forms of sexual aggression, including child sexual abuse, eve-teasing, sexual aggression toward adult women from strangers as well as men known to them, and more recently, from men at the workplace. While popular coverage on issues of sexual aggression may engender social awareness, it also generates uncritical, institutional discourses in the same instance. What is especially troubling is how articles and news reports on matters of child sexual abuse, sexual abuse, and harassment of adult women frequently begin with or highlight lurid vignettes without adequately analyzing why these incidents occur.

So, for example, an article in the widely read *Times of India* reports on a newly formed Forum Against Child Sexual Exploitation (FACSE), and a feature article in *Sunday* details the nature and consequences of incest.[7] These articles serve complicated functions. On the one hand, given the dearth of available information on issues of incest and sexual abuse of children, the estimate of 40,000 children who are the victims of sexual abuse each year reported in the first article, or the addresses and phone numbers of sources of help against incest provided in the second article, become important sources of popular information. Furthermore, the second article helps undermine popular myths related to the sexual abuse of children, such as the idea that it occurs only in poor and illiterate families. But, without any analysis or a sustained critique, the frequently used vignettes in each of the articles are more inflammatory than informative. In such articles, not only is a deeper social critique of gender, sexuality, and social class altogether absent, but the information that is presented is itself suspect.

Frequently, this information reinforces profound structural tensions that shape women's experiences of sexual aggression recounted in the life-history interviews. Lacking any sustained critique of sexual violence directed toward women, such articles run the risk of at best reinforcing, and at worst naturalizing deep-seated assumptions that women are sexually violated and men are the violators. Under the guise of information and awareness, this kind of journalistic language supports popular and questionable social norms of womanhood, female and male sexuality, and maleness. For example, the newspaper article "Every Lane a Terror for Eves" predictably begins with one vignette of sexual assault and another of imminent sexual threat. The next two paragraphs read as follows:

> These are not stray incidents, they form part of over 4.2 million women's everyday experiences in the Capital. Is Delhi safe for women? The answer is predictable: No. Has it ever been safe? Never.
>
> The situation does not seem to get any better. With the rate of rapes twice as high as the national average and eve-teasing incidents accounting

for 18 percent of the countrywide total, women in the Capital have never felt more vulnerable.[8]

Besides rewriting women as vulnerable victims who have never been safe, articles of this kind play a role in exacerbating women's perceptions of their vulnerability and insecurity. Indeed, if these incidents are historically pervasive and part of the daily experiences of this substantial group of women, then the information should lead to unrelenting demands for effective social change. In effect, the lack of a more effective social critique that moves beyond the descriptive is conspicuous.

Ironically, texts such as *Problems of Adolescent Sexuality, Growing Up . . . Facts and Feelings, Bloom and Blossom: A Girl's Guide to Growing Up*, or *What You Should Know About STDs and AIDS* are silent on matters of sexual harassment and sexual abuse. If anecdotal and journalistic evidence is at all indicative, then it is especially perplexing that issues of sexual aggression, intricately tied with the female body, are absent in the discussions. As the notable exception, *Teenagers Ask, The Doctor Answers* raises the issue of sexual aggression in the form of a question on the meaning of rape. It defines the meaning of rape as a woman being compelled to have sexual intercourse against her will; it is also unequivocally described as "one of the most serious of crimes." But, the limitations of this single question on sexual aggression are most obvious when the advice given is,

> The best way to guard against unpleasantness is to avoid men who are not well-known to the family; beware of heavy drinkers, never accept lifts or other invitations from strangers, and avoid being on your own in lonely or dark places.[9]

Coupled with descriptions that rape entails using physical force and that rapists generally are "mentally sick," the issue of sexual aggression is narrowed still further.

Given the limitations of the more popular and journalistic descriptions and the dearth of social research literature on issues of sexual aggression from the perspective of the putative victims, in this chapter the primary task is to explore the narratives of these middle-class, urban women on sexual aggression. The most striking contrast to the popular reporting on sexual aggression is that these women express their experiences and their perceptions without reaffirming the violence. Their narratives are extensive without being explicit. Perhaps out of self-protection, the women communicate the egregious nature of the incidents without going into the uncomfortable details; instead, they rely heavily on phrases such as "he tried to do something." Against the grain of popular reporting on sexual aggression, these women's narratives offer a useful starting point for social awareness, and they make visible the tensions of gender, sexuality, and class.

What, When, Where, and Why: The Accounts of Sexual Aggression

Fourteen of the 50 women describe incidents that could be termed child sexual abuse, frequently involving family members. As Anu, a 26-year-old, with a young son, recalls such incidents, she grapples with the term "sexual abuse." On the one hand, sexual abuse appears to connote penile rape in her narrative; thereby, she says, she was not sexually abused. On the other hand, the violence of the acts that stop short of rape, compel her to suggest that indeed they were sexual abuse. In a low but agitated voice she says,

> It happened to me when I was a very small kid. I don't know how many times it has happened. He used to live in our society [residential complex]. There was not just one person. I was the eldest, and we didn't have any servants. My mother used to tell me to go out and get something very often. These were the places. At that age your parents don't educate you. She told me about my periods very early, but she didn't tell me not to sit on somebody's lap. At that age you don't know there is something very strange happening. It wasn't sexual abuse . . . but to an extent it happened. Not intercourse, it stopped short of that. At that age it's too much. It was not abuse. . . . but it was all sexual abuse.

In her narrative, Anu captures the vulnerability of the young, presexual girl in an environment where she is thought to be safe. Elsewhere in the interview, she says that the abusers included family members.

In their narratives, women frequently recount multiple incidents over a period of time and incriminate multiple perpetrators. None describe sexual violations from fathers or brothers. Rather, the perpetrators are men who work in the house, who have access to them, such as neighbors, and the family members, such as uncles and older cousins. It would seem that especially through early childhood, these are the men who are likely to come into unsupervised contact with young, middle-class female children.

It is particularly ironic that parents may attempt to protect their daughters from strange men but ignore the threat posed by men known or related to the family, thereby putting their young daughters at risk. Even where they may be conscious of the threat of unsupervised male contact to their daughters (such as male live-in help), they may not be able to prevent it altogether. In some cases, such as Payal's, mothers may be aware of the threat posed by male live-in help and older male cousins, yet unable to fully protect their daughters. In her account, Piya describes what can happen when children are momentarily left unattended with male live-in help. From a distant perspective, as if she were talking about someone else, she says,

> I think I was about three to four years old. I have a vague recollection. We used to have a male servant. One day he took me upstairs. I don't remember what happened exactly, but he did something with me and I distinctly remember my panties being wet. My mother was downstairs. A few minutes of inattention and look what can happen to a little girl. These are the things that have a long impact. These things make you very insecure.

Piya's account is not only profoundly disturbing for the sexual abuse itself but for the grievous long-term effects on girls, including making them feel insecure. In each of their interviews, both Piya and Payal emphasize that they would not leave their children with unattended male help.

Sexual aggression at the hands of family members is described as particularly unnerving. Piya says,

> The worst is the cousins. Parents think they are very nice, everyone thinks they are very nice, and you get to share so much—share rooms, bed also. You wake up in the middle of the night that somebody is watching you, reach out and touch you. It's such a horrible, dirty feeling I can't tell you. I hated that part. Why cousins? Why not go out and do it? Why not get a girlfriend? Initially I was very close to these cousins. I used to feel repulsed. I hated the idea, I was not talking to them, I wouldn't spend time with them. I wouldn't sleep in the same room, whatever happened. I was scared, in the middle of the night a guy can do anything to you. I was very scared.

As the women describe incidents that occured later in childhood, their feelings of fear and anxiety are emphasized. In contrast to her account about the insecurity and the lasting impact due to the abuse perpetrated early by the male live-in help, Piya emphasizes the fear with respect to the incidents in later childhood that involve older male cousins. As Nipun suggests, a young child may sense there is something amiss but be too young to understand the meaning of such violations. In her account she describes herself as too innocent to comprehend what her older male cousin was doing to her. Fortunately, she mentioned it to her uncle, and her cousin was not permitted to have any further contact with her. But, as these women describe incidents of sexual aggression from cousins and uncles that occur in the latter years of childhood and into puberty, they emphasize the more wide-ranging effects of child sexual abuse and the mechanisms used to cope thereof.

Also implicating older cousins, Kavita, who has a young daughter, articulates the insidious and long-term effect of these experiences for herself and in her role as a mother. According to her, aloofness, guardedness, unrelenting vigilance are forms of protection born out of these experiences. She says,

> Elder cousins are the worst. When I was in the third standard [six or seven years old], I didn't know what it was at that time. When I used to be sleeping. I don't know how parents are so worried about the world but they don't think about what happens in the home. Somehow those things never tend to leave you, never let you relax; you are always conscious, tense for your daughter. Maybe those things build that reserve in you, you start staying aloof. Now a physical relationship is what I want, but at that time you have no conception. I didn't tell my mother. We could never talk about physical relations, about sex.
>
> There was also another cousin of mine who would make me sit here [indicating her thigh] and I could feel that thing. . . . He would tell me a story and make me sit on his lap. Even at that time I knew it wasn't pleasant, so I started avoiding getting close to him. He would do his best.
>
> I don't know what pleasure they get out of a child. It's their own restrictions, that they can't try it out in the open so they try it out on their younger cousins, sisters. Isn't open sex better than this? When a child couldn't talk about it? At that time I couldn't talk about it to anybody, not my sisters, not my mother. I just knew that something is wrong somewhere. It was too early. It weighs on your mind, on a child's mind. It takes a long time to get over these things. This is something you can't share easily with anyone. You would rather keep it to yourself.

According to Kavita, the profound impact of sexual aggressions within the family are compounded when a child is unable to tell her family. The experiences become her burden to bear. In effect, parents may be unwitting conspirators in ensuring the silence of young girls who cannot adequately grasp the meaning of abuse or as they get older are afraid to bring such matters to the attention of their parents for fear they will be held responsible. Instead, she describes patterns of self-reliance to protect herself from this kind of abuse—reserve, avoidance, keeping the incidents to herself. By way of another such coping mechanism, Kavita and others who experience sexual aggression early on also tend to repress the memory.

In the accounts, the initial coping mechanisms—reserve, caution, and repression of such incidents—are easily jarred when more aggression is experienced through later childhood, through or after puberty, when women become sexually active, or become mother's to daughters. For example, according to Piya, experiences with her older male cousins when she was 10 or 11 years old reminded her of the abuse by her male servant. Pranati, 28, agitatedly describes the resurfacing of abuse experienced when she was six or seven years old,

I was in my early 20s. I was going around with [dating] my husband. I told him that I didn't want to see him any longer. It had that impact on me. I said I don't want to see men any longer, and I hate men. That was when we were getting physically intimate, and I said, "No."

It was a serious issue with me because it was actual assault. It wasn't just anything, it was actual assault. It happened repeatedly.

According to Pranati, her brother noticed her responses and intervened by listening to her childhood experiences and then discussing them with her husband-to-be. So vigilant is Pranati about her two-year-old daughter that she is completely opposed to the idea of her daughter and other children in the household having rooms on the uppermost floor of the house. In Kavita's case, she concludes her account on sexual aggression with, "I had forgotten all this, but when I see her [daughter] it is all coming back."

Speculations regarding the causes of these incidents vary among women. Kavita and Piya say men who prey on their younger female cousins do so for lack of other alternatives. Kavita suggests that it is the result of restrictions related to sex and its covert nature. Sadhana, who works for the state and is currently single, reasons that in their roles as uncles, men target nieces due to sexual discontent. She says,

Because they are not very happy. In their sexual life they are not very content. So they keep looking for cheap thrills outside of marriage. They don't have the means to get excitement outside of marriage. This is readily available, they don't have to pay anything.

Clearly, notions of sexual repression and sexual dissatisfaction among men are suggested reasons for these aggressions toward young girls. Whether men do indeed prey on girls out of misplaced sexual tensions needs to be analyzed. But, what is immediately apparent is that from their vantage point as adult women, they challenge this kind of male sexual aggression. They also see the sexual vulnerability of young girls as a problem of maleness and male sexuality; inadequately channeled male sexual impulses make young, accessible girls the targets.

What is equally noteworthy are these middle-class women's perceptions of why young female children are the targets of such abuse. Sadhana suggests that with young female children, older uncles can count on their silence due to fear. She says that these men are smart enough to come hug you and put their hand on the wrong place without making anyone else aware of it. Piya elaborates that

A younger girl is easier to catch hold of, she is more tender, she can't say,

"No." Initially they are just trying to hug you, you can sense it immediately. A younger girl will not say. An older girl will be more careful, slap the cousin. I couldn't do that. I don't know why I was scared. Now it won't happen. If it does, I won't keep quiet about it.

In their narratives, women question the vulnerability of young girls that makes them the easy targets of older males, uncles, and cousins. According to them, the men prey on the fears, anxieties, and innocence of young girls. At the same time, these women see their vulnerability as children/young girls as the outcome of the lack of male protection, especially from fathers and brothers. Perhaps because fathers, brothers, (and grandfathers) are cast in their roles as protectors, they are not implicated as sexual aggressors in these accounts. Rather, these women implicitly question the failure of their fathers to intervene. As women narrate accounts of sexual aggression within the family, they seem to implicitly distinguish between male roles as sexual aggressors and protectors. Some men can prey only because other men are unable to prevent them.

Zeenia, who had married a few months before interviewing with me, captures this tension of maleness and male sexuality. She says,

When my Dad died it changed the whole world for me. The whole world changes towards you. We were staying somewhere else, the three of us [mother, brother, and herself]. A relative would come over very often to help. But then I started getting this uneasy feeling, he used to look at me and things like that and I was 12 or 13 years old. He would come when nobody was home. One day I was studying, and he was home. I was wearing my nightie. He passed and he touched me, he touched my breasts, and it was very scary for me. I didn't say anything. I didn't know how to react. I didn't tell my mother about it. The next time it happened again so I felt very very scared and somehow I got the courage to tell my mother about it. My mother was very understanding. She told me not to be scared about it, and the next time he came to our place, she gave him hell. She blew him up and said: "How dare you come to our place." It was a very, very close relative. It showed that nobody is caring. That brought back so many memories of when I was very young, things I did not remember. This same person had tried something with me earlier on when I was three or four years old. I was lucky to get away with it without any harm or anything, but when I think about it I get depressed. I got the courage to tell my Mom about it. There are hundreds of girls who cannot tell or are misunderstood. If one of us has to die, it should be me, not my husband. If you do not have a husband, or children do not have a father, the whole world is bad to you. I don't know how we managed to live but we survived.

Even though Zeenia says that she remembered an earlier incident that involved the same relative when she was much younger and presumably her father was still alive, she suggests that this relative could act because of her father's protective absence. Indeed, she worries about what would have happened had she not turned to her mother, and she emphasizes the significance of the protective presence of her husband for their (future) children.

Not always, but by the time women experience such aggressions in their early to late teens, they are more likely to tell their mothers, confide in a sister, or cope with the aggressor more directly. Women are the ones they turn to for help, even though the problem may be conceived as the tension between the threat of male sexuality and male protection. In her account, Ketaki says that she could come to terms with the aggression only after she confided in her sister who confirmed that she was not imagining the behaviors of an uncle. Similarly, Anita, who describes inappropriate sexual behavior from an uncle in her early adolescent years, says that it helped to talk to her sister and then later her mother. Perhaps the most outspoken on these issues, Meenakshi says that by the time she was in her teen years, she did not hesitate to threaten the offending uncle or cousin that she would inform her mother.

To summarize these accounts on sexual aggression directed against them when they were children, the women are more likely to implicate men known to or related to the family. Implicitly perceiving themselves as presexual in their childhood years, women seem to see their sexual vulnerability as the failure of parental protection against male sexual aggression. But, as they chronicle the sexual aggression from early to later childhood, it appears that they internalize the responsibility for preventing such transgressions. Where the incidents of early childhood are buried in memory, or in the case of Nipun brought to light out of innocence, it is troubling that by later childhood women are more likely to keep the incidents to themselves and develop individual coping mechanisms. Perhaps due to this assumed sense of responsibility, these middle-class women emphasize emotions of fear and anxiety with regard to sexual aggression experienced through later childhood.

The turn inward is only further exacerbated as women recount events of sexual aggression through and after pubescence. While some of them say they continue to contend with aggression from uncles and older cousins, after puberty they are also likely to face increased sexual aggression from male strangers. If the onset of menarche and outward bodily changes culturally highlights the transition into emergent womanhood and sexuality (Chapter Three), then it also makes pubescent girls sexually more conspicuous. Perhaps anticipating threats to their daughters from the unknown, parents are said to be particularly vigilant after puberty. Traveling to and from school, returning alone in the evening after extra classes or extracurricular activities, or running errands are part of those mundane activities where young girls may come into contact with unknown men. Culturally dubbed "eve-teasing," these forms of sexual aggression from male strangers in public spaces are pervasive in the accounts of these middle-class women.

Through the Adolescent Years: Here It Is Called Eve-teasing

Puja, who is currently in college, details eve-teasing from the perspective of a young, middle-class girl.

> Actually it's supposed to make you feel good, that you are looking good. I hated it. First time I felt it was when I was walking down with my younger sister, and this guy walking past slapped me on my bottoms, and I said "Oh, shit, why did he do that." I went home and cried and cried and cried. Now you can take care of yourself but as a kid I used to feel bad and cry. I used to feel I am going to get a hold of that guy and slap him, "What the hell does he think of himself." The first time I cried, and that was a stupid thing to do. One time I started to fight with this man on the road. You are alone, and you start fighting, that was absolutely stupid. Now I realize that's not the way you tackle things. Now I just ignore the guy and walk off.

In the way Puja describes it, "eve-teasing" is a form of sexual aggression. This kind of behavior—being slapped on the bottoms, being touched on the breasts, being whistled at, being deliberately brushed against, receiving cat-calls or sexually suggestive comments—consistently appears in the narratives of these middle-class women. Women's accounts also reveal the absurdity of the term "eve-teasing" to describe the invidious nature and impact of these sexual aggressions.

The women suggest that, especially when they were younger, these incidents provoked fear and anxiety for the physical/sexual threat posed to themselves and, curiously, for their parents' reactions. For example, Piya describes being terrified at the age of 13 by older and physically tougher men who would follow or verbally harass her. Mala, 16, says that she worries not only about the aggression but also about what her parents might think. Mitali, 22, who works as a textile designer, says that she does not fully recollect when this kind of aggression first began for her, but she does recall being afraid and reluctant to tell her parents that she was being followed home from school by strange men; somehow, she says, she thought they would not trust her. In her account, Preeta says that she was trembling with fear under the blankets when her father intercepted one of many anonymous phone calls, in which she thinks the man said, "I will fuck your daughter"; she was afraid of what the man would say and that her parents would think that she provided the phone number. Fearful of parents' reaction, instances in which young girls may seek the intervention of their parents, such as in the case of Puja, are relatively infrequent.

Such incidents can make girls rather ambivalent about growing up. In her narrative, Mala says that she did not like the changes in her body, which meant menstruating and wearing a bra. From women's viewpoint, the development of breasts, wearing a bra, and other manifest physical changes are closely associated with arriving at an adultlike state. In Mala's case, the wearing of a bra along with other changes, such as dealing with eve-teasing and getting anonymous phone calls, was quite distasteful; she wanted to "remain small [young]."

On the contrary, where this arrival into an adultlike state is welcomed, the physical changes may be positively interpreted. Indeed, women may even derive pleasure from becoming more "womanlike." In her account, Venita says that she took much pleasure in the physical changes of her body, especially wearing a bra. In the interview she says in a lively tone,

> When I started wearing a bra I was in Villa Theresa [school]. They used to have a white uniform. It used to be a big thing because the strap would show from the back, and I would feel quite proud that now I am an adult, I wear a bra. Plus there are a lot of people who don't start wearing bras because they think it's too adult, and their parents keep them as little girls, and it's physically very uncomfortable. But I remember feeling quite proud the thing was showing from the back.

Nonetheless, juxtaposed against her account of the sexual aggression she and her peers experienced when they were 10 or 12 years old, her narrative indicates the inextricability of physical changes and the sexualization of pubescent girls. She describes the experience with anger and distaste.

> We used to go swimming in the evening and catch this bus, and we were young—sixth, seventh standard. It used to be obscene! There were hands going inside our skirts and our breasts squeezed. That kind of thing is disgusting. Jostling, rubbing. Then it got routine. We would get in [the bus] last. But it happens to all young girls. It's really sad.

Further capturing the ambivalences associated with physical and sexual development, Ketaki describes how uncomfortable she used to feel about her breasts when she was younger. She says,

> Before marriage I used to feel very ashamed of my breasts. People are looking at you, passing comments. I used to get comments. But after the wed-

ding I felt that I have such an asset. Before I was shy about them. In school I was very shy, "What are these people around me thinking?" Later you realize they are an asset for ladies.

Ketaki's shame about her breasts when she was in school derived from her self-consciousness; people were aware of her breasts. What is clear is that her self-consciousness about sexual development is tied to her perception of being sexualized. In other cases, women describe becoming self-conscious about their girlhood as a direct result of the sexual aggressions. For example, in Anita's account, growing up with three other sisters and no brother, she was always reminded of her girlhood, but sexual harassment fosters an awareness of the embodiment of girlhood; to be a girl is to have a female body. For Mitali, a primary impact of this kind of sexual aggression is a persistent self-consciousness. She says that she is consistently aware of people, wondering whether they are talking about and commenting on her. Elsewhere in her interview, Ketaki says that she used to bemoan the fact that she is a girl due to the eve-teasing she experienced on the streets and public spaces.

What is equally of concern is how the self-consciousness and awareness of their female bodies and girlhood are further unsettled by the restrictions that sexual aggression or the threat of it imposes in their lives. For one, it seems to make parents more protective of daughters. Based on the narratives of the middle-class women, this is precisely what their parents fear; they want to shield their daughters from the threat of male strangers. As explored in Chapter Three, such concerns regarding their pubescent and adolescent daughters seem to trigger restrictions in the comings and goings of their young daughters. The threat of this kind of sexual aggression appears to entail changes in girls' lives. In the context of eve-teasing and harassment, in her account, Anjali quietly questions the restrictions imposed on women. She says that her parents fear that she may be physically harmed, especially late in the evenings. As a result, she is unable to stay late at work or further her education by attending late evening classes. This may be another reason why women appear reluctant to share the details of this kind of sexual aggression with their parents. Besides the fear of bringing up these issues with mothers or fathers, women seem to worry that these incidents will trigger further parental concern, and thereby more restrictions in their lives.

The reluctance to bring the sexual aggression directed against them to the attention of their parents is troubling but not inconsistent. When asked their reasons for keeping these kinds of incidents from their family, they cite a range of reasons, including—the inappropriateness of talking about these issues, doubts about being believed, fears that parents will doubt their behaviors, concerns that more restrictions might be imposed. Under these circumstances, these middle-class women appear to take on the burden of the aggressions, particularly when they are younger. A lack of awareness on the part of their parents, a failure to gain the trust of their daughters, make these women vulnerable. Perhaps the most conscious impact these incidents have left is a determination to protect their own daughters, not to fail them as they themselves have been failed. This is not to say that women do not ask for intervention in these problems, but especially when they are younger, they suggest self-reliance and personal responsibility for preventing further sexual aggressions.

In terms of their responses to sexual aggressions from strangers in public spaces, at younger ages these middle-class women describe what could be termed more defensive approaches. When she was followed home from school, Mitali started to take a new route to and fro. Similarly, when several men harassed her at the nearby general store, she stopped going there. In her account, Anita says that initially when she used to experience eve-teasing, she would react passively out of fear of making a scene. Only when she got older, after talking about it with friends, did she realize that making a scene was an effective strategy to get intervention from other people in that setting. In a similar tone, out of frustration at the inevitability of such incidents and the lack of more effective responses, Bindu, who travels by bus to attend design school, says,

> Even in a bus guys are brushing up against you. I don't know what to do. There are 10 people looking. They are sitting next to you and are practically on your lap. I keep my portfolio in between or I will get up and change my seat if there is place. I can't fight with these people.

Simply shutting out or outwardly ignoring such occurrences is one such defensive strategy adopted by these middle-class women to thwart sexual aggression in public spaces. Perfected over a period of time, this defensive survival strategy attempts to counter sexual aggression by pretending ignorance. In other words, if nothing is happening, then there is no problem. This strategy is culturally encouraged as women are advised by family members and schools to minimize any interaction with the men; it is seen as a way of discouraging the offensive behavior. This advice is often reinforced by circulating reports of backlash against women who seek to retaliate against male violators. That these reports serve as important mechanisms of gendered control is evident as several women in this study invoked cases of other women being harmed because they had retaliated against sexual aggression from a stranger. In other words, by retaliating they had encouraged the attentions of the men. For example, Pranati assumes the blame for the event described below because she openly retaliated despite the advice of her brother and father to ignore sexual aggression. She says,

> From the busstand to my house, it happened to me four times when in school. There were guys who would run after me, and I had to run for my life into the house. Partly it was my fault, I answered back. When you answer back, you call for danger. My father and brother taught me never to answer.

Giving a man a "dirty look" is another common but more interactive, defensive strategy. It is often used to quell any further violation. These strategies may also mask a profound sense of fear experienced by young girls of being hurt/assaulted, a fear that is all too often realized. These concerns are rooted in feelings of personal responsibility and self-monitoring of their sexualities. As explored in the previous chapter, women frequently express concerns that what they wear or how they carry themselves might exacerbate such forms of sexual aggression. They seek to minimize sexual harassment by monitoring their clothing and behavior. This self-monitoring proves to be inadequate each time they are verbally or physically assaulted despite their "impeccable" conduct. Even as women talk about getting used to it, they are periodically driven to retaliate aggressively, often despite themselves. The anger and frustration may yet spill over as women periodically "lose it." Especially as they get older, women seek to retaliate more explicitly by using verbal abuse or by reporting to family members, friends, and, sometimes, the police.

The women said that, as they approached adulthood, they tended to react far more angrily to such aggressions. Anita cites an instance when she caught hold of the hand that pinched her bottom and then hit the man. Similarly, Seema describes her changing responses to eve-teasing with these words:

> It happens so often. You see it happen so often that you adjust to it. I was standing at the bus stop, and this guy was singing.[10] I got his badge number and reported him to the police. They slapped him two or three times. He got the fright of his life and so did the other two men with him. I didn't want this to happen again. Now you learn what's there to get scared! Sometimes you can't take it. You get so sick of it that you give the guy two, three [abuses]. At a certain age you are scared; later you can handle it.

In the case of Venita, not only does she respond angrily but anticipates she will protect a daughter from this onslaught by sending her out with "huge sharp objects" and the advice, "If anybody gets near you, just shove it into his eyes if you have to, I don't care." In Payal's case, she says she retaliates with the help of umbrellas, stepping on the toes of the man standing too close to her, or screaming and abusing. Thirty-three-year-old Neetu says she has no qualms whatsoever about making a scene to retaliate against an aggressor.

Marriage appears to shift the nature of the sexual harassment and middle-class women's responses to it. After marriage, they are less likely to travel unaccompanied on public transportation. Based on these accounts, it is also probable that due to their adult status, they are less likely to be harassed face-to-face. Instead, anonymous phone calls and letters are more frequent in adult, married women's accounts. Indira, who is the principal of a school, describes such a an occurrence in a shaken voice,

> Two years ago I was getting blank calls from a man. It got very bad, so I talked to my husband. I was doing a play at the time. He seemed to have followed me, it was frightening. I never stopped doing anything, but the little bit of tension was there. It was awful. One night it was 40 calls. Then it stopped suddenly. It was bad.

Similarly, but in a more outraged tone, Meeta says,

> When in college it used to happen. Nowadays you get letters. I showed it to my husband. They were horrible, dirty letters. I must have got about 200 letters. I wrote back saying, "I am not that kind of a girl, stop writing or I will go to the police." Now I also get blank calls. I feel so horrible. I want to take it to the police. With these letters I felt really horrible. I was afraid that my children might read them or my family [in-laws]. Then I said "balls to [the men]."

Married women who describe such incidents after marriage also express concern about the reactions from their conjugal families and, in the case of Bella, about getting a "bad name" (translation from Hindi) within the new neighborhood. And as Meeta suggests above, women appear to see harassment as their responsibility.

Clearly such accounts are not to be confused with cases in which women say they seek male attention or when they describe feelings of mutual attraction. So, for example, Piya, who describes the trauma of sexual aggression at length, also speaks about the pleasure of interacting with male peers and, later, a boyfriend. Both Meenakshi and Jaya describe incidents in which they experienced mutual feelings of sexual attraction that, in the first case, involved a cousin, and in the second case, an uncle by marriage. In their interviews, these middle-class women distinguish between what they experience as sexually stimulating and sexually offensive.

But, they also recognize when that which can be defined as sexually aggressive and offensive may have contradictory effects. For example, Preeta says that on the one hand she did not enjoy the harassment which used to occur before she was married. Nevertheless, she did miss getting that kind of *bhav* [special attention]. According to Sheetal, she used to be subjected to comments on the streets regarding her physical size till she lost the excess weight at the age of 22. Then comments became more sexual. She describes hating both kinds of comments. Yet she adds, "It changed from being a negative catcall to a not-so-negative catcall. To me it was a sense of accomplishment. One day you call me 'Hey fatso' and now you want my body."

Meenakshi, married for about 15 years, was the striking exception who says that she not only enjoyed the harassment but indeed sought it out. "I go for attention. I would wear chiffon [saris] to expose more" (translated from Hindi). She adds that the attention made her feel good and that only the fear of her family prevented her from engaging actively in any interaction.

To recapitulate, in comparison to their accounts of sexual aggression experienced when they were children, the accounts related to their pubescent and postpubescent years are characterized by more heightened feelings of fear and anxiety, but also anger and retaliation. Perhaps because the perpetrators are more frequently unknown men, women tend to be afraid for their physical and sexual safety. But, what is especially odd is that they are not likely to seek parental intervention. Despite the fact that these are unknown men, women say they fear what their parents will think or are reluctant to bring such issues to the attention of their parents. Instead, they seem to take on the burden of such aggression and seek strategies best protect themselves. For the most part, women avoid interacting with these male aggressors, but periodically their anger spills over, and they seek to retaliate more aggressively. Especially as they get older, these middle-class women seem more likely to respond aggressively to sexual transgressions from unknown men. But what remains consistent is that they perceive such behaviors as sexual aggression and take on the responsibility of dealing with them.

Sexual Aggression from Acquaintances and Friends

When speaking of sexual aggression from acquaintances and friends, the women evince a heightened sense of personal responsibility and guilt. It is both troubling and contradictory that women appear to carry the responsibility of the ramifications of sexual harassment. The contradiction is particularly evident in Piya's account of being assaulted by a man that she knew vaguely. Compared with the other accounts, Piya's narrative is unique and disturbing. Nonetheless, her account is illuminating in the way she first assumes responsibility for responding to the aggression, and then its outcome. She says in Hindi,

> I was in my final year of college. This guy was always following me, writing letters. He was really creepy. We shared a friend. She said that he is in very bad shape. So one day I went to see him at his factory. He was all alone. On my part, I went there to do a good thing, to reason out with him and tell him that I was not interested. He tried to . . . force himself on me. Somehow I managed to run out from there. I immediately went to that friend and told her what had happened. I felt so embarrassed with what I had done, I felt there was no need for me to have gone to him, no need at all. My friend felt so bad that somehow she was responsible. We both took an overdose of sleeping pills. We collapsed and were rushed to the hospital. In that small town everyone came to know. It was wrong, I should have talked to my parents. They were very helpful after the incident, they really took care of me. For a while after that my life became hell. I brought a bad name to my parents, I couldn't go out anywhere. Then as people came to know the truth things got a little better.

Piya directly assumes responsibility for the sexual aggression; her embarrassment at attempting to reason with the man and thereby exposing herself to risk triggers the overdose of sleeping pills incident and all of this also gives a "bad name" to her family.

Similar feelings of guilt and self-blame echo in the narratives of the three women who say that they were subjected to sexually inappropriate behavior from male friends. In each of the cases, the women react strongly to the incidents and say that they refused to have any further interaction with these men. Yet, in comparison with the women who describe sexual aggression from male strangers, it appears that when sexually aggressive behavior comes from friends and acquaintances, women are more likely to be concerned that their own behavior may have encouraged these men.

At the Workplace

Women who have worked outside the home say that the men they encountered in their jobs tended to view them as somewhat dimwitted and sexually accessible. Their accounts emphasize their own abilities to forestall male transgressions by self-monitoring their conduct and attire, but they may also express residual feelings of guilt. Anjali, who works as a graphic designer, says,

> Working women experience more problems because they are more at hand. They [men] have more access to her, they can approach her. He may not have drastic attentions but is trying to get close to her. Today you should try to be safe, be careful, not wear very hep clothes to the office. Wear decent clothes, not showing off your body, and be careful about your attire.

Also girls who are very chirpy and bubbly. They think she's easy to convince. You should keep limiting yourself and have control over your excitement. Not that you should create a barrier but know what to talk when.

In her account, Anjali emphasizes the significance of women's clothes and conduct in the context of male sexual aggression. She feels strongly that in order to be safe, women need to maintain limits on their demeanor. Jennifer, a well-known fashion model, agrees with Anjali's emphasis on the way women dress and interact at the workplace. Although she refuses to change the way she dresses, she says that she is the target of male sexual aggression as a result of the clothes that she wears—including shorts, skirts, and dresses. Particularly in her profession, Jennifer says, men perceive women as easy and unintelligent sexual prey.

In her narrative, Venita further articulates male coworkers' perceptions of women working in particular professions, such as actresses and models. With regard to her career as an actress in Hindi films, she says,

> People assume you are not going to be so bright, but they will make a pass at you regardless of whether they think you are bright or not. Women are still viewed as sexual objects, not as an independent entity. . . . A producer I went to meet for work told me to call up my parents and tell them that he would drop me back the next morning. I was very naive; I didn't even understand what he was getting at. When I got it, I left. I think it works two ways. Women also use their sex to get ahead. . . . I was very upset. I kept crying, "Did I give him the wrong impression?" Most girls feel that terrible sense of guilt, but all girls should get rid of that, it's not your fault. You are viewed as a sexual thing whether you are sitting like a stone or sitting in a plunging dress, you are the same. You are an object. . . . Now I don't care. I feel I should have the freedom of doing what I want without it being seen as an invitation.

In contrast to Anjali and Jennifer, Venita contends that women are predetermined as sexual objects, regardless of their conduct or attire. Although most girls internalize the guilt associated with sexual harassment at work, she says, it is independent of individual control and more appropriately blamed on a social structure that encourages men to view women as sexual objects, especially so in the case of women who work outside of the home and therefore are not under the immediate protection of male family members such as fathers, husbands, and brothers.

In highlighting the contradictions of this embedded social structure, Venita also chronicles the contradictions of female sexuality. A woman is construed as the recipient of male sexual attention but bears the responsibility of self-surveillance. Within this framework, she also bears the responsibility of restraining the sexual aggressions of men through defensive strategies and avoidance mechanisms. But I would suggest that there is another, perhaps more deep-seated, tension that shapes Venita's narrative, namely, what women describe as sexually offensive, the terms in which they describe themselves and the men they indict. As she describes the incident when she was momentarily unable to understand the producer's intent, Venita raises questions implicit in all of the narratives: Under what conditions do women perceive a sexual threat or sexual aggression, and how do they characterize male sexual aggressors?

The above narratives represent what middle-class women collectively see as the range of male sexual aggression toward them. Since these narratives are recounted in response to questions about questionable male sexual behavior, clearly, they are all within the range of what these middle-class women perceive as sexually offensive. But, across the accounts of sexual aggression that occur at various times and implicate various men as sexual aggressors, there is a shifting language of self and other. The narratives of sexual aggression related to childhood or young adulthood are not the same. Male sexual aggressors such as unknown males in public spaces, versus male coworkers who sexualize the women, are not exactly recounted in the narratives. For example, when women speak about unknown, sexually aggressive men in their postpubescent years and family members in pre- and postpubescent years, they perceive them as particularly sexually deviant, and therefore, offensive. By the same token, the women appear to be more invidiously affected as a result of the sexual aggression. Beyond the politics of woman-hood and masculinity, the politics of female sexual respectability and social class are implicated in these accounts of sexual aggression.

How They Narrate Sexual Aggression: Perceptions of Self and Other

Where these tensions between male sexuality, female sexual respectability, and social class are most strikingly revealed is in the way that middle-class women express their perceptions of sexual aggression. This language crisscrosses their accounts of sexual aggression encountered through childhood within the home or neighborhood, as well as the accounts that detail incidents in public spaces, or those that involve acquaintances and friends or male coworkers. While there are significant contextual variations across these accounts, the most clearly articulated differences are encoded in the language used to define the self and the other, or the male aggressor. Through accounts of the incidents, the impact and meaning thereof, these middle-class women suggest specific perceptions of their embodied selves, genders, and sexualities.

Sick, disgusted, dirty, irritated, angry, and scared are some of the words that women use to express the impact of incidents of sexual aggression on themselves. More than anything else these terms raise questions about the context within which women recount their experiences. Sheetal, who is in the process of setting up a clothing manufacturing plant with the help of her father, describes sexual aggression in public spaces in these words,

> In Bombay, traveling in trains you can't help but be pawed. Quite frequently. It made me feel sick, literally sick. I would feel like throwing up: "How dare you do this to me." At a younger age, I used to feel really sick. I couldn't understand why is he touching me. I wasn't abused or anything, just pawed, felt. I detested it. Today when I am pawed, I understand it from one perspective. I think all men are frustrated. I scream at them, but one has gotten used to it. I remember recently when traveling. You are getting off and men are rushing on to you . . . I was pawed. I was screaming hysterically. At that point, I felt sick, I felt disgusting. I wanted to go have a bath.

The vehemence in Sheetal's voice, her anger and outrage are compelling. What is equally noteworthy is the way she describes feeling sickened by such experiences to the point of being physically sick. Speaking about a specific incident, Sheetal articulates the disgusting nature of the experience that makes her want to erase it from her body by having a bath. Her accounts also resounds with a sense of outrage—"How dare you do this to me."

Especially in the accounts on sexual aggression from unknown men in public spaces, women are remarkably consistent in expressing their feelings. Fear, anxiety, feeling sullied, dirtied, and violated are some of the emotions that organize these accounts and the perception of the self. Women recount intense anger at insolent men who dare violate them physically and/or verbally. Feeling physically sickened, dirty, and disgusted are the reactions provoked by men who transgress boundaries by singing suggestive songs aloud, whistling, slapping women on their bottoms, and elbowing them in their breasts. They struggle to wash off the stickiness on their wrists, the touch on their breasts, and the vicious remarks which are indicators of male sexual aggression. So dirty did Mitali feel after she was touched by a male stranger that she says,

> If they are just whistling I ignore them. If they get physical that really annoys me. You can't do anything about it. In school you are taught not to create a scene. Once this guy caught my wrist as I was walking by. I went home and bathed 10 times. I felt so sticky where he touched me.

Similar emotions of fear, anxiety, dirtiness, and anger mark the accounts of child sexual abuse, and of the women's perception of being harmed and damaged. In her account, as Nipun describes the incidents perpetrated by her older male cousin, she says: "I was never hurt in any way. It was stopped before any serious damage was done." Other women describe such incidents through terms such as *disgust, dirty, horror,* and *fear,* especially as they contend with sexually aggressive uncles and cousins. But as they speak of sexual aggression from male coworkers, friends, or acquaintances, women are more likely to feel upset, guilty, and angry but not describe themselves as being dirtied or sullied.

When describing unknown males who are sexually aggressive in public spaces, the women cast them as (sexually) frustrated, sick, cheap,[11] perverted, and frightening. Male perpetrators emerge as deviants in women's accounts. Women in this study imply that male perpetrators are sexually deviant because they are either unable to control the sexual frustration that exists in all men, or because they are fundamentally different from other men, who do not commit acts of sexual aggression. This is especially consistent with respect to unknown male strangers and sexually aggressive men within the family, and far less so in the cases involving male coworkers or sexually aggressive male friends of acquaintances. So, for example, characterizing men who are sexually aggressive in public spaces such as the streets, Seema says in no uncertain terms,

> Basically people frustrated in life, who get cheap thrills touching somebody. They have sick minds, no ambitions in life. I don't blame them in a way. They are frustrated and have no one to remove their frustrations with, this is how they do it. It's like this, you have to adjust, that's the way it is.

These characterizations of the self and the other are rooted in the relationships of gender, sexuality, and class politics. The women characterize the male sexual aggressors in these terms when they perceive a threat to their sexual respectability. This language of self is related to class-based concerns of sexual respectability that are expressed by women through feelings of disgust, dirtiness, and fear at sexual aggression from unknown men. Although men across socioeconomic classes are socially constructed as potentially sexually aggressive, those from lower socioeconomic class groups are perceived to be more actively seeking release for their sexual frustrations. When male sexual aggressors are perceived as deviant either because they are from lower socioeconomic groups or because they prey on children within their families, they are also more likely to be perceived as threatening; the characterizations of self and other are likely to be heightened in women's narratives.

In their narratives, the women suggest that unknown men who engage in sexually aggressive behavior are also from lower socioeconomic backgrounds. Phrases such as "roadside Romeos," "cheap crowd," "crowd not too good," reveal that these middle-class women are quite conscious of the differences in the class statuses of the male aggressors in public spaces. For example, Anjali uses the class-related phrase "crowd not too good" to explain the sexual harassment that she frequently confronts in the vicinity of her home. In another case, Nipun says that she lives in a "decent neighborhood" to suggest why she faces only "a little" sexual harassment from unknown males. Clearly, these middle-class women are conscious of the class differences between themselves and unknown male sexual aggressors.

From this perspective, male sexuality that transgresses not only normative codes of behavior but also socioeconomic lines appears sick, perverted, and cheap. Gender- and class-based divisions shape women's perceptions of men and their offensive behaviors, and provoke women's anger and disgust in these cases. To recall Sheetal's account, she is outraged that lower-class males who travel in the general compartments of trains "dare do this to [her]." Thus, sexual desire across class and gender divisions is pathologized in the accounts of middle-class women; and men from lower social classes are more likely to be perceived as sexual deviants or as immanently sexual. As a result, it is not surprising that women describe the impact on themselves in terms that express class-based perceptions of threat to their sexual respectabilities. In these cases, male sexuality is inextricable from lower socioeconomic status and respectable female sexuality from its middle-class status.

The incestuous aggressor also threatens middle-class women's sexual respectability. If male family members are seen as the protectors of women and of women's respectability, then these aggressors, who are unequivocally seen as sexual deviants, posit a direct threat to woman. Incestuous aggressors, in contrast to the strangers and known strangers, are likely to be from the same social class as the woman. Yet, women's reactions to sexual aggression from family members, including uncles and male cousins, are somewhat similar to their reactions to aggression perpetrated by men of lower socioeconomic groups. They describe feelings of repulsion, fear of the men, and fear of telling their parents. The women also describe the men as sexually frustrated, sick, and perverted. As expressed in their accounts, middle-class women's unequivocal perceptions of these incestuous aggressors as sexual deviants reflect their concerns with sexual respectability.

In contrast, although men who are perpetrators of incidents of sexual aggression at places of work are more likely to be from the same socioeconomic class background as the women who report it, they are not cast in the same light. In these cases, as Venita and Anjali suggest in the previous section, male sexual transgressions are attributed to the absence of male protection afforded to middle-class women through fathers/brothers/kin members/boyfriends/male friends rather than the perception of desire as perverse and uncontrollable, as in the case of men of the lower socioeconomic classes. Since male colleagues and coworkers are also not kin and family members, they are less likely to be seen as deviant or perverted. Their attentions may be upsetting to women, but not in the same way as those coming from unknown or kin-related male sexual aggressors. Not surprisingly, women do not describe themselves as sickened or feeling dirty by the transgressions of male colleagues, who are likely to be of the same socioeconomic class as themselves. They are more likely to be annoyed, uncomfortable, angered, or simply relieved at the resolution of the situation.

Therefore, although there are some variations in women's accounts related to the perceived differences among male aggressors, the largely negative and culturally specific experience of sexual aggression is clearly evident. Furthermore, the experience of sexual aggression is particularly exacerbated in the cases when the sexual aggressors are men of lower socioeconomic status. Matters of gender- and class-based inequalities seem to be especially relevant to threats against the sexual respectability of the women in this study. In a parallel to these women's narratives on menarche/menstruation, the experience is recounted through an essentially individualized lens. Both fear and disgust are internalized and personalized despite the social parameters of the forms of sexual aggression. Women in this study appear to internalize the burdens of protecting their socially constructed bodies that signify womanhood and sexuality but also make them vulnerable.

Conclusion

Based on the accounts of the middle-class, urban women in this chapter, it seems necessary to broaden the range of issues that are usually described as sexual harassment or sexual abuse. The term *sexual aggression* provides one way to expand the range of issues that are named by these women, and to see the links between the various kinds of sexual aggressions perpetrated against women. It seems especially useful to bring the issues of child sexual abuse, harassment in public spaces, at the workplace, and in social settings into the same field of critical examination. If women's narratives shed light on the nature of these sexual aggressions, then they are even more useful for revealing the underlying structural tensions that, such as those accompanying class differences, lend meaning to the recounted experiences of sexual aggression directed against them.

Although state-sponsored texts are relatively silent on issues of sexual aggression, popular literature has been replete with related articles, especially over the last few years. As sexual aggression as an issue is being so addressed and managed, feminist activism against sexual violence presents an important source of challenge. What the women's narratives provide is an especially useful site to not only challenge popular discourses on sexual aggression, but to consider the meaning, nuances, and effects of sexual aggression directed against them. These narratives indicate that although hegemonic discourses scarcely represent sexual aggression as a normal part of growing up as women, class- and gender-based notions of sexual respectability help identify and give meaning to experiences of sexual aggression.

In describing the effects that acts of sexual aggression have on them and their perceptions of male sexual aggressors, women express the tensions of female sexual respectability, male sexuality, and social class. Arguably, women's narratives on invidious sexual aggression are a result of more profound and questionable notions of what constitutes womanhood, female sexuality, and maleness. These narratives call for a deeper and more thoroughgoing social critique than the rhetoric of "male dominance" and "women's low social status." Instead, they turn the focus on the structural tensions of gender, sexuality, and social class as they are manifested as experiences of sexual aggression.

What is to be challenged as well are the ways in which awareness of the female body is heightened in the experiences of women on a daily basis as they make the transition from childhood into adolescence and adulthood. Through menarche, continued menstruation, and experiences of sexual aggression women contend with the ramifications of their sexed bodies. Their lives are framed in terms of femininity and sexual respectability, and their bodies, genders, and sexualities are social effects of a system that requires self-surveillance and internalization of responsibility. Perhaps most glaringly evident in these narratives on sexual aggression, women are encouraged to self-monitor and manage their behavior according to normative gender- and class-based standards of respectability. If these regulating strategies are implicit in women's narratives, then these strategies also indicate how the gender- and class-based tensions of sexual respectability thoroughly shape what may be experienced as the female body.

In women's narratives, the emotional cast of the experiences is emphasized, and broader links to transnational processes remain attenuated. These middle-class women's characterization of themselves and male sexual aggressors resonates more broadly—for example, in the dominant discourse on rape or the pathologization of male child molesters that appears to prevail in the United States. But, given the need to theorize sexual aggression, gender, class, and sexuality against hegemonic codes produced by the nation-state more extensively, I refrain from commenting here on the intersection of more wide-ranging transnational cultural discourses.

Chapter Five

Negotiating the Norm: Speaking of Heterosexual Desire

Nowhere are these middle-class women's narratives more eye-opening than in their accounts of heterosexual desire. They effectively dispel myths about sexual conservatism, passivity, and dutiful but reluctant participation in heterosexual sex. Instead, their accounts indicate a range of discourses that shape the meanings of pleasurable participation in sexual activity and experimentation. These discourses are predominantly shaped by the links between heteronormativity, nationalisms, and transnational hegemonic codes. That the narratives appear to be colored by the lens of heteronormativity is reflected in that women seem to conflate sexuality with heterosexuality.[1] What these narratives more explicitly indicate is how heteronormativity is inextricable from nationalisms and how the premise of heterosexuality is sustained through discourses of what is socially/sexually respectable. At the same time, transnational discourses—the fusion of love and sex and the use of English to tell the narratives—are so strong that they thrive across the accounts on aspects of heterosexuality. Women's accounts of premarital and marital sexual activity indicate how they cast and recast these complex normative discourses of sexuality.

If the link between heterosexual activity, sexual respectability, and nationalism is promoted in state-sponsored sex education literatures (see Chapter Two), then it surely colors popular discourses as well. For example, an article in a widely read English language newspaper proclaims that India is undergoing a sexual revolution.[2] Other articles suggest that the sexual mores and norms are being recast amid already destabilized gender roles.[3] The hallmark of the sexual revolution appears to be changing national cultural norms of (hetero)sexual behavior for not only men, but more significantly, for women. Women, especially those from the middle and upper classes, are seen as having more sexual choices. That older middle-class women now initiate sexual relations with younger men is considered culturally novel, newsworthy, and an indication of the changing sexual attitudes and behaviors of women.[4]

At first glance the discourse of an unfolding sexual revolution suggests that Indians, and especially (middle-class) Indian women, once constrained by either tradition or Victorian prudishness, are increasingly less bound by it now.[5] But a closer look at this discourse of sexual revolution is perturbing. Although the emergence of gay and lesbian identities are considered an important aspect of this revolution, the term *sexual revolution* encodes heterosexuality. Naming a sexual revolution, which indicates a transition from repression to sexual liberation, may obscure how an increasing number of options may not entail a radical critique of the constraints on, or a revisioning of, women's sexualities. Instead, the discourse of sexual revolution may simply mark a shift in the attempts to control and manage middle-class sexualities.

From a feminist, postcolonial lens, what is clear is that the language of a sexual revolution foregrounds not only questions of changing national cultural norms of sexual behavior but also the politics of middle-class women's sexualities. Compared to the previously cited articles on sexual harassment and abuse that write women as victims of male sexual aggression, these articles acknowledge women's sexuality through a more active, if less than complex, lens. Yet, the underlying premise of what Foucault calls the "repressive hypothesis" prevents a more nuanced and critical understanding of middle-class sexualities. This premise of repression also limits feminist analyses of women's sexuality in contemporary India. Speaking to the bulk of feminist literature on sexuality, in the Introduction to the collection *Social Reform, Sexuality and the State* Patricia Uberoi astutely notes that the literature focuses on male control over women's sexuality rather than more thoroughgoing considerations of the meaning of sexuality.[6]

In this chapter I explore and analyze women's narratives for the ways in which they reflect and negotiate discourses of heterosexuality. What is most striking about these narratives is the way they continue to reiterate notions of sexual respectability, especially as shaped by social anxieties of women transgressing the boundaries of what is considered sexually appropriate. Social anxieties of this kind include fears that these women will violate the rules of chastity outside of marriage; that, especially before marriage, they might engage in or agree to sexual intercourse and jeopardize their status as virgins. Yet the women also recast and contest notions of sexual respectability. This is perhaps most explicit when they challenge the normative expectations of premarital chastity.

I explore women's narratives on various aspects of heterosexuality including nonmarital sexual activity, the meaning of virginity, marital sexual activity, sexual satisfaction, sex and intimacy, and the role of pornography. A fundamental distinction between the accounts explored in the previous chapter on sexual aggression and the accounts in this chapter is that when women speak about sexuality and sexual relationships here, they are more likely to represent themselves as active sexual agents, capable of desiring and being desired. The narratives on sexuality and sexual relationships are rooted in assumptions of mutual heterosexual attraction, desire, love, romance, and sexual needs rather than perceptions of male sexual aggression.

•   •   •

I would like to begin this chapter with Kanika's (edited) narrative on aspects of heterosexuality. Her narrative is particularly useful not because it is typical in its content but because it highlights some of the themes that undergird the accounts of the other women in this study. The way Kanika, a 24-year-old married woman, recounts her experiences and perceptions illuminates the politics of women's sexuality and sexual respectability.

On a warm afternoon, Kanika's maid shows me into the living room. Kanika is seated comfortably on a low platform that probably doubles as a bed when necessary. Dressed in black slacks and a long white T-shirt, Kanika says that she has just showered after her aerobics class. Kanika was married six months ago and still wears a newlywed glow. She lives with her husband, father-in-law, mother-in-law, and her husband's younger brother. Her marriage was arranged by her parents only after horoscopes were matched. Kanika's in-laws are from a higher social class than her family. As Kanika describes it, with her light skin color and her long, dark hair, she is considered in her ethnic community to be very attractive. She says that she had wanted a husband who was professionally qualified, understanding, loving, and with whom she would have an equal relationship. Her in-laws and her mother did not want Kanika to work outside the home after marriage. As a result, she reluctantly gave up her prestigious job. Although her husband was not professionally qualified, nonetheless, Kanika says, he had status and money. She consented to the match in deference to her parents' wishes. Kanika also describes herself as a simple girl who can adjust easily. And as the interview progresses, she clarifies that although she may have been somewhat reluctant earlier, she does not regret the marriage. According to her, she now has all the amenities plus the love from her husband. "He loves me madly," Kanika says with a laugh in her voice.

Since Kanika and her husband were from different cities, through their period of engagement they interacted primarily over the phone. She remembers fondly their extensive conversations, which on one occasion lasted several hours despite the significant cost of the phone calls. Kanika and her husband did not have sexual relations until after their wedding.

> I wanted a kiss from him. In fact, that is what we had before marriage, nothing else. [Before marriage] I was not interested. It was a total new feeling about sex after marriage. I think a woman experiencing it after marriage will be more satisfied, and she will feel more good if she has not done anything before marriage. We tried [on the wedding night], but we couldn't; we both were new, and it took a little time for us to start that kind of relation, say three or four days [she says a little shyly]. It was totally new for both of us.
>
> I think my husband enjoyed more than me [she laughs]. It was very painful for me, of course. I'd always heard about these things, but experiencing it was totally different. Then I begin to like, of course . . . and it went on smoothly [giggling]. At times after my marriage I never let him touch me. I was always shy, very scared, but later on, of course, after a few months, living with him, I enjoy sex. He was very, very understanding. He was very understanding he never forced sex, never! [with emphasis]. He said "You should be comfortable, we can do it later on." That helped me a lot. My husband understands me very much, in all matters, not only sex.
>
> I think a husband and wife become closer with sex, become closer, and the love bond also increases. Physical is a part of our marriage, it is must and compulsory [giggling]. At times I tell my husband not to go to his factory, just relax and have a holiday time and then, we have fun [giggling happily]. He's looking forward to that opportunity. Most of the time he starts it, but at times even I do it, I don't feel ashamed telling you. When he starts it I feel very sexy, I feel good, that he really cares and loves me. That is the way a person shows his feelings towards the other person. If both persons in a marriage are not sexually satisfied they will not be able to get along well, even end up in arguments, and the marriage life will become a hell. I think [sexual satisfaction] is an important part of marriage.
>
> For me sexual satisfaction is to satisfy my husband. Being an Indian housewife, that's my answer. In the West it's not that, it's just your physical satisfaction. I cannot really comment on it because I do not know much. What I feel personally is that satisfying husband, making him happy as an Indian traditional woman is your own personal satisfaction. I feel that a woman must achieve orgasm, that is good for both of them. Otherwise . . . masturbating is not good. If you are enjoying sex both the partners must be satisfied completely.
>
> Sometimes when my husband comes back tired from his factory and he does not want to, he wants to in a way but he can't do it because he is very tired, . . . hugging, kissing, just caressing each other—he loves that.

Sometimes he tells me to suck [as she misses a breath]. He feels very good and in fact feels it better than going into an intercourse. He excites me or whatever, we do not mind doing anything at all as long as we are sleeping together. Sometimes we even get up in the morning 3 o'clock, 3:30 we start, get going [she laughs].

Sexuality for me is a sensuous feeling, touching, caressing, maybe just a simple kiss. Touching each other makes me feel very satisfied. I feel very secure that he is near me and I am touching him. It makes me feel very good, very happy. Whenever we sit next to each other watching TV, he tends to catch my hand or just put his arm around me. That is the feeling that I love, just touching.

We have watched blue films [pornography] together many, many a time [she says with rueful laugh]. It was my husband's idea. Before marriage I never had the opportunity, but now, since we have a separate TV in our own bedroom, we see them. He gets the films. Initially I never liked it because I thought it was very vulgar and what we don't even do in real life they show to extremes. But later on OK, I have accepted it. It has the advantage of teaching you new kinds of ways [her rising voice ends in a laugh]. I don't feel shy to tell you that we have started doing new ways from blue films only because there is no one else to teach you these things. So it's OK. We both enjoy watching the films. In fact sometimes I tell him to get it. "It's long time, come on, get it." It's from both ways, not only my husband. You get new ways of sex, learn how to do it. It does not excite me, but I just look from the view that I am learning something. . . . I like watching romantic scenes in Indian films. I daydream and place myself and my husband in a dance sequence, kissing sequence, or even a bed scene. Indian films are totally different from blue films. They are more emotional, you feel yourself in that place, and you enjoy more.

Before marriage I was closest to my mother. After marriage, of course, my husband. I tend to shed my tears on his shoulder and tell him everything. I don't hide anything from him because the way he asks me, the way he cares. He says, "We are very good pals in this world. I don't have anyone else besides you. You are the only one, and why do you want to hide anything from me?" And he tells me all his problems. So we both share everything to each other, every single minutest detail. That way we have an excellent relationship.

Kanika's narrative is frequently interspersed with self-conscious giggles, laughter, embarrassed glances, hesitations in the voice, and shifting postures. Throughout the interview, and especially as she discusses sexual issues, Kanika does not decline to respond to a single question posed to her. Rather, she strategically negotiates her way around the sensitive nature of this topic. Kanika is able to speak of intensely personal issues by resorting sometimes to ambiguous language and at other times to abstract language. For example, in the first paragraph of the interview reproduced above, the nature of the language is quite ambiguous. What provides meaning is not only the context of response, but also the tone of voice, facial expression, and body language. Indeed, compared to other women in this study, Kanika is relatively more direct in her responses in her repeated use of the word "sex" and other words such as "suck" and "masturbating."

Kanika's narrative locates the role of sexual activity for women, with the exception of kissing, within marriage. In her interview, she is decidedly clear that women should experience sexual intercourse after marriage. In fact, she suggests that women will feel better if they have not had any prior sexual experience. A kiss from her fiancé, Kanika admits, is what she wanted and no more. With regard to sex and marriage, she speaks to the initially unfamiliar nature of sexual activity and sexual intercourse. Kanika believes that an understanding husband enabled her to overcome her shyness and fear around shared sexual activity and eventually even abled her to enjoy sex. Kanika goes from experiencing sex as at first painful, to being shy and afraid of sex, and finally to enjoying sex. She makes a transition from being a passive part-ner while her the husband initiates and enjoys sex, to initiation of mutually enjoyable sex. The "understanding husband" is the enabling factor in this transition; had he been less than understanding, he could have forced sex upon her.

In establishing the role of sexual activity within marriage, Kanika simulta-neously separates and fuses it with love. Kanika believes that sexual activity is compulsory within marriage because it increases the so-called bond of love; by implication, then, they are intertwined but not redundant. Initiating sex-ual activity is a demonstration of the emotion of love, according to her. Moreover, sexual activity keeps the marriage together. Perhaps this is why Kanika says that no matter what kind of sexual activity she and her husband engage in, the important aspect is that they sleep together. Furthermore, sex-uality is not only a sensuous feeling that involves caressing or a simple kiss but it is rooted in the sense of security manifest in a mere touch between her-self and her husband.

The emphasis on the inseparable links between emotional love and sexual activity in marriage consistently shapes Kanika's narrative. In her account the bond of marriage is not only secured upon emotional and physical closeness with her husband, but on friendship and an unrestrained, communicative relationship that takes precedence over all other relationships. Specific forms of activity, such as watching pornography with her husband, are important to the extent they serve this sexual/emotional marital bond. Kanika says that she does not enjoy pornographic videos in the way that she enjoys romantic Hindi films, but she qualifies that pornographic videos have the advantage of teaching new kinds of sexual techniques. In the absence of other such avenues, pornographic videos can be partially enjoyable because they ultimately promote the sexual/emotional marital bond.

What is especially puzzling is the way Kanika invokes the issue of nationality when speaking about sexual satisfaction. She suggests that her sexual satisfaction is predicated on satisfying her husband sexually. Indeed, not only is this an aspect of being a traditional woman or housewife but about being an *Indian* woman. In so doing, she associates the issue of women's sexuality with national cultural differences. Yet, doubtlessly, both partners must be equally satisfied because this is integral to the "love bond" within marriage, and, arguably, the opposite could lead to masturbation. This tension between sexual satisfaction, womanhood, male sexuality, and Indianness, on the one hand, and mutual, seemingly egalitarian sexual relationships within marriage, on the other hand, further complicates her narrative on sexuality.

In effect, Kanika's narrative raises several analytical issues: the location of sexual activity—specially, forms of sexual intercourse within marriage; the centrality of sexual activity to her marital relationship—the fusing of heterosexual activity with emotional intimacy and the expectations of mutual, egalitarian sexual relationships within marriage; and the link between gender, heterosexuality, and discourses of nationalism manifest in the assumptions of sexual respectability. Extending our focus to include the narratives of other women in this study, allows an analysis of each of these issues in turn. Of particular interest is how women describe these various aspects of sexuality in the context of the interview and the ways in which they reiterate, negotiate, and contest the politics of sexual respectability from the viewpoint of the middle class. I will also explore the links between these narratives on heterosexuality, respectability, the contemporary nation-state, and transnational processes.

Sexual Respectability: Chastity and Premarital Sexuality

If a predominant expectation pertaining to middle-class women's sexualities is pre-marital chastity, then it is only appropriate to explore women's perceptions on the meaning and impact it has in their lives. Available literature on sexuality emphasizes the contemporary importance of premarital chastity for women. For example, in his book *Intimate Relations*, Sudhir Kakar argues that social norms seek to channel women's sexualities within the institutions of marriage and ultimately motherhood.[7] Sujata, a 29-year-old who has been married for eight years, confirms the importance of premarital chastity in no uncertain terms. Although she and her husband-to-be dated for more than three years sex was never an issue, she says,

No, no. There was no question of it at all. In the sense . . . we didn't either of us think that way. Like he says now—"That was my initial intention," he tells me that, he tells my mum for that matter! But, no, not at all. It didn't reach to that point at all, maybe giving kisses but further than that, no!

[Why not?] Because I was not brought up that way for me to give myself up or give up my virtues or whatever you call it. Before marriage it was implanted in me, it's maybe not sinful but it's wrong. Not that I had any friends who had gone that way, but it was inbuilt into me. I am positive even if he had coaxed me and taken me somewhere, it would not have happened. I was not mentally prepared for it. Maybe physically I would respond, but you also have mental preparations. You will stiffen up and say "I can't do this." And I guess he knew it and respected it. Maybe a year later he broached the subject and said "Can we?" and I said, "No," but at no point did he pressurize me. When I ask him he says, "I was serious at the time. I respected you for that." And I said, "Good, when I get married, I will get something different."

What is most striking is Sujata's vehemence to what I would consider a fairly straightforward question. Then again, perhaps it is not so straightforward. As Sujata suggests, at heart, the question of premarital sexual relations is one about how she was raised, the kind of values that were instilled in her, and, arguably, her sexual behavior as a woman. Given the circumstances, her sexual response may have been strong, but her mind would not let her proceed with it. In her account there also appears to be a division of labor regarding sexual intercourse. Her fiancé is the one who initiates and intends the possibility, but she is the one who quells it. Indeed, this is what distinguishes her, conceivably, from other women, and earns his respect, according to Sujata. What is perhaps most telling about Sujata's narrative is the way she sees the issue of premarital abstinence from sexual intercourse as a matter of her "virtues or whatever" that secure her mental resolve against male sexual intentions. Kisses are OK but anything further is unthinkable.

Meena gives similar reasons for not consummating her relationship prior to the wedding. About her fiancé and the period of their engagement, she says,

I was against it. I was totally against it. Because I have this upbringing in me, my culture, that I didn't want to have sex with a guy before marriage. I was stern about it. . . . He was not of the point that we should do it before marriage—go all the way. He would not agree to that also. We were quite stern about it.

Not only does Meena, like Sujata, invoke the idea of upbringing but she more clearly links it with the notion of "culture"; that is, the cultural belief that one should not "do it before marriage" or "go all the way." Elaborating on this premise of premarital sexual abstinence and culture, Chandni succinctly says that she and her fiancé did not consummate their relationship prior to the wedding because "We are not of that mental outlook, being Indians." In her narrative, Nipun further spells out this connection between heterosexuality and national cultural tradition,

> The impression I get is that Indian women are becoming bolder with the Western influence. We are becoming bolder in the wrong sense. They are becoming more conscious of AIDS. We are in reverse. We are having more sexual partners. I don't see it becoming better in India. We take the wrong things at the wrong time.

Nowhere is the question about sexuality more clearly associated with the issue of national cultural tradition in these interviews than when the women speak of premarital sexual chastity. By mandate of their cultural upbringing or being Indian, anything more than a few kisses belongs within the institution of marriage. Recall Kanika's narrative where she says that all she wanted before marriage was a kiss, and that's all she had. As many as 34 of the 53 women who were asked about premarital sex implicitly or explicitly invoked a similar set of meanings—the importance of chastity for women before and outside of marriage *in keeping with a national cultural tradition*. As the women cited above suggest, sometimes vehemently, and at other times more dissmissively, there is little ambiguity regarding this issue. Respectable sexuality does in fact belong to the domain of the nation-state.

But what is less apparent from these narratives is that the lines between sexual chastity and "going all the way" are blurry and that what counts as sexual respectability is by no means unambiguous. As is more clearly established by literature regarding premarital heterosexual activity within the United States, sexual chastity and virginity are not the same;[8] there are a myriad of sexual possibilities between kissing and sexual intercourse. *Teenagers Ask, The Doctor Answer* provides a useful glimpse into the distinctions between chastity and virginity.

> *Question:* What do you mean by the term "a virgin"?
> *Answer:* By definition, a virgin is a girl whose hymen is intact. The hymen is a fleshy, thin membrane which partially closes the mouth of the vagina. The closure is not complete and it is possible to introduce a finger through the opening without breaking the hymen.
> When the girl first has sexual intercourse, the hymen is stretched and ruptures and this is accompanied by some discomfort and bleeding. As the shape, texture and size of the opening differ considerably in different

women, the discomfort and bleeding will vary. However, there are cases where even in a virgin the hymen is not intact, and may be so stretchable that it may not bleed at all even at the first intercourse.

In other cases, the hymen can rupture as a result of operations, injury, masturbation or excessive physical activity although the girl is still a virgin.[9]

Alongside the obvious problem of the gendered explanation of the term virgin—by definition, the virgin is a woman—there is an attempt to specify its meaning technically and behaviorally. On the more technical side lies the intact hymen, which is the litmus test of virginity or lack thereof. However, the test, as the doctor suggests, is not infallible. It is conceivable to be sexually active and have an intact hymen, either due to a resilient hymen or digital penetration. Hence, according to this explanation, although the intact hymen defines a virgin, more accurately a virgin is a woman with or without an intact hymen who has not had sexual intercourse. While both the intact hymen and abstinence from sexual intercourse prescribe the virgin, only abstinence from sexual intercourse is a necessary and sufficient criterion.

For these middle-class women to engage in sexual activity outside of marriage—to create an oppositional set of meanings as it were—they would need to overcome two societal barriers in their lives: the technicality of the hymen and, more importantly, of nonmarital chastity. Kissing, petting from the waist upward, mutual masturbation, and oral sex are all forms of sexual activity that circumvent the technical importance of the hymen. Through these forms of sexual activity, it is conceivable to be sexually active without overtly challenging the prevailing cultural construction of the hymen, merely undermining its connection to chastity. Forms of sexual activity that preclude penetrative vaginal sex lie in that ambiguous domain of sexuality, blurring commonly held distinctions such as sexually active/inactive, chaste/impure, virgin/nonvirgin. Sexual intercourse prior to marriage, however, enables the explicit and irrevocable repudiation of the ascendancy of the hymen. Thereafter, one is no longer sexually chaste.

Twenty-five-year-old Anita's story perhaps most compellingly illuminates this ambiguous realm of sexually active virgins with intact or ruptured hymens. When she was dating the man who is now her husband, they were sexually active for several years before having vagina-to-penis penetrative intercourse. She elaborates,

> Initially you are a little shy because of your upbringing that a woman is supposed to be a little more subdued, but if it gives pleasure to the other person you love so much, why not! Then I started taking equal part in everything, and it really helped. You feel good about it. Initially for the first three years

it was normal hugging and kissing, stuff like that. You are a little worried about other things. It's stupid but waist upwards is okay. You feel good about things, and you have trust in that person. For two, two and a half years I was against penetration. Maybe for the first one and a half or two years I was against anything waist downwards. Then I got a little used to it. Some friends said that when you are in love with somebody, and he can give you that kind of pleasure, it's nice. So you think that's OK but not penetration. So for about a year, year and a half before penetration we would do other things, mainly oral sex. Today I feel very foolish, but you have these taboos and these stupid mental blocks in your head.

It is notable that Anita describes hugging and kissing as normal, but all else appears taboo and, by implication, deviant. Her account reads like a gradual progression to increasingly sexual activity. At the end of the continuum lies vaginal-penile penetration. Based on this account, the question of when Anita became sexually active is moot, to say the least. What appears to be critical here is that she is in love with the man whom she is sexually active with. At first, she invokes the significance of his pleasure, but later, when referring to oral sex, she expresses her sexual pleasure. Whether oral sex is less sexual than vaginal penetration is difficult to determine. But it is clear that vaginal penetration is more charged; it is the most enduring taboo in Anita's narrative.

Anita is one of the 12 (or 20 percent) women in this study who describe experiencing sexual intercourse before marriage. Seven are now married. Of them, six married their sexual partners; the remaining married woman says that her first sexual intercourse was with a man other than her husband and that her prior sexual experience was not an issue for either her or her husband. None of the five single women who have had sexual intercourse indicated that they have plans to marry that male partner or anyone else.

Based on the descriptions of these women, the number of sexually active women prior to marriage is probably greater than 20 percent. Yet, it cannot be fully ascertained since women engage in a range of sexual behaviors. They describe forms of sexual activity ranging from kissing, petting from the waist upward, and in some cases, gradually easing into sexual intercourse. Curiously, in the accounts of women who engage in premarital or nonmarital sexual activity, a gradual progression into what are perceived as more sexual behaviors is evident. This progression into successively more "sexual" forms of activity distinguishes the women who describe having sexual intercourse before marriage from those who first have sexual intercourse after marriage.

Yet, 20 percent of the women in this study say that they have had nonmarital or premarital sexual intercourse. Anu and Pranati each elaborate on the reasons for their initial inhibitions toward vaginal sexual intercourse and then for eventually shedding them. They both describe being initially uncomfortable with the idea of progressing beyond the "normal" hugging and kissing. Anu says, "Initially I was so scandalized." The chances that they would not marry the men that they were dating and seeking to be sexually active with scared them both. Cultural prescriptions on women's premarital virginity partially inhibited them. But, as Pranati expands, "Initially one was a little scared. . . . then you realize that you love a person. If you are all for the person, you are all for the person." Eventually within a context of heterosexual romance they are able to overcome their cultural inhibitions. For all 12 women, the decision to be sexually active was based on the fact that they were in love with those men at the time.

Similarly, the seven married women link and justify their decision to have premarital sexual intercourse with the fact that they were in love with their male partners. For six of the seven married women, the assurance that they would marry the men they were romantically involved with eased their decision to ignore the cultural norms of premarital chastity. Rati explains, "I didn't want to sleep with someone I wouldn't marry. I wanted to be totally sure that this is the guy I am going to marry; then I could give myself to that person." Romantic love and the promise of imminent marriage together justify the repudiation of dominant cultural inhibitions in the accounts of the women.

In retrospect, these married women remember their premarital sexual activity with humor. Anu and Pranati recall being sexually active with their husbands-to-be despite their mothers being present in the house, and in Rati's case, her grandfather. They were also convinced that these adults knew about their sexual activities but did not confront them. The humor is tinged with regret, perhaps most dramatically in Rati's account. She says about her premarital sexual activity,

> I think that's another thing that put me in their [in-laws] black books. I've never been able to live it down. That's probably the most impulsive thing I've done all my life . . . but now that I've been through some things in life I've learned that certain things you can't get away with.

The other point of regret expressed by six of these women is the decline of postmarital sexual activity due to structural constraints, such as the effect of their husbands' jobs on their marital relationships.

The five single women who describe having had first sexual intercourse also base their sexual activity on romantic or emotional involvement. For Monica, a 28-year-old, it is important that she was in love with her male partner, that it was special because it had happened only two or three times. Otherwise, she says dismissively, "It's just sex." In her account, Sheetal echoes the significance of emotional love. She says,

> It was wonderful. I thought myself in love. It was the first time I slept with
> someone, and it was a great confidence booster. I slept with him after a
> year of wooing. After kissing, caressing, etcetera. I couldn't do it in India
> the first time. I couldn't let myself go. I did not have a room, we did not
> have any privacy. . . . He came to New York, and we stayed together for a
> month.

Sheetal did not travel to New York for the sole purpose of having sexual
intercourse with a young man, but it appears to have helped her to shed cultural inhibitions and also provided the necessary privacy.

Across the narratives of currently married and single women, the decision
to engage in sexual intercourse outside of marriage is justified upon the
premise of heterosexual love and romance. In some cases it is partly based on
an assurance of marriage to the male sexual partner. But, in all 12 accounts,
love and romance are the factors central to the decision. Being in love, trust-
ing and feeling comfortable with the male partner, justifies sexual intercourse
prior to marriage. Gradual progression through culturally charged forms of
sexual activity helps these middle- and upper-class women to negotiate prevailing cultural inhibitions and the mandate of chastity. Premarital and nonmarital sexual activity is articulated through a language embedded in the discourse of heterosexual love and its attendant aspects, such as emotional and
sexual attraction.

This is not to suggest that women who do not describe first sexual intercourse as yet or prior to marriage are committed to the ideology of premarital chastity. Two of the 32 married women and five of the 17 single women
who say that they have not experienced sexual intercourse, do not believe in
this premise. In the case of the married women, sexual intercourse seems to
have occurred only after marriage for situational reasons; for example, the
lack of opportunity. The five single women say that although they have not
experienced sexual intercourse thus far, their decisions are likely to be based
on the situation at hand rather than a strongly held belief in premarital
chastity.

The narratives reiterate notions of sexual respectability. Normative prescriptions of premarital chastity appear to be central to what counts as sexual respectability for these middle-class women. Not only do these normative
prescriptions shape women's narratives on sexuality but they are overtly
linked to the premise of national cultural identity. As *Indian* women, premarital nonchastity is unthinkable. On the other hand, this link between
women's sexuality and sexual respectability is extended and reshaped in other
narratives. What counts as sexual respectability is itself reshaped by linking
premarital sexual activity, including but not limited to sexual intercourse, to

notions of heterosexual love and emotional affinity. Within this framework, if you are in love, then premarital sexuality, if not requisite, is at least not inappropriate. Even as these narratives undermine one normative definition of middle-class sexual respectability linked to national cultural tradition, they invoke another prescriptive model that cuts across the parameters of national cultural tradition—the fusion of love and sex, or the eroticization of love and the romanticization of sex.[10]

The Sexually Respectable: Marital Sexuality, Intimacy, and Transnational Cultural Discourses

In contrast to coverage of premarital sexuality, the literature on marital sexuality has reinforced notions about the lack of women's agency and willing participation in sex. Available studies on marital sexuality suggest that because of prevailing attitudes on sexuality in general and on women's sexuality in particular, women do not have much agency in the realm of sexuality. In a study of Hindu women of a village in south-central India, Dhruvarajan suggests that women perceive sex as a man's pleasure and a woman's duty.[11] According to her, women believe that men have stronger sex urges and that it is unwomanly to be interested in sex; nonetheless, women have a duty to accommodate men and bear their children. Das extends this theme in her study of the relationship between femininity and the body among urban Punjabis.[12] Das argues that women are expected to be sexually accessible to their husbands, to extend the lineage, and to absorb the pollution of sexual intercourse, including its attendant sin and danger. Reporting on the lives of married middle- and upper-class women, Kakar paints a more dismal picture in which the majority of women are sexually deprived and unsatisfied.[13]

By contrast, middle-class women's narratives on sexuality within marriage do not support either the picture or the notions of absorbing pollution, simply being sexually available to their husbands, or describing sex primarily as an avenue to motherhood. Rather, in their narratives on sexuality and marriage, these women draw on prescriptive notions of the centrality of sex within marriage in ways that are likely to heighten women's anxieties as well as their expectations. If marriage is where women are able to be sexual persons, then it is probable that sexuality would be seen as a central aspect of the marital relationship. Within this framework, marital sexual activity is as closely associated with concepts of romantic love and intimacy as is nonmarital sexuality. The quality of one determines the quality of the other.

Initial Sexual Experiences

The narratives of the 24 middle-class women who describe their first and early sexual experiences within marriage tell about heightened anxieties but also expectations of pleasurable and enjoyable first sexual experiences. In her account, Sheila, who was engaged at age 18 and married at 19, says that she was a little excited but also anxious. In her words,

> A little excited, a little anxious because it was something very new. A little anxious, excited, scared also. So it was all mixed. I felt very scared, very ashamed. I felt very embarrassed to go in front of him. It was all very new. So, I felt very embarrassed first few days.

Perhaps Payal, who was also married at a young age to a man she met through her family, best captures the anticipation around sex after the wedding. She says humorously about the day of the wedding,

> We were very comfortable with each other. We were waiting: What's going to happen! You want to know about it. It's such a big hitch. I remember being in school and saying, "We can't die before knowing what it's all about!"

In her narrative, Chandni, who married a man she was engaged to for three months, further elaborates on the anticipation of sex after marriage as well as what it took to make it a positive experience. She says,

> I was looking forward to it. I didn't read any books or see a blue movie to excite me. That's what one of my family members said. She said you will feel more excited. I said, "Sorry I don't feel it necessary to excite me through those media. My husband will be enough to excite me." He was very nice to me, very considerate. Although he had done a lot of reading, he wanted to know what I would feel like. He read it for me. He knew that I didn't have any serious boyfriends so I was basically ignorant about these things, although in today's age and generation nobody can really be ignorant about it. It was just the fact that it was new for me, I had never been through it, and he was very nice and not only through the act but even after that, that felt even more nice.

If Chandni was looking forward to her first sexual experience with her new husband, then what seems to be the critical factor in making it a "nice" experience is his considerateness and responsiveness to her. In these narratives, husbands frequently bear the onus for the quality of the first sexual experience.

In her account, Sarita, who married after what she calls a whirlwind romance, says of her first sexual experience after marriage,

> The night we got married we were not able to consummate it; the penetra-
> tion was not complete. I think it happened two or three nights later. But he
> was very caring, very loving, and I think he is still very caring.

What is curious about Sarita's account is that even though they were not
able to have sexual intercourse the first time she and her husband tried, she
emphasizes the caring, loving role that he played in these events. Put differently, her first sexual experience is recounted in terms of her husband's role.
By the same token, Indira describes physical discomfort at first sexual intercourse only to emphasize that "nothing else was wrong, everything else was
all right. We have never been anxious about each other. There was a lot of
curiosity what it would be like, one wondered, but no anxiety."

If women's anxieties related to first sexual experience are mitigated or their
anticipations fulfilled as a result of considerate, understanding husbands, then
husbands can also cause less than pleasurable sexual experiences. Meenakshi,
who consented to marry a man she met through her parents some 15 years
ago, says in Hindi,

> It wasn't much fun. I didn't enjoy at all. Before marriage I didn't have a rela-
> tionship with anyone. I was very much excited, and it was as if something
> incredible was going to happen. . . . But nothing of that sort. It was two or
> three years after that I started enjoying. He was not too interested. He was
> not too confident about himself, his sexuality. He was very nervous. To
> swallow that also took some time. Today we are mentally and physically
> close to each other, but it took some time. With respect to the physical also
> it took a long time for me to adjust to him.

What is clear from these narratives is that the women were anxious but
also anticipated and expected to enjoy these first sexual experiences with
their husbands. Nonetheless, the onus of the pleasurable outcome and quality of these experiences is contingent upon the husbands. Even when physical pain is described, it is subordinated to the understanding and considerate
husband. On the flip side, that kind of a husband can make the difference
between expectations met and those disappointed. Whereas a considerate
husband is pivotal to Chandni's account on a positive first sexual experience,
for Meenakshi, the account centers on the failed expectations of sexual
enjoyment, but also the failing husband.

The Eroticization of Marital Love and the Marital Romanticization of Sex

As the 31 married women recount the meaning and role of sexual activity within marriage, they stress not only the role of their husbands but the overall quality of the marital relationship. Based on their accounts, sexual relations play a pivotal role in forging and maintaining marital bonds.[14] Anita tells about how her understanding "sweetheart" of a husband not only helped bring sexual pleasure to her but enhanced their relationship. Since Anita could not enjoy sexual activity to the point of orgasm, her husband was concerned for her; a rare quality in a man, especially an Indian man, she says,

> It is rare because most men don't give a damn, most Indian men. I don't know whether all men but most Indian men. So it was important for him that I have pleasure too, so we tried other things and it didn't really work. I don't know if it was my concentration or I don't know what. So I spoke to this friend of mine and she said try orally, and you will really like it, and it worked! It was a wonderful experience, and of course it was intimate. It brought us a lot more closer.

This premise that sexual activity fosters closer emotional relationships is consistent throughout the married women's narratives. Elaborating on the link between sex and the marital relationship, Piya suggests that she and her husband share a lot more because of the sexual activity. She says emphatically,

> Once a day, we will talk about it and much more. This is very important, very important. If I am away, I think about him. I think about him sexually, not just as a person. I think about him touching me. Till date it is very important. I don't know whether it is right or wrong, but it's important.

As she talks about the role of sex within marriage, Indira sheds further light on its significance. According to her, only then is it possible to have "the emotional and mental closeness." Ketaki, who has been married four years, sees sex with love and sex without love as oppositional. She says,

> When you are having this thing you should feel good, wonderful. You should feel your husband loves you so much. The love should be there. That's the thing. But if the feeling doesn't come, you don't feel close to each other, then I feel you don't truly love each other. It's like you are just having it, it's like eating food, going to the toilet or something like that.

From their perspectives, sex and emotional love are inextricable, and if the emotional bond is seen as lacking, then these middle-class women are likely to express concerns with sexual activity. Since sex is seen as instrumental to a more fulfilling emotional relationship with one's husband, without its emotional connection, sex would be seen as lacking in this framework. Payal, who married a man eight years her senior when she was 18 years old, expresses her dissatisfaction in so many words.

> Strangely enough the physical part was very good for both of us. That would upset me even more because I used to say OK . . . you feel comfortable and have a nice time, but there's more. Maybe men and women differ on this. I would say, "Why don't we talk" but men like to get it over and done with. He was very good to me when he was feeling physical and everything, and then he would say, "Don't disturb me." That used to really annoy me.

Similarly, for Kavita, who has been married 14 years, sex continues to be less than an enjoyable experience because the emotional connection with her husband is lacking.

> I think for a person like me mental happiness is very important. I need to be mentally relaxed. So I never wanted it. It is my duty to please him, and so I do it. Otherwise, given a choice, I don't mind living without it so far. I am not saying I have never enjoyed it at all or enjoyed it ever. Maybe when I am happy. Then of course when we come closer, it's fine. But not otherwise and not very frequently.

What is curious about Kavita's account is not only that she invokes the concept of sex as a "duty" to her husband despite her own reluctance but also how infrequent this concept is across the narratives of the middle-class women. Only one other woman, Bella, reasons in her account that even though she does not particularly enjoy sex, it is her duty as a wife, so she might as well do it with love.

The framework within which the 31 married women tell their accounts is undergirded by notions of mutual enjoyment, pleasure, and emotional intimacy rather than duty and an unambiguous subordination of their sexuality to that of their husbands. Within this framework that secures marital sexual activity to normative ideals of companionate marriage, the understanding husband is vital to accounts of sexual pleasure. Thus women are less likely to describe feelings of sexual deprivation and dissatisfaction—to do so would be a reflection on the quality of their husbands, their marriage, and their lack of pleasure. In Chapter Six I will further explore why these women are unlikely to implicate their husbands. But, here it is important to note that where women perceive sex as integral to the marital bond, a source of pleasure and emotional intimacy, they are more likely to describe ways of enhancing it rather than to dwell on its inadequacies.

Pleasure and Sexual Satisfaction

In their accounts, the 31 married women stress the importance of mutual sexual satisfaction. Physical pleasure is central to what is perceived as sexual satisfaction. With the exception of Bella, the one thing that these women seem certain about is the importance of sex as pleasure in marriage. Sex in its procreative function appears to play no part in the meaning of sexual activity and desire. Speaking on this link between pleasure and sex, Piya says in a clear, even tone,

> If it gives pleasure, I can do anything. It means touching, kissing and orgasming as well. You need both, some start—kissing, hugging and then orgasming. At least I need both. I can't just start up like a machine, and I can't end without reaching climax. The reason women are not sexually satisfied is that they haven't been able to talk about it. Mostly in India they don't talk about such a thing or don't feel it's important. Or they feel that men don't think it's important for them to reach climax. I don't know about this generation but especially the last generation, I don't think they would tell their husbands whether they enjoyed it. You both should be comfortable about it because it is like a normal part of life like eating, bathing, drinking, sleeping. It's the normal need of a body, so it should be satisfying for both, and you should talk about it.

If Ketaki had separated sex from the mundane activities of life in her narrative quoted above, then Piya suggests that sex is about pleasure and enjoyment for both partners precisely because it is a normal part of life. In this account, Piya also suggests that part of the satisfaction and pleasure to be derived from sex is based on the ability for a woman to talk about it with her husband, to express whether it was satisfying.

So central is this expectation of sexual satisfaction and pleasure in these women's narratives, that sexual satisfaction, or the lack thereof, is expected to affect every aspect of a woman's life. In Anita's words,

> I think it is very important. One friend of mine, her husband is well educated but not sensitive about her. As a result she has such a mental block, and she doesn't enjoy sex at all. She just doesn't bother, but I told her, "Why don't you speak, you must speak in these things." Eventually it does make a difference in your personal life. It does make you irritable. You have a guy, but you are still a little lonely. You are not a complete woman. You are not cheerful if you are not sexually satisfied. I have another friend who is sexually satisfied. She is totally confident. She has a mind of her own and is totally confident about it.

What is consistent about Anita's account is the way she emphasizes the importance of talking to one's husband when one does not enjoy sex. What is equally remarkable is Anita's emphasis on the kind of toll this lack of sexual satisfaction will eventually take on a woman's life. On the contrary, a sexually satisfied woman is totally confident and sure about herself. Similarly, Nipun expects a wide-ranging impact of the lack of sexual satisfaction and pleasure in a woman's life. She says,

> In my opinion a woman is happier if she is sexually satisfied. Otherwise she has always got a feeling of craving or disappointment. You never know what it may grow into and make her bitter. To my little experience once you start liking it the more you want it. And if you don't get it, it may come out in some other form of behavior. I think it is an important part of life. I wouldn't take it lightly. She can feel satisfied without having orgasm. But we just got pleasure from the act. That's all.

Based on these accounts, the lack of sexual pleasure and satisfaction will manifest as psychosomatic ill health, irritation, frustration, and general unhappiness in the life of a married woman. In effect, not only is sexual pleasure normalized as the centerpiece of sexual activity but also framed as a factor of the quality of one's marital relationship. In these accounts, pleasure is expansively defined. It may include, but not be limited to, orgasm. According to Indira, while orgasms are nice, they do not exhaust the definition of sexual pleasure.

Speaking of and otherwise communicating about sex is thereby necessary to ensure the smooth functioning of sexual and, more importantly, married life. Rati succinctly captures these aspects that thread through the various narratives,

> It is important to be sexually satisfied. I don't know many women who are. I don't think that many women achieve orgasm by normal sexual intercourse. You have to be stimulated orally or some other way to achieve orgasm. I've never had orgasm just by direct physical intercourse. With me I've learned to live with things. There are times when I have not been satisfied but I don't make an issue out of it, but there are times when I have, and it makes up for the other times. Actually I don't think it's necessary to get an orgasm to feel satisfied. It's just that you are close to each other, doing this together means a lot more than achieving orgasm. It's just that your husband loves you, he's holding you, kissing you. There are other sensations of the body besides orgasm.

The ambiguity about whether this is a narrative about sexual climax, sexual pleasure, emotional intimacy, or the marital relationship only illustrates the ways these strands are woven together in women's narratives on marital sexuality. Moreover, where sexuality is about pleasure within the context of intimacy, women are also likely to describe ways of enhancing these experiences.

Watching Pornography, Improving the Marriage

Counterintuitively and contrary to some feminist literature on pornography, the women describe pornography as a significant way to improve their sexual relations with their husbands, and their overall marital bond. In most accounts of these married, middle-class women pornography serves to improve their sexual and marital relationships. But not all see pornography in a positive light. Indeed, a few of the women say that they are completely repulsed. Yet most of them support the role of pornography within the context of their sexual relations with their husbands. Even those who say they did not initially enjoy watching pornographic videos do see some benefits. Others are more candid about the kind of pornography that they enjoy and the stimulus that it provides to their sexual lives. In these accounts, pornography specifically refers to what are called "blue films" that circulate in the forms of videos to be watched in the privacy of homes and bedrooms and films that are broadcast over a mushrooming cable system.[15]

In her narrative, Indira explains the conditions under which she and her husband watch pornography. She says,

> Our cable guy used to show it. And it came on late in the night so we said, "Let's see what it's all about." It was a big joke. It was not the first time we were seeing it. We enjoy soft porn because it makes more sense—there is something happening, there is a reason for whatever happens. Here you just have a girl, and she just takes off her clothes, and beyond a point you say, "Forget it. Disgusting." It's the same old thing, you see it once, fine. We enjoy something if it is light. Because even in our relationship there's a lot of lightheartedness in the sexual part.
>
> I have no hassles. I don't think there's anything wrong. There's nothing negative. If it gives you any satisfaction, great. But I believe it because I have seen a lot of change here in India especially in a big city like Bombay. I don't think the men have to be coerced, and if the wives don't agree, it's more out of conditioning. It's something that one should pretend not to like. You look at *Playboy* and say, "Sheee" [disgust]. Sometimes they are very beautiful, and I think it's great. A lot of that is going on with the higher middle class and the upper strata.

To read Indira's account on the role of pornography, it appears that "soft porn" promotes sexual interaction with her husband.[16] Whereas she emphasizes elsewhere that soft porn creates a sexually playful setting, Indira also suggests that hard-core pornographic films are "disgusting" and repetitive. If Indira sees no merit in hard-core pornography, her description of the purpose of soft porn is markedly similar to other women's description of hard-core pornography.

Describing hard-core pornography, Payal says,

> We first watched them when we got married. These cousins of my husband's had got them for us, and we were all four watching. Highly embarrassing. We had just got married, and we were flying off to our honeymoon. We are very close to that couple. They put it on, and I didn't know where to look. If it is just the two of you then it's OK.
>
> You enjoy it when you feel you have run out of ideas, it's the same. Then I tell him. It acts as a stimulant. Gives you an idea of what else can be done. It does have an effect. If you watch two people making love, it makes you feel you want to. It arouses you. Just the act is arousing itself. It works with everybody the same way. I think women feel the need to have sex but because of the conditioning that you are not supposed to or only loose women are supposed to, you are not supposed to enjoy it. It's not spoken out, but it runs through your mind. It can make you feel, am I very aggressive?

What appears common to these accounts is more than one narrative about women's sexuality with respect to pornography. On the one hand, women are not supposed to enjoy this kind of stimulation, but on the other hand, it is instrumental to sexual play, sexual arousal, and sexual stimulation. Both Indira and Payal express notions about the nature of women's conditioning, yet in their cases, they do not feel bound by them. Perhaps related to the conditioning, in their accounts, these married women suggest that their husbands or others initiated watching pornographic films/videos.[17] But, as Preeta suggests in her account, the women may start to take equal initiative.

> Starting, he [suggested]. Now I always tell him, "See we are not doing [sex] . . . let's see a movie." The last time we saw it, I had to call for it. I asked for an adult movie, I wanted triple x, but I said single x. You feel like doing it or whatever. I feel like if you watch a movie, if husband is tired, it's like an initiative. I don't know, I think every couple must need it after marriage.
>
> Actually it's very good for a newly married couple. You learn. Once in a while, once in a month or two months is good. But the worst is when I have to call for it. At least with these stupid Indian people. Actually triple x is dirty, some are very dirty. Single x or double x are OK. When you watch a blue film together you feel [sexual].

In her account, Preeta expresses that pornography acts as a stimulant for married couples; in fact, every couple must need it after marriage. Moreover, like Indira and Payal, Preeta also suggests that watching pornography is a dimension of the more private aspect of their sexual/marital relationship. Indeed, with the exception of one woman, women describe watching pornography alongside their husbands. When it ceases to be a private event, as in the case of Payal or Preeta, it also becomes embarrassing, in their accounts. Therefore, not only did Preeta feel awkward about calling for the video, but she settled for one rated single x.[18]

Of the 25 married women asked about pornography, only two say they have never watched a pornographic film or video. Rather, nine women describe enjoying it because pornography acts as a stimulus, creates a setting appropriate to sexual activity with their husbands or because they learn sexual techniques. Recall Kanika's narrative at the beginning of this chapter, which is reiterated by Preeta and others. Additionally, two women emphasize the thrill of watching something taboo; they stress the illicit content of the videos. Four of the 25 women also describe preferences for sexually explicit films or videos that have a narrative plot over what they define as hard-core pornography; for some women, it is the degree of explicitness, whereas for others, it is important that sexual explicitness be in a narrative context. As Manisha explains the difference, "I don't really enjoy blue films. I enjoy something not quite as explicit, which starts off more subtly. Blue films can be too mechanical. You don't get a sense of building up." And Piya adds, "I don't like the triple x movies. My husband suggested it, I didn't like it at all. Something which is more romantic, like a romantic story which is explicit, that arouses me. I really like single x movies, I find them erotic." However, six women say they do not enjoy blue films. As Sujata bluntly puts it, "I am glad I never saw it before [marriage], maybe it would have turned me into a frigid fish, if that was sex."[19]

What remains curious is not so much the surprising number of women who describe their enjoyment of soft or hard-core pornography but the terms under which they do. Their accounts of pornography are further reflected in Rati's narrative. She is the striking exception to this group of women in that Rati describes watching "blue films" by herself. Nonetheless, her account is strikingly similar to those of the other women. She says,

> I have watched alone, like each time when my husband may have got it at home, he will say, "Let's see it tomorrow but I am very interested, I cannot wait till tomorrow." Hard core, not necessarily with story line, made abroad. Actually, it's really sick, we shouldn't watch it. Those guys are doing it, and we are enjoying it like a spectator sport, which in a way is not good, but it turns you on. It turns you on or maybe the way they do it, the positions. Sometimes it's the positions, sometimes when you have been married so long, it gets quite boring. The same thing again and again, the same body. When you try something different, it may add a little zest to your life. You can maybe learn something . . . how to please your partner. I get turned on, I get sexually aroused. There are times when I am really turned on, and there is no way I can get to my husband, he's not in the mood to do it, I do it. I've never masturbated while watching a blue film. If I have watched it, I have

put it off and gone to sleep. If I have ever masturbated it has never been after I watched or in the process of watching, no! Most likely I watch a blue film with my husband.

Even as she discusses the impact of pornography, Rati questions her practice of viewing pornography. And her account is somewhat contradictory. Unlike other women in the study, she initially separates pornography from her marital relationship. She expresses that she enjoys viewing pornography on her own. But, this separation is immediately followed by her assertion that viewing pornography is mainly part of her marital relationship—to add excitement, to teach new sexual techniques. Although Rati's narrative is exceptional, in the last instance she also subordinates the role of pornography to her sexual/emotional/marital relationship.

Based on these narratives, it appears that what is most compelling are the expectations that frame their accounts of sexuality and marriage. Within the context of marriage, these narratives are clearly framed by what Steven Seidman calls the eroticization of love and the romanticization of sex.[20] Expectations of mutual and simultaneous orgasms, emotional intimacy, better marital relationships are fused within this framework. Viewed in this way, this language of sexuality is both enabling and limiting. It provides these women with ways of speaking about and relating to sex. It provides that normative language of sex or what is deemed sexually normal which frames how to speak about sexual enjoyment, satisfaction, and sexual pleasure.[21]

At the same time, this framework also clearly limits and constrains the possibilities of the narratives on heterosexual desire. Anything that falls outside of these parameters may well be seen as deviant or unrespectable. Perhaps most clearly reflected in Rati's account on her perceptions of pornography, she momentarily steps outside this domain of acceptable sexual possibilities only to then retreat from the risk. Watching pornography is more or less acceptable within this framework only as long as it is by way of increasing sexual/marital intimacy. In these women's language of sexuality and marriage, their responsibility lies not so much in being sexually available to their husbands but in partaking and ensuring mutual sexual pleasure. From the parameters of this framework women are not likely to describe sexual dissatisfaction or do so somewhat defensively as in the case of the two women who say that they do not enjoy sex (with their husbands). Put differently, this language of sexuality and marriage becomes another way of regulating and managing middle-class sexual respectabilities.

Surely this language is not limited to the premise of the Indian nation-state. To recall the narratives of single women who describe sexual intercourse prior to marriage, the link between sex and emotional affection is equally persistent. As suggested earlier, to undermine the expectations of premarital sexual respectability these women invoke another set of cultural prescriptions. Not only does this link between sex and love cut across national boundaries but it is exacerbated by the flow of pornography or blue films. When these women, married and single, speak of these films or videos, they refer to pornography that is produced elsewhere, in countries like the United States and Holland.

English Only!

The English language figures prominently in these women's articulation of concepts of sexuality, romantic love, and marital intimacy. Although it is possible to express these concepts in Hindi, for example, these middle-class women relied on phrases and sentences in English to tell narratives on matters of sexuality.

All of the interviews were more or less bilingual; they were predominantly in English, interspersed with words and phrases in Hindi. Some women shifted comfortably between Hindi and English to express themselves. In general, the language of sexuality tended to be somewhat abstract and allusive rather than formal and concrete. For example, no woman spoke directly of the first time she had sexual intercourse or had sex with a man. The language was largely metaphoric, with the words such as *sex* and *orgasm* being somewhat sparingly used by all of us. Instead, we use phrases such as *physical relations* and *doing it*.

In her interview, which was conducted mostly in Hindi, Meenakshi explained how sex is discussed on a day-to-day basis. She says that sexual matters, be they about health or sexual humor, are spoken of obliquely—through allusion. The tone of voice, its softness, are used to indicate that sexuality is the topic of conversation. Meenakshi says that within her kin setting sexuality is never spoken of directly. Jokes and light discussions occur through metaphors and choice verbs, such as the verb *Karna*, which translates in English as "to do." To say to another family member in a specific tone of voice that her husband has an infection adequately conveys the sexual nature of the problem, according to Meenakshi. Terms in neither Hindi nor English are appropriate to the conversation. Yet, she adds, when it is necessary to carry on a serious discussion related to sexuality with a friend, then English is the language of choice. In other words, when issues of a sexual nature are to be directly named, then it is done through English, even though it is not her first language.

In his work on the study of sexuality in India through a psychoanalytic framework, Kakar analyzes the use of English by college-educated women to describe the sexual parts of their bodies.[22] According to Kakar, because strong sexual taboos are prevalent in the culture as well as the ignorance generated by silence, women experience tremendous discomfort about sexual matters. English allows women to speak of these culturally forbidden matters; in some Hindu communities, women do not have a name for their genitals. "At the utmost, the genitals are referred to obliquely—for example 'the place of peeing,' though even this euphemism carries a strong affective charge," Kakar writes.[23] He cites the example of a woman who could easily mention the sexual parts of her body as long as she did so in English.

In their narratives, women talk about sex through relatively allusive forms of spoken English. Perhaps this is why only one woman declined to answer a question about her first sexual encounter; there is little need to refuse responses to questions about sexuality. For example, descriptions such as the one below are fairly typical. In her interview, Nipun, married 10 years, says after a slight hesitation,

> Once you start liking it, there are times you want it, but you are not very sure. Oh! What will your husband think about it? OK, you get good feedback, then you start becoming comfortable. Basically because we talk openly, freely, so I feel now I am not scared if something were to disturb me, or if I want something I would voice it.

If not immediately apparent, Nipun is speaking about her and her husband's level of comfort with Nipun initiating sexual activity.

Somewhat in contrast to Nipun, Sheila responds to the same question with assurance and laughter in her voice,

> Now sometimes I also start it first, sometimes he also starts it first. When sometimes I want it he'll say, "I'm tired," like that. And when he wants it, he'll make me get up also from my sleep and have it—because it's very less that I avoid telling him something if he wants it. I feel I should give him the best of everything that I can give him. When I want something, when he gets . . . that time I get very hot [angry]. I say, "When I want it I can't have it."

It may be argued that Sheila is less ambiguous than Nipun, but not less abstract. What is reflected in these two quotes in spoken English is more starkly visible when compared with three narratives on heterosexuality that occur primarily in Hindi.

These three interviews are Meenakshi's, Bella's, and Nirmal's. They were conducted in Hindi because the women expressed comfort in speaking Hindi over English and probably because of my lack of familiarity with other possible languages such as Sindhi or Marwari. Rather than being atypical, these interviews foreground a tendency that runs through the other interviews, especially those in which women constantly shift back and forth between English and Hindi. To illustrate the point, it is useful to attend to the way in which Meenakshi speaks about sexuality in her interview. In response to a question about the role of sex in her marriage, she says,

> *I thought* pehle ke iska bahut bada *role* hota hai *but* jab mein dekhti hun apni *personal life* to merko nahin lagta ki iska koi *role* hai hi nahin. Mere *relations* mein to iska bahut chota, *minor role* hain. Baki *major role is our sentimental attachment, how much we care for each other.*

> Translation: At first I thought that it has a very large role, but when I look at my personal life then it does not appear to me that it has any role at all. In my relations it has a very minor, minor role. In effect, major role is our sentimental attachment, how much we care for each other.

A few minutes later Meenakshi volunteers:

> Aaj ki baat batati hoon. *Living in a joint family*, jo bacche bade ho gayen hai, *they are sleeping with me, teenage* . . . bacche bade ho gayen hai, *teenage* mein aagaye hain. *Like* woh log nahin hote hain, *mostly school* mein hote hain . . . *like our sex relation is very much minimized because we don't have privacy* to *we enjoy it more* kyonki kabhi kabar karte hain. *Second thing, we are tensed also.* Darwaje pe *knock* nahin ho, kuchbhi, us *time* koi *comfortable quite* to nahin rehta hai.

> Translation: Let me tell you about these days. Living in a joint family, the children are grown up, they are sleeping with me, teenage. . . . The children are grown up, they are in their teenage years. Like, if those people are not there, they are mostly in school. . . . Like our sex relation is very much minimized because we don't have privacy so we enjoy it more, because we do it now and then. Second thing, we are tensed also. Should there be a knock on the door, anything, at the time one is not quite comfortable.

In the first instance Meenakshi refers to sexual activity by substituting a pronoun for it. In the second instance, as she discusses her sexual relations with her husband currently, she uses the words "sex relations" to adequately communicate her thoughts and then in the same sentence describes being sexually active as "doing it" in Hindi. In the second case, as Meenakshi searches for the words to be able to talk about sexuality in a direct manner, only the phrases "sex relations," "we don't have privacy," "we enjoy it more" are adequately able to communicate her experience. Many of the other English words that Meenakshi uses are also noteworthy—role, personal life, sentimental, and attachment, among others. Meenakshi or any of the other women in the study could have substituted other words in Hindi when necessary such as sharirik bandhan (physical relations), kaam (sex, sexual desire), but "sex relations" appears to be the obvious choice.

The recourse to English to name aspects of sexuality in these interviews is obviously a dimension of the larger presence of the English language especially in the lives of middle-class, urban, educated women who have access to English. In his book *The Cultural Politics of English as an International Language*, Alastair Pennycook traces the significance of the language under colonialism.[24] In the Indian colonial context, Pennycook argues, the expansion of English under the British Empire occurred at the insistence of local elites who recognized its links to social and economic power. He also observes that relationships between English and globalizing processes such as capitalism, democracy, and development are neither coincidental nor structurally determined. Instead, Pennycook argues,

> [T]here is a reciprocal relationship that is both historical and contemporary. . . . Particular global and local discourses create the conditions of possibility for engaging in the social practice of using "English," they produce and constrain what can be said in English. At the same time, English creates the conditions of possibility for taking up a position in these discourses.[25]

What is striking about Nirmal's account is precisely this use of English to both enable and constrain a discourse on sexuality from a specific vantage point. Speaking about her reaction to watching a sexually explicit film on cable, Nirmal says,

> Us din ulta maja aiye mujhe. Dekh ke jaise na, mujhe aise laga jaise dekha ya *English music* chal raha ho, *then you enjoying more sex.* Pata nahin. Mera ye hai. Ya thoda mujhe *dance* wance ka thoda hai. To inko pata chal gaya. To jab hum log karte hain yeh *English music* chala dete hain. To laga *film* ki wajey se maja aah gaya. Aur humne teen-chaar baar uske bad kiya...Humne *continuous* teen-chaar gante kiya us din. . . . Karta to aapna hi hai banda par chad jata hai.
>
> Translation: Instead, that day I enjoyed. Watching it I feel, or if English music is playing, then you enjoying sex more. I don't know. That is the way it is with me. Perhaps I have this thing about dance etc. He came to realize that. So when we do it, he puts on English music. It felt as if because of the film it was enjoyable. And we did that three or four times after that. We did it continuously for three or four hours that day. One does one's own but one becomes sexually aroused.

Within Nirmal's narrative in Hindi the selective integration of English helps her express some meanings to the exclusion of others. Like Meenakshi, Nirmal uses words such as "English music," "enjoying more sex," to express her account about sexual activity. At the same time, Nirmal also says that she better enjoys sex with English music or a sexually explicit English film playing in the background. In effect, Nirmal relies on choice words and phrases in English rather than Hindi to express herself, but she also invokes music and sexually explicit films in English to define what is sexually arousing to her. Not only is an English language–related stimulus sexually more effective but the account on sexuality can be better expressed within the same language.

For middle-class, urban women in this study, English is a way of negotiating the politics of sexuality. To all of us associated with the study, especially when speaking of sexuality, the words come more easily in English. In Hindi, we speak through metaphors. We are unable or unwilling to name the discourse of sexuality in Hindi. In Hindi, especially in its spoken, colloquial forms, the same words sound crude. Swearing in English is possible, in colloquial Hindi, unthinkable. English eases narratives on sexuality but also constrains them. We need to speak about sexuality, to name it, and to define it in meaningful ways, simultaneously framing and limiting that discussion. English fulfills that role within the culture for this socioeconomic group. For example, the Cambridge English-Hindi dictionary translates the meaning of the word *sex* as *ling, yoni,* and the word *sex* in Hindi script. So, it is no coincidence that this chapter is in English, with a similar discussion of the issue of sexuality in Hindi virtually impossible.

This is not to suggest that the transnational, globalizing flow of English is necessarily homogenous, for English is never quite the same.[26] In his article, "The Local and the Global: Globalization and Ethnicity," Stuart Hall considers the politics of culture in an increasing global environment. Hall argues that the process of globalization is due to the surge of capital in an international, global market, the process of decolonization, and increasing international financial and environmental interdependence. Within this context, Hall argues that global culture is "centered in the West," but not quite in the same way.[27] According to Hall, English is the new international language, which hegemonizes other languages, but also makes English diverse and unstable.

Indicating this diversity and instability of English, Bella, in Hindi, deploys the English word *sex* to express herself, but in a way that cannot be adequately translated back into English. In our conversation about women's sexual desire, Bella recalls this incident in her narrative,

Meri ek *cousin* hai, woh thoda na *mentality weak* hai. Hum log do, char saal pehle gaye the kisi ki shadi mein, to raste pe hi ja rahi thi hamare saat hi. To usko ek aadmi ne khade ho ke uske *balls* aise daba raha tha. To woh achhe se us se karva rahi thi. To us se lag raha tha ki usme bhi jo ye sex ki bhavana hai, hai. To woh *time* usko dekhke itna *feel* ho raha tha, bahut ajeeb lag raha tha.

Translation: I have a cousin, she is a little mentally weak. A few years ago we were going to someone's wedding, she was with us. A man stopped her and started to press her balls [breasts]. She was letting him. From that it was apparent that she also has the emotion of sex within her. I really felt badly about it at the time, it felt very strange.

Much of what is cited from the narratives of Bella, Nirmal, and Meenakshi does not easily lend itself to translation without, as others have pointed out, changing meanings. Yet, "*sex* ki bhavana" as used by Bella or Nirmal's phrase "*sex* chad jata hai" translate especially inadequately into "the emotion of sex" or "sexually aroused," respectively. In its specific form, English appears to shape women's expressions on sexuality. To that extent it serves to normalize and constrain discourses of sexuality without determining how they may be cast in women's narratives.

Conclusion

The women's narratives of erotic sexuality destabilize stereotypical assumptions about the nature of sexuality in the lives of middle-class women in contemporary India. By not posing these narratives within a framework of sexual repression, I hope to enhance understanding of the proliferation of discourses of sexuality, desire, and pleasure and their normalizing effects. More specifically, this perspective also raises crucial questions about how these narratives on sexuality are being normalized as heterosexuality and regulated through the discourse of sexual respectability. If the regulation of heterosexuality is indeed through specifications of normality, pleasures, sensations, and sexual expectations, then it is clear that the "deployment of sexuality" may not be limited to the "West" nor easily circumscribed within the boundaries of the contemporary Indian nation-state. To that extent these narratives reveal much about what may be specific and what may be more general in the social regulation of womanhood across diverse social locations.

If these narratives foreground the nationalist discourses, then they make the effects of transnational cultural discourses equally visible. The imbrications of heterosexuality, nationalisms, and transnational discourses are no less than striking in the narratives. They raise questions about the ways in which the politics of sexual respectability, heterosexuality, womanhood, and nationalisms are deeply intertwined. Furthermore, perhaps because these narratives describe women when they are at a relatively later stage in their life cycle, they also suggest how these women negotiate and recast notions of sexual respectability and chastity in their lives albeit within a heterosexual framework. In so doing, they invoke more transnational cultural discourses of sex and romantic love and spoken English to accommodate and challenge the constraints on erotic sexuality in their lives. To that extent, these transnational cultural discourses simultaneously enable and limit the expressions of sexuality in the lives of these middle-class women. Put differently, this language on sexuality both normalizes what women express as sexuality and sexual experiences, and helps them negotiate other constraints, such as countering social expectations of sexual chastity outside of marriage and invoking the romanticization of sex and the sexualization of romance to secure their marital relationships.

Chapter Six

Rethinking the Requirements: Of Marriage and Motherhood

The literature addressing marital issues in women's lives is descriptive but not easy to reconcile with the narratives of the 54 middle-class women featured here. Based on these studies of marriage across social classes, a more general picture of marriage emerges. From this literature it appears that marriage is both socially mandated and riven with problems. Marriage may be seen as necessary to ensure the chastity of women and leash the threat of their sexualities, but especially the early years of married life are not trouble-free.[1] That women have to contend with the demands of marriage and problems of adjusting into conjugal families, defer to their husbands, and where applicable, juggle the demands of marriage and paid and unpaid work, is described as an outcome of the subordinate status of women.[2]

This literature paints a dismal picture of marriage for women because of their subordinate status and a lack of intimacy. The lack of intimacy is attributed to nationally based cultural distinctions. For example, although Kakar refutes the full-scale oppression of women, he suggests that, contrary to Western patterns, in Indian marriages, intimacy is an outcome of parenthood.[3] In another example, Caplan suggests that ideals of marriage are not based on expectations of companionship between wives and husbands among elite women in Chinnai (formerly known as Madras City).[4] Precisely because Caplan attempts to analyze the meaning of marriage from the perspective of these elite women, by noting a lack of intimacy, she is not only measuring their responses against an external yardstick but also reinforcing cultural stereotypes.

In this chapter I explore middle-class women's narratives on marriage and motherhood in part because they illuminate aspects that remain obscure in much of the available literature. Frequently, there appear to be significant dis-crepancies between sociological and anthropological findings especially about marriage and middle-class or elite women and the narratives of women in this study. Where there are some parallels between the existing research and women's narratives, the literature disputably imputes these as changes due to westernization and modernization.[5] In this literature, women's chang-ing perceptions on marriage and marital adjustment are erroneously evaluat-ed on a scale of modernity. With regard to the issues of motherhood, there is a greater degree of confluence but also important points of difference between the literature and the narratives included in this study. From the viewpoints of these women, the literatures on marriage and motherhood con-found rather than illuminate the issues, and worse, they reinforce the social regulation of middle-class, urban women in marriage and motherhood.

On the contrary, middle-class women's narratives on marriage are clearly shaped by discourses of companionate marriage.[6] Their narratives are ground-ed within a framework of marriage as companionship and marital relationships as egalitarian and characterized by mutual respect. Especially in the narratives of the 31 married women, what is especially striking is how they attempt to negotiate the uncertainties as wives and daughters-in-law. Unlike the literature, their accounts are not rooted in assumptions of subordination, but in their agency. Their narratives call for an analysis that addresses both the ways in which hegemonic discourses of marriage produce and normalize parameters of womanhood and how women negotiate the mandates of wifehood. It is in this respect that their narratives on motherhood are especially instructive. Although these middle-class women do not narrate motherhood as a social mandate, they suggest how they use their status as mothers to assert themselves as wives and daughters-in-law within the conjugal extended family.

From a cultural standpoint, marriage and motherhood are considered the primary gender roles for women across social classes. Indeed, motherhood is seen as the essence of womanhood, and marriage, the context within which a woman should bear children. To the extent that these statuses are consid-ered normal and essential aspects of adult womanhood, they also serve to limit and regulate women's lives. As Venita, an articulate woman of mar-riageable age indignantly says, marriage and motherhood give women the "good girl" status in society. Any deviation from these roles is considered inappropriate and is negatively sanctioned. In their narratives, as women speak about aspects related to marriage and motherhood, not only do they express their viewpoints but also implicitly indicate how these social man-dates help reinforce the premise of womanhood and gender identity in their daily lives.

Perhaps reflecting the deeply ingrained and pervasive social expectations of marriage, middle-class women may be ambivalent about marriage, but none of the marriageable-age women indicates that she does not want to ever marry; nor do any of the currently married women suggest that they would prefer not to be married. Nargis, who is currently divorced, says that after a period of time she too would like to remarry. While there is no prescribed age for marriage, women are expected to marry young. Among the women in this study, the youngest to marry was 18 and several were in their late 20s. The oldest single woman is 31 years old. Also indicating the importance of motherhood, 23 of the married women have children and other married and marriageable-age women expect that they will bear children.[7]

From a sociological perspective, marriage and motherhood mark adult womanhood in a woman's life cycle. Triggered by the onset of menarche, an evolving and emergent womanhood culminates with the birth of the first child. Especially because women may marry young, such as 18, the status of motherhood, rather than marriage, more distinctly heralds womanhood. Put differently, if marriage marks the transition into womanhood, then motherhood solidifies it. Menarche, marriage, and motherhood, in that order, normatively define the various stages in the social status of women. But, as social markers, marriage and motherhood are somewhat different from menarche. Although the onset of menarche, marriage, and motherhood each define important cultural turning points and involve widespread changes in the life of a woman, unlike menarche, marriage and motherhood are social statuses that also entail social responsibilities and rights.

Marriage heralds sweeping changes in a woman's life including changes in her residence, her kin affiliation, the rights and responsibilities of being a wife—including participating in sexual activity, bearing some or all household responsibilities, and maintaining kin relations within the conjugal family, among others. Not surprisingly, this is also generally considered an uneven phase in women's lives. The first flush of marriage is offset by the broad-based adjustment that is expected of newlywed women—to their husbands and their conjugal families. By the conjugal family I refer to the familial unit within which women marry and live which may include members of the husband's family. This is also popularly referred to as the joint-family arrangement. For the most part, prior to marriage women live with their families of origin; upon marriage they live with their husbands and/or their husbands' families. Only four of the 22 single women live away from their families since they are based in Bombay as air stewardesses, and as many as 25 of the 31 married women currently live with their conjugal families. Before she was divorced, Nargis was also living with members of her husband's family, and two more women say they established independent households with their husbands only recently.

If marriage entails such extensive changes in women's lives, then mother-hood is expected to involve not only additional child-care responsibilities, but also a more secure position within the conjugal family. As Dube suggests, marriage is seen as the gateway to motherhood.[8] Motherhood is expected to smooth out the rough edges of the marital/conjugal relationships as well as provide a more clearly defined position for a woman within this setting. This is why I choose to juxtapose middle-class women's narratives on marriage and motherhood. Probably because these are culturally mandated statuses for middle-class women, what is striking are the parallels in how these women strategically and effectively negotiate these statuses. Women's attempts to mitigate the uncertainties of adult womanhood are not only reflected in their narratives on motherhood, as is suggested in the salient literature, but also in their accounts on marriage.

In the first section of this chapter, the focus is on middle-class women's narratives on marriage, including those who are married, divorced, or of mar-riageable age. This section deals with women's narratives on their marital relationships with their husbands as well as the narratives on their conjugal families. I consider these narratives against some of the scholarship on mar-riage more generally, and specifically, on middle-class, urban women. The next section is devoted to the accounts on motherhood, both from women who currently have children and those who anticipate them in the future. To this purpose I focus on the narratives of three women regarding motherhood. If the first narrative expresses motherhood as an integral though not essential part of womanhood, the second narrative dismisses it as an added burden on women. What is equally intriguing is how the third narrative details mother-hood as the means to ensuring the rights of responsibilities of womanhood within conjugal families. This narrative poses the greater analytical challenge in that it both draws upon and circumvents hegemonic codes of gender iden-tity that are imbricated in cultural discourses of the nation-state and those that cut across national boundaries.

"When I Get Married": Narratives from Marriageable-Age Women

Nowhere do discourses of tradition versus westernization and modernization obscure hegemonic codes of gender and sexuality more than in the literature on marriage. For example, arranged marriages are probably more associated with India than any other national cultural tradition. It is claimed that as many as 95 percent of the marriages in India are arranged.[9] In popular wisdom, "love marriages," associated with westernization and modernization, mark changes in this enduring national tradition. Where romantic love and companionate, mutual marital relationships are seen as the markers of "love marriages," "arranged marriages" are associated with practices such as girl-viewing, practical considerations of a prospective husband's occupation, and his family's status, and deferred marital intimacy, if any.

Aside from the necessity of establishing the historical context for the tradition of arranged marriages, these distinctions are questionable for two additional reasons. First, from the point of view of middle-class women in this study, distinctions between love marriages and arranged marriages are more ambiguous than clear-cut. For example, parents may legitimize mutual attraction between a young woman and man of the same social class by arranging the marriage. On the other hand, it is equally possible that women will emphasize the instantaneous mutual attraction when they first met then husband-to-be as per prior arrangement. Second, and more contentiously, it is not clear that love marriage connotes mutual, spontaneous attraction and companionate marriages in contrast to arranged marriages. Neither of these suppositions is borne out by the narratives on marriage in this study nor the putative national cultural differences so constructed. Instead, it is more useful to explore the hegemonic codes of marriage from the viewpoint of these middle-class women.[10]

Unencumbered by notions of westernization and modernization, these marriageable-age and married middle-class women's narratives about meeting prospective husbands on their own and through family members articulate qualities of ideal husbands and marital relationships in the following sections. Distinctions between "arranged" and "love" marriages shape women's narratives, but only in ambiguous ways. Particularly in their narratives on ideal husbands and marital relationships, these middle-class women describe the meaning of marriage in ways that are neither traditional nor Western, that are neither easily categorized as "love" nor "arranged" marriages. Furthermore, as reflected in the comparisons that they make between their parents' marital relationships and what they would like for themselves, these women raise the possibility that there may not be the distinct generational changes in marriage and marital adjustment reported in literature. Finally, in their narratives on aspects of marriage, these middle-class women suggest ways in which their perceptions of marriage help them strategically negotiate the cultural mandate of marriage for women.

A Little Bit of This and a Little Bit of That: Destabilizing "Love" vs. "Arranged" Marriages

From a cultural standpoint, the unmarried women in this study, with the exception of the two youngest women, are of marriageable age. Those women in their 20s and the one woman in her early 30s expect to be married over the next few years. Indeed, some of them expect to meet their marriage partner whereas others are in the process of meeting men through their relatives. As they speak of the process of meeting prospective husbands, the women invoke distinctions between "love" and "arranged" marriages in ambiguous ways. Bindu, whose parents are keen that she marry, had recently met a man through her parents. She describes the sequence of events,

> I met this guy a few months ago. My parents met this guy and called me saying that I should go over to the hotel. I didn't want to dress up. I wanted to go normally. He turned out to be really good. He was very polite, and he got up and said "Please sit down." Made me feel as if he had called us over. It was as if he already knows me and made me feel very comfortable. My parents left us alone and we really spoke. We met one evening, and my parents said, "Don't meet. Let things work out properly."

According to Bindu this meeting did not come to fruition because her parents were later warned against marrying her into that family. What is notable is that although it may appear that Bindu is describing a characteristic aspect of "arranged" marriages, her language is not so easily categorized. Confounding such categorization, shortly into the interview, Bindu says, "If the bells don't ring, I know this person is not for me." Precisely because she sensed a connection with this man that was not realized, Bindu adds that she went through a period of depression thereafter. Though the meeting with a potential husband was arranged by her parents, her language is clearly romanticized.

Out of the 20 marriageable-age women in this study, two indicate that they have met the men that they would like to marry. While they could indicate imminent "love marriages," these two narratives are also riven with the practical considerations typically associated with "arranged marriages." Both Seema and Jaya anticipate parental objections to these marriages, and each of them asks that I switch off the tape recorder when they describe their feelings for the men. In Seema's case, she believes her father may not approve because of the ethnic difference. In the meanwhile, as she continues to see this man, who at 30 is nine years older than her, the uncertainties make her anxious; if he decides not to marry her, she would have fruitlessly opposed her parents. Meanwhile, Jaya, 21, is quite serious about a man who is one year older than her but she is ambivalent about his lower socioeconomic background and his responsibilities toward his mother and sisters since the death of his father. Like Seema, Jaya is unsure about the outcome of this relationship and unable to separate the practical considerations of ethnicity or class status in potential "love marriages."

As these middle-class women describe anticipated marriages, their narratives are both shaped by, but destabilizing to, distinctions between "arranged" and "love" marriages. These women sometimes invoke the distinctions only to achieve similar outcomes. For example, Jaya goes on to say that she would prefer to have a "love marriage" because one knows the person who is the marriage partner. "Arranged marriages" by contrast are more based on the luck of the draw. Yet, given the drawbacks of "love marriages," such as making clouded judgments, Jaya says that perhaps the best compromise is to have a "love marriage" as long as you are practical about issues such as finances, individual personalities, and mutual understanding. On the other hand, perhaps shaped by her negative experience, Bindu is in despair about the outcome of "love" and "arranged" marriages. She says that since there are no guarantees, the only thing that can help is to know the person prior to marriage. Unlike Jaya, Bindu believes that she has a better chance of getting to know her marriage partner through an "arranged marriage" as she can take her time. If Jaya and Bindu use these distinctions to achieve the same outcome—to know the person and ensure their compatibility prior to marriage—then Puja undermines the distinctions altogether by emphasizing the importance of her role in the decision-making process. According to Puja, the important aspect is not whether it is a "love" or "arranged" marriage but her ability to choose her marriage partner in conjunction with her parents.

Understanding Husbands and Mutual Marital Relationships

Despite these ambiguous, questionable differences, the women are remarkably consistent in their expectations regarding the husbands and the relationships that they would like. When describing ideal qualities of husbands, the single women emphasize what could be considered material and psychological characteristics. The expectations about religion and ethnicity are less well articulated. When noted in the accounts, the women expect to marry someone of their own religion, such as another Catholic or Hindu, and in only a few cases do they specify that it is important to marry someone within the same caste or subcaste ethnic category. But, these women consistently specify the class status of their potential husbands; none of them expects to marry a man with a lower-class status. They suggest that, at the minimum, he will be of the same social status, or possibly higher. Where others are more expansive on the psychological aspects of the potential husband, Anjali melds the material and psychological considerations in her narrative. Expressing some concern that she has preset expectations that might be difficult to meet, Anjali has this to say about the prospective husband,

> Very nice, simple nature. Needn't look smart, but has to be smart. The world should not be able to outsmart him. A gentleman, where you feel you've met a nice person. No pseudo-inhibitions, not very showy, not very rich, my class. Probably with a vehicle for us to move around. Probably a good sense of understanding of the other person. [He should] understand me well.

In her account, Mitali, who expects to be married over the next two years, specifies the following criteria for a desirable husband:

> As I don't want to change, he should be able to adjust and to understand me. I don't want to explain each step of mine in life. I want him to respect me. I want to look after my parents. Don't want to go outside of Bombay. [I want] to be close to them, no restrictions about visiting them. I want the responsibility of taking care of them.

If for Anjali and Mitali it is also important that their prospective husbands own a vehicle or reside in Bombay, then these criteria are fused with expectations of understanding and adjusting husbands. Across the narratives of these middle-class women, the most consistently used term to describe desirable qualities in a husband is "understanding." Repeatedly, and eventually predictably, across the narratives, being understanding of them and their needs is the indispensable quality they want in a husband. Speaking of this and related qualities, Jaya says in no uncertain terms,

> Very understanding, caring. Where there is a lot of mutual understanding. I don't like the dictatorship kind that "I am the male." He should try and understand the female's way of thinking.

Similarly, Radhika emphasizes the importance of the understanding husband as a friend rather than solely as a husband. Characterizing the marital relationship and the husband, Radhika says,

> A relationship that will last. That is difficult nowadays. It should be someone not too filmy [flashy like film heroes], cares about me and looks after me. Friendly. It is a husband-wife relationship, yes! But, we should be friends and . . . he should be understanding.

Besides articulating the essential qualities of the desirable husband, through her narrative Radhika also illustrates the inextricability of desirable husbands from desirable relationships. In the narratives, there is a constant shift between the characteristics of ideal husbands and marital relationships. In this vein, Bindu says about the marital relationship and the husband,

> Based on friendship. He should understand me, value my work equally. Don't be jealous about my relationships at work. He could be from a different field. I would prefer service [professional], working in a respectable firm. We should understand each other. The initial clicking has to be there. You can tell him what you feel like.

Echoing similar themes but speaking more clearly of the marital relationship, Puja, who does not expect to be married until she is financially self-sufficient, says,

> Total understanding. It shouldn't be that the woman has to listen to the man or has to be under the man. It should be a mutual sort of thing. I don't want anybody bossing over me. If you love somebody, you want to do things for that person, but I don't want to be forced into doing things. So it has to be mutual. If and when I do get married, I want the kind of relationship where I can tell the guy anything, there's no hiding between people. Total understanding. I don't have to think before I say anything. I can say anything, and he will understand.

Clearly, what is consistent in these accounts are the requirements of understanding prospective husbands and mutual, egalitarian marriages based on friendship and respect.[11] For these middle-class marriageable-age women it appears to be equally important that they know their husbands, establish emotional connection with them, and be able to express themselves and their needs. Repeatedly, these women note the importance of being able to speak their minds, to be candid, and unguarded with their prospective husbands. Undergirding these expectations are assumptions about the social class and, to a lesser extent, about the religious and ethnic affiliations of their husbands. Put differently, these women can express notions of gender equality within marriage because they assume parity of social class; it is about "equality among equals." These are the aspects that the women stress in their narratives, rather than the distinctions between "love" and "arranged" marriages.

Reflecting on Generational Differences in Marital Relationships

Counterintuitively, what is also somewhat consistent in these narratives is that these single middle-class women would like to have marital relationships similar to those of their parents. Implicitly countering the research, when asked to compare their expectations with their parents' marital relationships, for the most part, these marriageable-age women suggest that they would like husbands like their fathers and relationships akin to those of their parents. For example, Jaya says that she is ambivalent about the man she is considering marrying because, unlike her father, he seems a little chauvinistic. Mitali is equally certain in her comparison. She says,

> Similar, very similar. I want my husband to be like my father. My father has been an excellent husband, especially compared to my uncle. [My father] is the best husband! My mom had it easier. I am looking forward to it. I haven't paid much attention to my marriage. But when I was staying with my aunt she said that I have to alter myself, but I am very positive that I will get someone with whom I don't have to change.

Anjali addresses the parallel between her parents' relationship and the one that she expects to have. She says,

> My parents get along well. They are emotionally very dependent on each other. They choose to spend time with each other. My mom disagrees about some of his habits, but they are pretty compatible. My relationship will be on similar grounds. I would give him certain liberties and would expect the same.

The few women who are less positive about their parents' marital relationship blame a mutual friction between their parents rather than their mothers' subordinate status. Both Puja and Bindu describe their discomfort with their parents' relationships because of the arguments. Puja says that sometimes her mother's ego and her father's rigidity leads to their arguments. Although she does not believe that women should give in to men and she does not appreciate her father's inflexibility, she hopes to have a marital relationship that is free from these conflicts. In her account, Bindu says that the mistake that her parents make, which is not to be repeated in her own relationship, is that they both get angry and flare up simultaneously. Seema is the exception to the extent that she perceives the imperfect marriage between her parents as the outcome of their hierarchical relationship. She says,

> I wouldn't make the same mistakes that my parents have made. I would not give in the amount that my mother has. I would prefer walking out. I would not handle the situation the way that my father did. My mother has done a lot, she gave so much that he kept expecting more. If a person is demanding more from me and not giving me back, I would walk out.

These accounts are illuminating and provocative. They describe marital relationships and prospective husbands within the parameters of gender-egalitarian, mutual, companionate relationships, and unlike much of the literature on marriage and women, do not suggest that these expectations are generationally specific. Even if women describe their perceptions of their parents' relationships in the latter rather than earlier stages of marriage, it is remarkable that they do not see sharp differences. At the same time, since they are projecting and anticipating the future, these accounts also raise questions. Perhaps the most immediate of these questions is related to the differences between expectations and realities, between desirable qualities of husbands and marital relationships and the marital lives that these middle-class women have to contend with. To this purpose, it is helpful to turn to the narratives of the 32 women who have experience with marriage, husbands, and aspects that the marriageable-age women have less to say about.

"It Was Magic": Narratives from Ever-Married Women

From the vantage point of a year-and-a-half-long marriage, Chandni describes the first time she met her husband and how they were engaged:

> The first time when we met in a hotel we were sitting in a gathering of 18 people and we did not even say hello to each other. Before that I had met two guys and spoken for hours with them. One guy kept asking me whether I knew how to make this and that, and I asked him if he had applied for a cook. With my husband I didn't utter a single word, and when I went home I could not recall his face. These people called up at 12 o'clock at night and said, "Yes" and my father was not here. The decision was up to me and my mother and my mom's mom. His looks did not match up to what they had in mind. My main condition, I did not want a service-class family where there is restriction of money. My Mummy said, "I don't know what to do," so I said "Say yes." I don't know what came over me. She said, "Your father is not here." I said, "My father is not the one getting married," and after three days we got engaged.
>
> It was just a feeling of peace, it was a feeling of . . . it was magic. I don't have any regrets. I am very happy with my husband, and married life with him has been a beautiful life. I always wanted someone who would never get angry because my father was a very short-tempered person. I did not want a man who would scream and rant at me. I used to always pray to God for this one thing. From the first day itself I felt I have never been away from him, there's no shyness or coyness. From the first it was as if we have always known each other. He knew where I wanted to go, what I wanted to eat. It was beautiful.

As Chandni recounts their first meeting it is less remarkable that she cannot recall her prospective husband's face than the fact that she describes her feelings through a romanticized language. As she says, her major criterion, that her husband belong to a well-to-do business family, was confirmed prior to the meeting. To these class-specific considerations, Chandni weaves a language colored by romantic ideals—magic, peace, a sense of knowing each other forever, beautiful. Her hope not to get a short-tempered husband like her father was fortunately realized.

On the issue of desirable husbands, Jennifer compares her husband with the qualities that she hoped for prior to marriage. Married for two and a half years, Jennifer says,

> Most people like him instantly. He is very much like my father—steady, romantic. He completely swept me off my feet. He's very organized, totally the opposite of me. I don't know how to save. He's secure, steady. . . . I wanted someone to have a lot of fun with, to enjoy life. Somebody I could talk to about anything and have fun with. Someone on the same wavelength, the same social class. I definitely did not want to marry someone much lower than me, I couldn't survive.

In her account, Jennifer stresses the significance of a romantic but steady husband. Being on the same wavelength and social class are equally important to her. Similarly, Indira, who has been married the last five years, favorably compares her marital relationship with the one that she hoped to have. She says that she met her husband at the insistence of common cousins. Thereafter they met a few times and decided that they should marry. In her words,

> The relationship I was looking for is based on the one that I have now. An equal relationship where there is no one dominant partner. I need a lot of space, I can't have a claustrophobic relationship. A lot of respect for each other. You may not agree, but as long as you can accept the other person's views that this is where I am, it's all right. These were the basic requirements, and it has been like that.

If these married women suggest that they expected to marry understanding, caring, companionate husbands, then for the most part they also suggest that their expectations have been met. Much like their single counterparts, these women emphasize similar characteristics for husbands and marital relationships prior to marriage. In a marriage that she describes as 50 percent "arranged" and 50 percent "love," Piya categorically says that she got what she wanted. She says that she wanted someone very caring whom she could also care for, and above all, a friend in whom she could confide and with whom she could share everything.

Women who are more ambivalent or negative about either the husband or the marital relationship tend to highlight particular faults in the husband or the lack of compatibility: Notably absent are suggestions that they have to suffer less-than-ideal husbands or relationships because of their subordinate status. Instead, the marital unhappiness is seen as a result of personal conflicts. Neetu, who had reservations about her compatibility with her husband before their marriage 10 years ago, says,

> His nature, it was too much to accept. His temper is too much. The way he used to [verbally] abuse anyone was too much. His father and grandfather are like that. They don't think anything is wrong with that. We used to really have fights where he used to insist that I drink [alcohol]. One day my father-in-law said, "Why don't you give him company, it's your duty to give him company." I was surprised because he was a Radhaswami [religious sect].
>
> My husband always felt that I should try to put him up in front of other people [praise him], and I couldn't do that all my life. He wanted that I should agree with him and never say that he was wrong. But I could never say it. He would really dislike this.

Neetu also says that their relationship is much better since this time period. She attributes this improvement to a mutual change in their attitudes toward each other and the relationship.

When describing the problems with their husbands and marital relationships, Meenakshi and Kavita are both critical and conciliatory toward their respective husbands. Meenakshi says that there was a difference between what she expected in her husband and what she got through marriage. Although her husband is considered good-looking, unlike her expectations he was not very self-confident or outgoing. She also adds that since this early period of their marriage, her husband is more self-confident, he gives her a lot of respect and support, and they share a communicative relationship. In her account, Kavita says that although her husband was nice to her, he never gave her parents due respect, which was of utmost importance to her. After 13 years of marriage, Kavita adds that they still do not have a relationship whereby she can express her thoughts and opinions quite comfortably without ending in an argument. For Preeta, married at the age of 18, her husband's social reserve is a problem that is offset by his love and caring for her.

Protecting Understanding Husbands and Mutual Marital Relationships

What is perhaps most striking about these narratives is that the women appear protective about their husbands and marital relationships. Narratives of prior expectations of understanding, caring husbands and mutual, companionate, and egalitarian marriages are juxtaposed with rather positive characterizations of reality. Even the women who are more ambivalent or negative about their relationships or husbands tend not to be critical of their husbands. Where they may share considerably intimate details about their lives, arguably there is a censoring of the kinds of accounts that can be narrated in this context. Against the grain of these women's narratives on conjugal families, this difference is even more noticeable. When speaking about their conjugal families, especially in the first few years of marriage, these women are not only more loquacious but also far more critical.

This tendency for middle-class married women to protect their husbands may be explained by prevailing cultural sanctions. Upon marriage women are expected to uphold the social appearance of their husbands and conjugal families at all costs.[12] In her analysis on "dowry deaths," where women are killed or harassed to suicide by husbands and their families ostensibly because of insufficient dowries, Rajeswari Sunder Rajan analyzes the refusal of the dying woman to testify against the husband. Rajan suggests that deep-seated sanctions against "naming" the husband act to silence women.[13] These taboos deter a woman from either literally saying her husband's name or, more figuratively, implicating him in the crime perpetrated against her. Frequently, when women are able to, in their dying moments, they will acquit the husband and his family. Arguing that the antidote to silence is not necessarily speech, Rajan suggests that within the constraints of protecting the husband and his family, for women both testimony and silence work to protect the husband. Analogously, middle-class women's narratives are shaped through what they omit to say as well as what they do say about their husbands. In either case, they attempt to shield their husbands. But they are far less protective of their conjugal families.

This difference between the women's narratives on their husbands and on the conjugal families is grounded in a woman's position as wife and daughter-in-law. A woman's status within the conjugal family is dependent on the status of her husband. Depending on the relative security or insecurity of the husband, a woman's position is stabilized or jeopardized. For example, Meenakshi describes and illustrates a beleaguered new bride's enthusiasm to please her husband's relatives, to win them over, as it were. As the wife of the third son in the family who was dependent on the family business, she was not well-regarded in the new environment. In this context, the model of companionate marriage, with its ideals of intimacy, mutuality, understanding, and love serve to reinforce these middle-class women's ties to their husbands. Indeed, where this tie is not secure, women can find themselves totally isolated and unsupported in an alien environment. Therefore, this language of understanding husbands, and egalitarian, companionate marriages is strategic, not superfluous, to women's roles as wives. It is easier and more effective to direct issues of marital difficulties to conjugal families rather than the husbands. In these narratives, husbands are to be protected, and conjugal families can be criticized.

In her account, Nargis, who is the only woman in this study to have divorced, illustrates these tensions between husbands and conjugal families in the narratives. After a period of nine months, much deliberation, and the support of her natal family, Nargis initiated divorce proceedings. Most of the narrative focuses on the difficulties that she had to face at the hands of her ex-husband's relatives. Especially focusing on the role of her ex-husband's mother, Nargis details the day-to-day trials of living in that house. While she does not single out any issue as especially egregious, Nargis describes the problems related to their misrepresentations before marriage and their lifestyle, financial burdens upon her, unreasonable demands and restrictions, and often incomprehensible behaviors that emerged after marriage. In contrast, Nargis focuses much less on the role or inadequacies of her ex-husband; the mother-in-law accounted for 75 percent of the problems. Although Nargis questions the ex-husband's lack of support and his role in the misrepresentations prior to marriage, she says that the crux of the problem was her ex-mother-in-law's influence over the son and his inability to establish intimacy and affection based on trust with Nargis over the period of the marriage. Within this framework of marriage and women's roles as wives and daughters-in-law, Nargis, who perhaps had the least investment in protecting either the ex-husband or members of the conjugal family, unequivocally implicates the role of the conjugal family and holds the husband responsible insofar as he is unable to participate in an intimate and mutual marital relationship.

"As a Daughter-in-Law": Narratives on Conjugal Families

As mentioned in the introduction, 25 of the 31 married women currently live with their husbands and conjugal relatives, and three other women say they lived with conjugal families until recently. In an unusual situation, Jennifer and her husband live with her parents in Bombay to save money to buy a home of their own, while her husband's family resides in New Delhi. Only three women say that they have never lived with conjugal families since marriage. As suggested by the literature, since marriage is patrilocal, most women start their married life amid strangers. In women's narratives, these changes account for the more troubled part of their early married lives. Payal, who was 19 years old when she married nine years ago, captures these tensions of the first few years of marriage. She says,

> The first one to two years are the worst. Living with a person and going out with somebody is different. We were engaged for six months. We would

meet every day. Once you get married . . . it took me three to four years to find my bearings. The hardest was the loss of freedom. There are these norms, you can't go out alone, you are expected to behave in a particular way. They like it if you are sitting in the house, just sitting in the house. I could never understand if I am not doing anything what difference does it make if I go out? My husband is not very expressive, and I can talk about anything I feel. He doesn't communicate very well with his father. So if there was a problem, me in the middle, and they on each side. He is shouting at me that I listen too much to his parents, I am trying to please his parents to please him. The parents feel that now that he is married he doesn't listen to us so maybe she is the one who is making him like that. Where do you go? I used to tell him, "They will forgive you murder," but as a daughter-in-law, if I tell them something, it would be harder to forgive.

Many women feel the loss of freedom after marriage and the constraints of living in conjugal families. Elsewhere in the interview, Payal notes that with marriage, the bride is suddenly thrown into and expected to deal with a range of things including running a house, family, relationships, and sexual relations. Not surprisingly, the first few years are troubled.

In her narrative, Preeta expounds on the loss of freedom and the kinds of restrictions placed on her by her husband's parents after marriage.

In my mom's house we were free. Here it was like a cage. Normally I didn't tell [her mother] her where I was. Here you have to tell everything, where you are going, you have to account all the time. You have to adjust because you don't know which family you will get. The bad part was I couldn't finish college, I had two years left. You need their cooperation. You are newly married, so you can't argue much. It creates a bad impression.

We get along well, my mother-in-law and I. But there are differences. She doesn't like my going to my mother's house because I shouldn't leave my husband. He will get bored. I like going to my mother's house. You can freak out without your husband, do what you want, get up late, go out with my sisters to discos. He doesn't like that. I went with him, and there was tension. Then I stopped going.

In this transition from one's home to the patrilocal, conjugal family, several issues become important in women's accounts. The loss of freedom and the imposition of restrictions and new norms are deeply felt. Yet, the restrictions, which are emphasized in women's accounts, do not seem fundamentally different from those imposed in their families of origin or natal families. Elsewhere in the interview, Preeta describes the restrictions imposed on her by her father when she was growing up. Furthermore, arguably her regret that she was not able to complete her bachelor's degree is equally related to her natal and conjugal family; her parents did not think it inappropriate to interrupt

Preeta's education to marry her off at age 18. Two factors are likely to shape their perceptions of the loss of freedom and restrictions in the conjugal families. First, forms of control in their own homes, mitigated by parental love and affection, are structurally exposed in their conjugal families. Second, new norms of behavior, specific to the statuses of daughters-in-law and wives are imposed, exacerbating the perceptions of restrictions and loss of freedom— e.g., not being able to work for pay after marriage. In describing the transition from their natal homes to conjugal homes women use a language marked by sharp dichotomies—freedom/loss of freedom, lack of responsibility/responsibility, relaxed/tensed, true self/guarded self.

Echoing these dichotomies, Pranati describes the difficult adjustment with her in-laws and how it affects and interrupts her marital relationship, this despite the fact that she and her husband dated prior to their marriage. She says,

> Before nobody could tell me what I have to do. If I want to do it I will, if I don't nobody can force me. But after marriage certain things you have to do. Simple things in the kitchen—put this here, keep that there. My husband is not like that, but my in-laws are. With time you adjust. That really irritated me. . . . If you are going out you have to say bye to my mother-in-law and father-in-law separately, it's not natural . . . I think it does affect your relationship with your husband. When they pass comments on you, your husband feels that you are not bothered. It's not easy; it's not easy for my mother-in-law either. . . . I think it is important to live with your in-laws so that a bond develops. But it is also important not to let it reach the breaking point where you can't live together anymore. It is better to separate before that.

In the narratives, adjusting to the conjugal family is expected but far more difficult than adjusting to the husband. In Pranati's account, her husband is not demanding, but her in-laws' requirements are exacting. Difficulties with in-laws can strain the marital relationship eventually, she says.

In her case, Sheila, who has been married for two years, speaks of the difficulties of living in a household as a daughter-in-law rather than as a daughter. She says,

> I am not used to doing work. I did not even know how to make tea before marriage. We had cooks in our house, servants to do everything. My grandfather did not allow us in the kitchen. He used to say, "Girls have no work in the kitchen." My husband used to say, "Get up early in the morning and help my mother." It was very difficult for me. I just do what I think is right. Afterwards I get scolding for it, but if I want something I will get it or I will do it my way. You can't talk many things to your parents, these things will pass. It's difficult for them to know that their daughter is not happy. I try to solve things at home.

Despite her husband's role in enforcing responsibilities upon her, Sheila is quite uncritical of him. Instead, she describes her unhappiness in the context of the transition into the conjugal family.

Implicit in these narratives on conjugal families is the perception that the women were cared for more as daughters than as daughters-in-law. Caplan and Kakar report that middle-class parents tend to bring up their daughters indulgently and with affection.[14] This also serves to heighten the disparity in their experiences before and after marriage. Through the duration of her still-troubled relationships with her husband and his family, Kavita describes being imbued with a precious feeling of peace when she could quietly lay her head in her mother's lap. Married six and a half years, Ketaki says that she is at her happiest when she is able to go out together with her sisters and her parents, and her husband, she adds almost as an afterthought. Parental love and affection are not uncomplicated but are fondly remembered against the grain of conjugal families. For example, although Chandni was certain that she did not want a husband like her father, who was short-tempered and unpredictable, she summarizes her position in her natal home as: "I was the queen in my house. I was given a lot of love and importance."

For the three women, including Nargis, who no longer live with their in-laws, relief is the dominant emotion. The two currently married women consider themselves very fortunate to be physically separated from their in-laws. Both Rati and Neetu suggest that their relationships with their husbands have improved considerably since their residential separation from the conjugal families. The stories of the three women who have never lived with their in-laws are marked by issues of adjusting to husbands, to a marital relationship, to a new home and a new life. For example, in sharp contrast to the women who live amid conjugal families after marriage, Richa says that the first year after marriage was like an extended honeymoon. It was only later, due to the mundane exigencies of life, that married life became more complicated. Nonetheless, she, like the other two women who have not lived with conjugal families since marriage, strives to cast her husband and their marital relationship in a positive light.

In comparison to the single women in this study, the married women seem to be more invested in drawing upon and maintaining a conceptual framework of caring husbands and marriages characterized by mutual affection and intimacy. Not only do these expectations shape notions of marriage in the narratives, but they seem to be strategic to women's roles as wives and daughters-in-law. Put differently, within the context of patrilocal marriages which exacerbate women's vulnerabilities as wives, these ideals for husbands and marriages are more likely to be effective.

Instead of being somehow superfluous or merely extraneous for their "Western" connotations, these ideals for husbands and marital relationships are more likely to offset women's subordination in marriage. Put differently, "westernization" does not account for enhancing women's status as wives but is the effect of hegemonic codes of gender identity. Neither do these narratives appear to be "traditional" in any sense. Instead, these narratives evince hegemonic codes that reinforce marriage as an integral aspect of womanhood. But, if these middle-class women draw on notions of marriage as companionship and partnership, then it is crucial that their husbands be understanding and accommodating of their needs and that the intimacy of their relationship be enhanced by open and candid communication. In their emphasis on marriage as an intimate relationship based on friendship and open communication, these middle-class women's narratives are shaped by and strategically draw upon transnational cultural discourses.[15] This language of understanding, caring husbands and marital relationships that are rooted in expectations of love, intimacy, egalitarian gender roles, clearly cuts across national cultural boundaries. Viewed from this perspective, these narratives are both enabling and limiting. They suggest a kind of normalization of the criteria for spouses and marital relationships, while also showing how women attempt to use these criteria strategically in their lives.

Clearly, the women seem to take for granted the social mandate of marriage for women. At the same time, this understanding of marriage seems to enable them to set expectations of marital intimacy and companionship that help secure the allegiance of their husbands, and in turn, their positions as wives. These expectations also help them set standards of gender-egalitarian and mutual marital relationships. This is not to suggest that these women may cease to be subordinate or realize gender equity in the face of pervasive and entrenched forms of inequality. Instead, these ideals help them negotiate the deep-seated inequalities in their roles as wives and daughters-in-law. To that extent, their narratives also suggest how discourses of subordination or "westernization" and "tradition" can mask rather than reveal these complexities.

The Significance of Motherhood

Motherhood is the other role through which middle-class women attempt to secure their positions as wives and daughters-in-law. In the narratives of these women on the meaning of motherhood, or its aspects such as pregnancy, childbirth, and breastfeeding, no monolithic account emerges. Instead, they express themselves in ways that draw upon, qualify, and question hegemonic notions of motherhood and womanhood. In contrast to these prevailing hegemonic expectations, these women's narratives on aspects of motherhood are more nuanced, complex, and not easily categorized. What do seem nonetheless consistent in the narratives are the ways in which motherhood provides added security to women and mitigates their vulnerability after marriage. But, most compellingly, these narratives also suggest ways in which motherhood may be a means to subvert the limits of their positions as wives and daughters-in-law. It is in this respect that these narratives more clearly deviate from prevailing notions or scholarly literature on marriage and womanhood.

Prevailing expectations of motherhood, marriage, and womanhood are perhaps most concisely reflected in a question in the text *Teenagers Ask, The Doctor Answers*.

> *Question:* I am just out of my teens. We have been married only six months. Both of us do not want a baby for at least three years. My mother-in-law is persistent that we should have a baby now. What is your advice?
>
> *Answer:* Having a baby is both a pleasure and a great responsibility. It should be the personal choice of the couple, based on sound reasoning, to decide when they are ready to start a family. Purely traditional views as expressed by your mother-in-law should not be the only criterion.
>
> After all, a couple must consider many practical factors. Will the coming of the baby affect your husband's plans and ambitions for his future? Do you have adequate finances? Have you a home of your own or would you be comfortable with the baby in a joint family? If you are a working woman, how would this affect you emotionally and financially?
>
> Generally doctors recommend that a couple start a baby within two years of marriage, so that if there are any factors that prevent conception, corrective measures can be taken at an early stage. Since you are very young, you can wait longer if you desire. To ensure that you use the most suitable contraceptive method, consult your doctor or visit a family planning clinic.
>
> I would advise you to discuss the subject frankly with your mother-in-law.[16]

Reflected in this account are cultural notions that motherhood is a certainty for women within the context of marriage. Furthermore, this account also captures widely prevalent notions about the past and the present, about traditional versus more rational contemporary views. Thereby, the mother-in-law is seen as the emissary of traditional cultural views about motherhood, but the young, newly married woman can be encouraged to see motherhood as a rational, planned event. Where the hypothetical mother-in-law may be insistent only six months after marriage, the daughter-in-law is advised to make this choice ideally within two years of marriage. What is assumed is the role of women in raising the question of children, planning through contraception, and making rational choices about when, not if, to have children.

The Meaning of Motherhood

Available scholarship on matters of motherhood confirms the primacy of women's roles as mothers. With respect to her work among urban Punjabis and their notions of kinship, Das notes the two fundamental aspects of biology with which kinship must reckon, namely, procreation and copulation.[17] Describing the centrality of motherhood for the procreative aspect of kinship, Das suggests that although children are supposedly linked to the father by the relationship of blood, they are considered to be closer to their mothers due to the extensive contact through pregnancy and the child rearing. Furthermore, women may be replaceable in their roles as wives and sexual partners but not as mothers, according to Das. Kakar, summarizing the importance of women's status as mothers in his psychoanalytic study of childhood in India, says that regardless of a woman's caste, class, or regional background, and whether she is a young bride or an older woman who has experienced repeated pregnancies and childbirths, an Indian woman knows that motherhood confers upon her a purpose and identity that nothing else can.[18]

That this view is prevalent and shapes the narratives of the middle-class women in this study is clear in some accounts but far more ambivalent in others. As noted in the introduction, 23 of the married women are mothers and others, with the exception of Neetu, both married and unmarried, expect to have children at some point. In their narratives, mothers frequently describe having children as the nicest part of being women. According to Anu, having given birth is a source of much pride to her. She says,

> The time I was a girl and really proud of [it] was when I had my baby. I am very proud of it till today. Very proud. Till today. When I gave birth, I am a woman, I can do it. A man can't. I am giving birth to life.

For Anu her capacity for giving birth is an integral part of her womanhood and the pride that she takes in being a woman. While some women may be less zealous, nonetheless they see motherhood as a natural part of life.

In her narrative, Preeta expresses far more ambivalence than Anu about having children but is certain that it is only natural to have children. Having been married just over two years, this 20-year-old says,

> After one or two months I will plan. My best friend is getting married in September. After that. It's high time. By the time I get [the baby] I will be 21 and a half. My in-laws are very much interested . . . I get real scared of delivery. I've heard so much about it being so painful, getting up in the night, all that. My mother-in-law will take care, or I will hire a maid. My husband will be cooperative because he is very fond of children. I get irritated when they

cry. You have to have children. In my family you do. I don't mind because I am not working. I feel you should have a child, you feel more complete. If you can't have you should adopt a small kid. It gives meaning to life, you have something to look forward to.

In this rather fragmented narrative, Preeta shifts constantly between the problems of bearing and raising children, familial expectations, and the advantages of having children. Even as Preeta describes the pressure from the proverbial mother-in-law and the familial expectation that she will have a child, she expresses her reservations about the process. Yet, she concludes this part of her account by saying that having or adopting children not only gives meaning to life but it makes a woman more complete.

In contrast to Preeta, Chandni rejects the possibility that having a child could make her more complete. What she does stress, however, is that it can help consolidate her marital relationship. She says,

As a woman, a child cannot make you complete or incomplete. I am my own person. A child is definitely an endorsement in India that you are a complete woman, but I don't go by those beliefs. But a child is important to me because I would like to give to that child what my parents have given me.

It gives you a certain discipline in marriage when you are living independently. I have heard of some cases when you reach a certain point, you go astray from one another. There's nothing to hold you. The child is that cementing pact which is important but not a necessity . . . so, I would like to have a child.

Chandni both expresses and rejects the prevailing beliefs that motherhood endorses womanhood. Not only would she like to have a child to pass on what her parents have given to her but to enforce the marital relationship and its responsibilities onto a married couple, especially one that lives independently. In a parallel narrative, Anjali, who expects to marry and have children over the next few years, says that children are a binding source that add to your marital responsibilities and relationship in a positive way.

Encountering the Responsibilities of Motherhood

Especially in the cases of women who say they married young, having the primary responsibilities of child care thrust upon them soon after marriage makes the experiences of pregnancy and the first few months after childbirth particularly hard. According to Ketaki, who married when she was 22, getting pregnant immediately after her wedding was a source of great distress.

I got pregnant immediately after my marriage. I didn't want to be pregnant. I couldn't believe it had happened. I had not got my period, I thought maybe after marriage my chums had become irregular. So I waited 15 to 20 days, and when I went to my mother's house, they had an [entertainment] unit, and I jumped from the unit. I said, "If I am pregnant something will go wrong." My mom gave me a yelling. I didn't want to get pregnant, I wanted to enjoy life more, wanted to be free. My older daughter, she was cranky all the time maybe because I was so unhappy in my pregnancy. To take care of her all the time. . . . The whole thing happened so suddenly. I got engaged, married all of a sudden, came to a new place, and got pregnant. I didn't get any pampering from my in-laws, they don't believe in it. My husband did, but he got a scolding for it. My mother-in-law felt that he is spoiling me, she thought I was acting. My mother and father really pampered me, specially my father. He took care of me.

So draining were the pregnancy and child care responsibilities, according to Ketaki, that her daughter seems to have been affected. And to make matters worse, Ketaki says, she was not pampered or attended to by her in-laws, and her husband was prevented from showing her any special attention.

Based on her fieldwork among elite women in Chinnai, Caplan suggests that women are more cosseted during and after their pregnancy than at any other time.[19] In the narratives of these middle-class women who describe pregnancy, childbirth, and early motherhood, such expectations appear to be present but not always met. Where women describe being appreciated and attended to by their husbands or in-laws during and after pregnancy, they are more likely to describe these experiences in positive ways. In her narrative, not only does Sujata say that she received much attention from her husband and members of both of their families, but she speaks at length about the positive nature of the pregnancy and the joy that their child brought to all of them. On the other hand, Ketaki and Sheila emphasize their dismay at being pregnant as well as being unappreciated by the members of their conjugal families.

That motherhood entails responsibilities toward children is also noted in the available literature. Characterized by physical closeness, constant attention, indulgence, sleeping with the toddler, the first four to five years of a child's life mark an intense attachment with the mother and a unique sense of maternal obligation to the child. According to Kakar, this maternal obligation to the child is heightened because the child has triggered the change in the woman's social status.[20] Confirming both the importance of motherhood and the maternal relationship, Caplan argues that since babies and children are much valued and treated with a great deal of attention and indulgence by all members of the household, mothers are expected to put the needs of their children first.[21] They are rarely separated from adults, especially their mothers, and are generally taken everywhere, according to Caplan. Therefore, not only does motherhood enhance the status of women in their conjugal family, but it also makes child care a mother's primary responsibility.

The close relationship between mothers and their children is reiterated in the narratives as well. Despite the availability of hired help, women say that they are the ones who take care of the needs of their children. Of the 23 women who have children, only two women work outside the homes; coincidentally, each of them owns and runs a clothing store near her home. Another woman runs a day-care center out of her home so that she can work without neglecting her son. As mothers, they emphasize that they are the primary caretakers of their children; they bathe and feed their children and children sleep in close proximity to them. According to the mothers, the children may share their beds, or they may sleep in their children's beds for part of the night. Yet in the narratives this close relationship between them and their children is emphasized alongside, instead of against, their marital relationships.

Motherhood as Security

What seems indisputable in the literature and the narratives on motherhood is that women's status is not only significantly enhanced but also made more secure once they become mothers. Kakar suggests that women may be accorded more security as mothers.[22] That motherhood, established by the birth of the first child, is the most secure status for a woman, is also confirmed by Caplan.[23] Documenting prevailing cultural preferences for sons rather than daughters, Kakar and Caplan, among others, also suggest that women's statuses are most secure as mothers of sons. Among the middle classes, although girls are much loved and indulged due to their departure from their natal homes at the point of marriage, both Kakar and Caplan suggest that there is a gender bias in favor of bearing male children. In her cross-caste study of a village in south-central India, Dhruvarajan makes similar observations that women are accorded deference as mothers but that male children are preferred.[24] According to Dhruvarajan, the living hell of the first few years of marriage, as described by women, is alleviated only by the birth of a son; the birth of sons evokes elation, and daughters, pity.

A prominent aspect throughout the narratives of the middle-class mothers in this study is that bearing children helped improve their positions within the conjugal family and their relationships with their husbands. Supporting the above literature, these women also suggest that motherhood promoted their integration into conjugal families. They are accorded more respect and a role within the family upon the birth of their children. In her narrative,

Payal, who has a five-year-old son, describes the significant changes that occurred in her life after the birth of her child. She says that not only did taking care of her son give her a lot of self-confidence but it considerably improved her position with her in-laws as well as with her husband. Thereafter, she had more of a say in important matters and was treated more respectfully by her in-laws and her husband. She describes the improved conjugal and marital relationship in these words,

> You get linked to your husband. Then you feel that you have a family. They [husbands] don't think that wives are family because you are not related by blood. That made a lot of difference. It gave me more authority in the house, more say.

Therefore, aside from more secure positions in the conjugal families, middle-class mothers in this study also indicate enhanced marital intimacy with their husbands. Husbands reportedly tend to be more responsive and concerned through the pregnancy and after childbirth. These mothers say that they become closer to their husbands upon the birth of their children. Children become the irrevocable link they have with their husbands. As Manisha reflects on the birth of her six-month-old daughter, she describes what it means to her as well as her marital relationship:

> Till today I often think about it in the night before I go to sleep, the experience of giving birth. I take pride in it. It's an achievement. It's a beautiful experience of giving birth. I cried for 20 minutes after I had her. It gives me a lot of satisfaction. You go through it alone. A man can worry, but fathers lie if they say they have gone through it. But the bond between the two of you gets stronger. Now you are bound together because of the child.

Rethinking Son-Preference

Against the literature documenting prevailing cultural preferences for sons in conjugal families, these middle-class women are far more ambivalent. Indeed, several women say that they would rather have girl children.[25] Among the women who have children, Hansa stands out as the exception for how she articulates her profound disappointment at bearing two daughters. She describes her reactions after the birth of her younger daughter,

> Initially I felt bad I didn't have a boy. I was miserable for 40 days. I've got everything but not this. Heart of heart everyone wanted a son and me also. For my husband, I never wanted for myself. It will be nice for him, he doesn't have a brother or a father. My mother-in-law did not say anything, she did the same for my children [as her other male grandchildren]. I was miserable

for 40 days, and I ask forgiveness for that even today. My brother-in-law can't have a child, they asked me for my second child. I actually thought about giving her up. Then I could conceive again. My husband said, "I will disown you now. How can you give up a child because she is a girl child? You, an educated person?" Now it's fine.

In her account Hansa expresses her deep personal disappointment, which may have been shared but not articulated in her conjugal family. It took the strong words of her husband to change her mind, and now Hansa expresses profound embarrassment that she ever felt this way. What seems clear from Hansa's account is that even though there may be some preferences for at least one male child, it is not without a sharp sense of guilt.

Describing her reaction at the birth of her second daughter, 30-year-old Madhuri speaks of how others' preferences can color a woman's perceptions:

I was disappointed when I first had my daughter. People make you feel like a victim. When I was pregnant the second time I desperately prayed for a son. I would do anything that anyone said to get a son. I would pray to God, "God, either give me a son or give me peace of mind." My second daughter is really attractive. I took one look at her and said, "Balls to the world baby! We are going to have a ball." It's not that there is anything special in having a son, but everyone makes you feel really bad if you don't. People would come over to see my first daughter and sympathize. It got to the point that I did not want to see anyone or that anyone should come over to see the baby.

In striking contrast to Hansa, and to a lesser degree to Madhuri, some women in this study say that they have no clear gender preference or would prefer to have girl children. Neetu, who says that she is unable to bear children, has promised to throw a celebratory party should her sister-in-law have a girl child, but not if it is a boy. Nipun, who has a four-year-old son, explains the lack of clear gender preferences for children among the middle classes. She says,

My husband wanted a daughter. We just prayed that the baby would be healthy, normal. We would have accepted a handicapped child, but you first pray for normal child. I don't agree when people say this but want a boy. I feel a child is a child. Each child has parents' blood, how can they differentiate between girl and boy? I have seen my friends suffer, it's more in the poor and in the rich. Middle class people don't bother too much, they can afford the same thing for both children. The rich want the money to stay in the family through the son, and the poor don't want to give dowry but want to get it through their sons. The friends from my class, they are not bothered.

In her account Kavita articulates a preference for girl children that is echoed by others in this study. The mother of an 11-year-old daughter, Kavita says,

> I wanted a daughter. I love girls, somehow that bond is there. I could never adjust to a boy. I wanted my husband to face having a daughter. For him to realize someday what the problems are to get your own daughter married. That rebellion was there. I wanted him to realize that having a daughter doesn't mean that she can be treated like mud. So I wanted very strongly my firstborn to be a daughter.
>
> I was very happy. My mother-in-law and husband were very disappointed. My mother-in-law took it better. It's still important for him [the husband] to have a son.

In Kavita's account and those of many other middle-class women, there appears to be a preference for girl children based on the perceived bonds between mother and daughter. There is an equally strong perception that as adults girl children are much more caring and considerate toward their parents, particularly their mothers. But in Kavita's account yet another reason is articulated. Due to her husband's disrespectful behavior to her parents, Kavita wanted to have a girl child. As the father of a girl or adult woman, Kavita's husband will be forced to empathize with her father, according to Kavita. In effect, not only does she express a preference for girl children based on the bond between herself and her daughter, but also as a means to subvert her husband's lack of respect toward her parents.

In this respect, the narratives of middle-class women in this study significantly deviate from the available literature on the meaning and significance of motherhood in the lives of women. What is unique in Kavita's narrative is that as a mother of a girl, she can challenge the inequity of her marital relationship. She is required to be respectful to her mother-in-law, but she cannot enforce the same requirement on her husband. But what is more consistent across the narratives is that motherhood may be used not only to secure women's positions in conjugal families and establish irrevocable bonds with their husbands, but also to change, question, or undermine particularly the conjugal relationships. This is perhaps the most striking point of difference between the literature that establishes the significance and security of motherhood in the lives of women and the narratives of middle-class women—that the women deploy their status as mothers to subvert their marginalization within conjugal families. In her study, Das suggests that the relationship between mother and child is used to secure the individual allegiance of the child but not to subvert the authority of patriarchal rules.[26] But, as reflected in the narratives of the women in this study, what they are sometimes unable to challenge as wives, they attempt to do as mothers.

The next and concluding section of this chapter further explores these links between marriage, motherhood, and subversion. I present three narratives, those of two single women and one married woman, that succinctly capture the contradictions of womanhood, marriage, and motherhood that crisscross the narratives of other women in the study as well. Each of these three narratives addresses the role of motherhood in the larger context of life. In so doing, these three women provide diverging accounts of the meaning of motherhood, raising important questions about the limitations and possibilities of their status as mothers. Through the role of motherhood in their lives, these three women also bring to a head the hegemonic codes of gender identity. Whereas Venita invokes ideals of gender-neutral persons and the importance of making rational choices regarding marriage and motherhood, associated with modernity, Vani is much more ambivalent about pursuing this path for women that she associates with Indian national culture, though she is unable to reject it altogether. In contrast, without invoking either notions of gender-neutral, rational persons or the advantages and constraints of womanhood in Indian culture, Rati describes how she uses her position as a mother to demand accountability from her husband and her conjugal family on behalf of herself and her children.

Venita: The Rational One

Venita is a 22-year-old actress in the Hindi film industry in Bombay. Articulate and self-assured, throughout her interview, she emerges as the quintessential rebel. At the age of 19, Venita walked out of her home to live by herself rather than concede to parental opposition to her becoming an actress. She says her parents simply could not accept her choice of profession and the fact that she was disregarding their opposition. She lived by herself for more than a year, lying to her neighbors that her parents had moved out of Bombay. Since then she has moved back with her parents at their insistence and because, she says, it is difficult to live without your family. Throughout the interview she registers her indignation at the double standards and the subordination that women are subjected to. In no uncertain terms Venita expresses that people should be judged on their worth, not based on their gender, class, or family background. Questioning the way many of her friends have complied with dominant social expectations of marriage and motherhood, she believes that through her choice of profession, her self-reliance, and individuality, she challenges the social system. She captures these beliefs in these words:

I believe in free thinking. If somebody puts restrictions on me, I won't stand it. Maybe it was OK till I was 18. After that even if I make mistakes, they are my own. I am very independent. To me that means a lot—that I can go out and do whatever I want to. I have too much respect for my own abilities and intelligence to fall into someone else's norms or dictates. I have a lot of confidence in myself.

Venita's story emerges as a passage into adulthood, characterized by her ability to exert her independent will and rationality. It also appears to be about the ambivalence of modernity. For Venita, walking out of the house to live one's life and exerting her free will are associated with modernity. That she is somewhat ambivalent about the ramifications of this rational, free-thinking position is evident elsewhere in her narrative when she says she used her position as a young woman from a "good family" to make it on her own. Venita seems clear that gender and family background should be irrelevant, that individuals should be treated for their own merit, but she is also unable to fully repudiate the privileges of her social background. Nonetheless, Venita privileges the notion of the rational, gender-neutral person to challenge a world in which women are treated unjustly because of their gender. To this issue she says,

You shouldn't think of yourself as a boy or a girl or a man or a woman because ultimately it's in your mind. You have to go beyond your physical limitations or advantages to try to make a life for yourself. I don't think of myself as a woman in this society, and I don't feel I am handicapped because I am a woman. I don't feel I am at an advantage because ultimately I am using my mind to get ahead. It's all individual, it doesn't depend on your gender, it's all in the mind.

In a consistent vein, on the issues of marriage and motherhood, Venita says that she is not so ambitious to not want these experiences. But in her narrative she suggests that the difference between her and those women who seek social respectability by becoming someone's wife, daughter-in-law, and mother, is that she will decide when and whom she should marry and with whom she should have children. Venita suggests that getting married and having children are natural parts of life. However, in her narrative it is her ability to exert control over these, instead of simply complying with social requirements, that makes her desire to get married and have children consistent with her sense of herself as a rational, free-thinking, gender-neutral individual. At one point in the interview she says,

I would love to have children, but I want to be more in control of myself before I do. I would love to have a family of my own someday. I don't want to be one of those spinster types. I am not so obsessed with my career. I should not be regarded differently just because I am a woman for my interests and pursuits. Marriage and having children is a part of life, it's natural. But, you have control over when that can happen.

By insisting that there is nothing unusual about the desire to have children and to marry, that these should be reasonable expectations rather than choices imposed on women to ensure their social respectability, Venita's account on marriage and motherhood is potentially subversive. In effect, Venita undermines prevailing double standards for women and the imposition of marriage and motherhood by recasting the requirements in ways that are reminiscent of modernity—as "natural" but rational choices to be made by self-directed individuals. On the other hand, as she defensively suggests that she is neither too obsessed by her career nor does she want to end up a spinster, also suggests the limits of taking the position of the rational, free-thinking, and gender-neutral person. Elsewhere in the interview, as Venita details issues such as sexual aggression directed against her, she also reveals that rational, gender-neutral positions may be potentially subversive and not free from contradictions.

Vani: Different and Better

In striking contrast, 23-year-old Vani's narrative is told through a more nationalist, gender-conscious perception of marriage and motherhood. Since graduating with a bachelor's degree, Vani has lived with her parents and shares household responsibilities with her mother. Although she is quite ambivalent about getting married and having children, she expects it will happen over the next two years. In the meanwhile, Vani says, she spends much time participating in a religious group that has much bearing on her life. This religious group is drawn from, but critical of, Hinduism, and has a wide, geographically dispersed national following. Vani takes inspiration from this group's religious teachings to integrate spiritual life with mundane responsibilities. But since this integration can be impractical and insufficient, especially for women, she wonders if she should reject the possibilities of marriage and motherhood in order to pursue an autonomous, spiritual path.

Challenging the way marriage and motherhood serve to bind women into household responsibilities, kin relationships, sexual desires, and maternal affection, Vani says that not only do these day-to-day responsibilities limit a woman's choices, but they prevent her from gaining spiritual fulfillment and autonomy. This is what makes her ambivalent and anxious about getting married and having children. In her narrative, Vani outrightly challenges the ways in which women are constrained as wives and mothers.

> In the Indian society not much freedom is given to women, and after marriage you can't do what you want to do. It's not just the household work, that is there in my mother's house also, but it's the relations. You have to do something that they like. I feel if I get married such things will come in my way.

A little later, Vani also worries about how sexual relations with her husband might further distract her from a life devoted to spiritual upliftment. If Venita tries to subvert the limitations of womanhood by emphasizing herself as a rational individual, Vani seeks to undermine them by rejecting marriage and motherhood altogether. Nonetheless, she emphasizes the importance of being a woman and being part of a national culture with its strengths and limitations.

From Vani's perspective, women are stronger than men, and the Indian culture better than the Western. Where Venita attempts to transcend the limitations on women by emphasizing the gender-neutral individual, Vani notes and values the characteristic strengths of women. She says that women are stronger and more self-reliant because they are taught to sacrifice, compromise, and work hard from childhood. Furthermore, if the Indian society imposes limitations upon women after marriage, it also does so because the desires, such as sex and bearing children, are natural and necessary. Indian culture, according to her, is more sound, spiritual, and scientific in comparison to the more degenerate culture of the West. Thus, in her narrative, Vani sees the issue of marriage and motherhood for women as part of a larger context marked by differences between men and women, between the West and Indian culture.

Caught between what is unique to women and Indian national culture, Vani is unable to forsake the possibilities of marriage or motherhood. She worries about unfulfilled natural desires as well as the chance to raise children as good strong human beings, imbibed with the values of Indian culture. Without marriage, she also wonders about being emotionally and sexually deprived, of seeking the natural pleasures of sex outside of marriage later in life. With regard to motherhood, Vani says,

> I feel it is important to be a mother. Depends from person to person. It is said that you can't feel complete without being a mother, but it depends. I would like to be a mother. If I successfully venture onto another path, then I won't miss it. But I would love to be a mother if I am married. I really love kids. I would like to be a mother, love them, and teach them. I've left everything on the situation, as it comes up, even with marriage.

What is partially subversive is also deeply ambivalent. Vani says that she is not sure how things are going to turn out, but in the meantime, her parents are looking for a suitable match.

Rati: The Struggle to Recover the Self

Thirty-one years old and the mother of two young children, Rati speaks about the ways in which she used her position as a mother to make her marital relationship more effective and assert herself with her in-laws. Rati describes the ways in which she was marginalized within her conjugal family over the 10-year period of her marriage, and how that affected her relationship with her husband. She believes because she and her husband were dating and had sexual intercourse prior to marriage, she was never able to fully get her in-laws' approval. They see her as an outsider, she says, and constantly question her intentions and her advice. Despite the 10 years in which they have all shared the same roof, her relationship with her in-laws is still contingent on her husband's relationship with his parents; she has no separate entity, according to her.

Rati describes how she was unable to voice her opinions in the conjugal family as she had been brought up to by her parents. Using terms such as *suffocating* and *pressure*, Rati describes the kind of impact living in this environment had on her. She says,

> I had no confidence left in myself. Whatever I said had no meaning. Over years, it brings a kind of pressure on you and you start feeling, "No, I am worthless." . . . I was a positive-thinking person. I totally changed. People could not recognize me.

Rati says that unlike the pampering that she was given by her parents, she was responsible for all of the housework after marriage. Despite the affluence of her conjugal family, she and her husband were given a relatively small sum of money out of the family business on a monthly basis as pocket money. All of this took a toll on her marital relationship. Her husband stayed out late for parties, and the in-laws would direct their disapproval toward her. Later, when she started to accompany him out of despair and loneliness, the situation with her in-laws became worse. Rati says that this led to much conflict between her husband and herself but that he was not the problem. Her husband was dependent on the family business, and therefore, unable to establish a separate household for the two of them or assert himself with his parents.

What changed the situation quite dramatically was the birth of her twin children. As per convention, she went to stay at her natal home after childbirth. But Rati refused to return from there until her husband made substantial changes in their lives. She describes the way she negotiated changes to an intolerable situation,

My husband was not earning any money, I had to ask my in-laws and my parents for money. I went through a very bad time financially. That is when I told my husband, "You are in a joint family, you are an equal partner. I am not coming back unless you earn your own money, you support me and your children." That's when I pushed him into demanding a share of his grandfather's business, and I pushed him into standing on his own feet. For him, it might be OK to ask his parents, but not for me. I didn't want to depend on my parents. Somehow it was our responsibility to look after our children. I pushed him, he did it, and that's when I came back.

Rati as a mother is able to make demands on her husband that she couldn't make as a wife. As a mother, she was able to push her husband into being financially independent. Rati was able to demand that she and her husband establish a separate residence. When it came time for her children to enter school, according to Rati, where they lived with her conjugal family, there were no acceptable schools. Refusing to make compromises in the education of her children, Rati insisted that they move for the sake of the children's future. A month before our interview, Rati and her family had established a separate residence.

She summarizes the events and the positive impact this separation from her conjugal family has had on herself and her marital relationship.

I felt the children have to be put in a proper school. That's the one thing I insisted on. I may not be able to give them a lot of property but at least I can give them a proper education, like what my parents gave me. So I felt that I should give them the education, although my in-laws were totally against my shifting out of the house.

Till now they are jealous that I am staying independently and have my husband to myself. They can't control me. I am my own individual. I am known as myself, not their daughter-in-law. I am me. In fact, I am more known around here than my husband is. He always teases me, "I am known as your husband, not the other way around." After a long time I am feeling this way, after a long time [she repeats with a smile].

Rati's narrative is told along multiple vectors—of past and present, of daughter and daughter-in-law, of individuality, its loss, and its recuperation. She was nurtured as a daughter but vulnerable as a wife and daughter-in-law; only through her status as a mother can she make necessary demands. Unlike both Venita's and Vani's, Rati's account of marriage and motherhood defies facile analysis. It is not clearly about notions of modernity or national cultural traditions nor does it lend itself to a narrative about the coherence of womanhood or gender identity. Instead, Rati tells about how she negotiates the devastating obligations of kinship, related to marriage and motherhood, without completely repudiating them. For example, toward the end of the interview, she describes how she still attempts to have a cordial relationship with her in-laws and urges her husband to respect his mother despite all of these conflicts and differences. But, what is most compelling about Rati's narrative is the way she tells a story of the struggle to recover some autonomy and a sense of her self under formidable circumstances.

Conclusion

Based on middle-class women's narratives and salient literature, the social mandates of marriage and motherhood are incontrovertible in the definition of womanhood and in women's lives. What is more debatable is how to understand and analyze marriage and motherhood as integral roles and markers of womanhood. Clearly, the literature that approaches these issues in women's lives, rooted in the vectors of women's subordination, "westernization," "modernization," and "tradition," ends up masking the complexities and reinforcing stereotypes about Indianness and, to some extent, womanhood. On the other hand, securing this exploration and analysis in women's narratives and critically engaging hegemonic codes that sustain the significance of marriage and motherhood in women's lives reveals a much more complex picture of women's agency in their roles as wives and mothers.

Middle-class women's accounts on aspects of marriage and motherhood reveal much about the ways in which the premise of womanhood is sustained in women's lives. The powerful, persistent discourse of companionate marriage sustains not only a model for marriage but, in effect, the premise of womanhood. It is in the mundane anxieties and pleasures—for example, of courtship, expectations of husbands, and marital relationships—that the premise of womanhood is reproduced. At the same time, the narratives also suggest the ways in which hegemonic discourses—such as companionate marriage—are simultaneously limiting and enabling in women's lives. The discourse of companionate marriage sustains, rather than unsettles, the social mandate of marriage. It ends up normalizing and regulating women's roles as wives and marriage as an essential component of womanhood. But, women also deploy this framework of marriage more strategically to negotiate and secure their positions within the marital relationship and in the larger conjugal family. In this way, they are able to partially gain from their compliance to wifehood.

What they cannot achieve as wives, these women seem to supplement through their roles as mothers. Their narratives suggest how motherhood promotes their integration into the conjugal family and secures their positions as wives and daughters-in-law. Listening to women's accounts on motherhood also sheds a different light on aspects such as their perceptions of motherhood, how they negotiate the attendant responsibilities, and the relevance of son-preference among their social class. If these narratives tell us much about how women negotiate the requirements of motherhood, then what is also clear is that women only occasionally disrupt the hegemonic link between motherhood and womanhood. For these women, motherhood and marriage may carry different meanings, but their narratives are deeply shaped by these hegemonic codes. Nonetheless, their narratives do not easily lend themselves to explanations of subordination, disempowerment, and tacit compliance.

Finally, I turn to narratives from three women to illustrate the importance of approaching women's accounts from a position that allows for their complex participation in maintaining and possibly disrupting markers of gender identity. Venita complies with the social requirements of wifehood and motherhood while appearing to cast them as liberal choices. She attempts to disrupt the link between marriage, motherhood, and womanhood by erasing gender. In her narrative, Vani foregrounds gender and nationalisms to question the limitations and constraints of wifehood and motherhood in women's lives. She sustains the premise of womanhood and nationality to question how it is regulated through the mandates of marriage and motherhood. Venita's and Vani's narratives also highlight how the hegemonic codes of gender, womanhood, marriage, and motherhood are complexly imbricated with questions of nationalisms, tradition, and modernity. Their narratives also suggest how the discourses of nationalisms, westernization, and modernity may not be causal factors in women's narratives on marriage and motherhood. Indeed, the reverse may be true—that these discourses are the effects of hegemonic codes on marriage, motherhood, womanhood, and gender identity. But, by sidelining the discourses of tradition and westernization, on the one hand, and muting the premise of subordination and victimization, on the other, Rati tells a story of agency. What is intriguing in her narrative is how she foregrounds agency and opportunities for subversion that arise within the parameters of marriage and motherhood. Neither based in unequivocal discourses of womanhood nor nationalisms or modernity, Rati recounts a compelling story about how she made her life more bearable on a day-to-day basis.

Chapter Seven

Hybrid and Hyphenated: Reading Queer Narratives

Even at the end of the twentieth century, the Eastern culture is untinged in its tradition of high morality, monogamous marriage system and safe sex behavior. Our younger generation and youth still practice virginity till their nuptial day. The religious customs and God-fearing living habits are a shield of protection against many social evils. It will be difficult even for the HIV to penetrate this sheild except in certain metropolitan populations.[1]

Question: What is "homosexual"?
Answer: A homosexual is a man who is attracted to other men rather than to women and derives sexual pleasure from them. Women can also develop a sexual attraction for their own sex. Such women are called lesbians. Some experts think homosexuality may be connected with the way people develop in early childhood although this view is not upheld by everyone.
In any case all boys and girls pass through a "homosexual" phase during their school years when boys hero-worship stronger or cleverer boys, and girls develop a strong sentiment towards other girls. Sometimes boys in their early teens experiment with other boys of the same age. This is a normal phase and is soon outgrown.[2]

Trikone is a safe place, a home for lesbians, gay men, and people of alternative sexualities who are of South Asian descent. We understand that you need a place to be yourself, to be with people like you. We know what it is like, we have been there ourselves. Come and join Trikone—you are not alone.[3]

In the last decade, gay, lesbian, bisexual, and transgendered people of Indian background have become increasingly visible within India and in countries such as the United States. In her address at the tribunal on human rights violations against sexual minorities, sponsored by the International Gay and

Lesbian Human Rights Commission in October 1995 to coincide with the 50th anniversary of the United Nations, Anuja Gupta, activist and representative for India, testified on two accounts.[4] She detailed the persecution of lesbians and gay men, and their consequent vulnerability to HIV infections. Gupta also described the emergence of a gay and lesbian movement in India, which she says exacerbates state-sponsored and societal violence against gays and lesbians. This increasing and contentious visibility of a gay and lesbian movement is reflected in the publication of numerous gay magazines, reports, and newsletters; the organizing of related seminars and conferences; and television programs and films that address the issues of being gay and lesbian in India.

As emergent gay and lesbian groups attempt to gain visibility while countering prevailing forms of homophobia within contemporary India, they face an immediate challenge in allegations that homosexuality is external to Indian culture and society. As partially reflected in the quote that opens this chapter attributed to a state AIDS programme officer, strongly held moral assumptions about the nature of sexuality, and particularly homosexuality, continue to prevail.[5] This quote is cited and countered in a unique and therefore definitive study, *Less Than Gay: A Citizen's Report on the Status of Homosexuality in India.*[6] In the collection, the authors counter such notions about homosexuality in India, including the idea that homosexuality is merely a westernized, upper-class phenomenon. Challenging the credibility of the claims of the state AIDS programme officer, the authors of the report write, "Typically this Professor of Medicine, like many others, has not cared to learn about indigenous texts, concepts and traditions which revered and even celebrated sexual ambiguity, whether in the Kamasutra, through sexual dualism, in mysticism, or in female kingdoms."[7] What is immediately apparent is how questions of homosexuality are riven with discourses of nationalisms.

The excerpts from what could be considered competing truth claims on sexualities cited above help set the stage for this chapter. Taken together, these quotes foreground not only the issues of gay, lesbian, bisexual sexual identities, but also discourses of the post-colonial nation-state. If in the first quote by a state AIDS programme officer anything other than heterosexual, monogamous, marital sex within the Indian/Eastern context is refuted, then the second quote acknowledges the possibility of same-sex sexual attraction and desire. Taken from the text *Teenagers Ask, The Doctor Answers*, the answer in the second excerpt posits the possibility of sexual attraction among women or men but also the likelihood that such kinds of attraction may be widely pervasive and merely a passing developmental phase. Whether this answer by framing homosexual attraction as a normal but transitional part of development has the effect of expanding the realm of same-sex attraction or neutral-izing it is not easily determined.[8]

Unlike either of these two quotes, the third excerpt is taken from a pamphlet put out by Trikone, the oldest surviving queer South Asian organization. Based in San Francisco, Trikone celebrated its 10th anniversary in 1996. This excerpt is different not only in that sexuality is framed as a matter of sexual identities, but it appears to complicate the questions of nationalisms and sexualities. Founded by first-generation Indian immigrants in the United States and shaped by Indian cultural nationalisms, nonetheless there is a consistent emphasis on Trikone as a South Asian, instead of a solely Indian, organization. Related to the fact that Trikone consciously positions itself as a South Asian organization, the excerpt cited implicitly problematizes the limitations of nationalisms and raises the possibilities of supportive communities that cut across narrow national affiliations in favor of more transnational alliances. But because these tensions of sexual identities, nationalisms, and transnational discourses are widely pervasive, across queer narratives within India and those of Indian affiliation elsewhere, in this chapter I would like to consider both sets of narratives—queer narratives produced within India, as well as those that are shaped by questions of Indianness produced in the context of South Asian organizations like Trikone.

Thus far, the primary task has been to consider and analyze normative aspects of gender and sexuality reflected in the accounts of 54 middle-class women in contemporary post-colonial India. While the normative aspects of gender—menarche, marriage, and motherhood—have received more attention, the literature on the normative aspects of sexuality—heterosexuality or homosexuality—is only gradually being theorized. If there is one overarching insight that emerges from sexuality studies related to countries such as the United States and England, then it is the importance of considering not only the seemingly deviant aspects of sexuality, such as homosexuality or gay, lesbian, bisexual orientations, but also the dubiously self-evident nature of heterosexuality. The importance of unraveling the construct of heterosexuality, which unlike homosexuality appears to require no explanation because of its arguable normality, is compellingly argued by scholars such as Jonathan Katz, who traces the coeval, inextricable emergence of the constructs of homosexuality and heterosexuality in Western medical literature in the second half of the nineteenth century.[9] Having considered the more heterosexually charged aspects of gender and sexuality in the previous chapters, in this chapter my aim is to turn the lens onto narratives on homosexuality, gay, lesbian, and bisexual orientations.

It is useful to bring middle-class women's narratives on normative aspects of gender and sexuality and the more self-consciously oppositional queer narratives into the same analytical field.[10] Unlike the narratives on gender and sexuality by middle-class women, the narratives considered in this chapter are produced from the margins of dominant cultures. Precisely because of the intense isolation of self-acknowledged gay, lesbian, bisexual, and transgendered women and men in India, and frequently among Indian immigrants elsewhere, the focus shifts from personal narratives to narratives produced by formal and informal groups that seek to challenge the exclusions and affirm what is positive about these sexual identities.[11] These narratives—taken from collections of writing, status reports, magazines—thus are not only informative and shaped by personal experiences, but they also collectively indicate what get authorized as gay and lesbian accounts.

Aside from these stated differences, there are sociological commonalities across the narratives related to gay, lesbian, bisexual, and transgendered identities and those told by middle-class women in previous chapters. Much like the accounts included in the previous chapters, these gay, lesbian, bisexual, and transgendered narratives are also upwardly class-biased. In his essay, "Sexuality, Identity, and the Uses of History," in the collection titled *Lotus of Another Color*, Nayan Shah notes how South Asian gay and lesbian discourse is shaped by assumptions of educated, middle-class affiliations.[12] Shah also questions the ways in which class differences and inequalities are often elided in South Asian gay and lesbian discourse. I suggest that gay, lesbian, bisexual, and transgendered narratives also tend to evince an urban bias and to be less conscious of ethnic differences, similar to the narratives included in the previous chapters.

Perhaps the most compelling reason to focus on queer narratives in this chapter, alongside the narratives on heteronormativity included in a previous chapter, is the parallel role of the post-colonial nation-state in producing and reproducing hegemonic codes of sexuality and gender. Unlike middle-class women's narratives, where the normative framework often is implicit or taken for granted, queer narratives have arisen in organized contexts where truth claims are structured in competition with hegemonic discourses of the nation-state. In these queer narratives, and as tersely reflected in the quotes at the start of this chapter, not only the politics of nationalisms but also transnational cultural discourses are evident.

Based on these tensions and contradictions, from the viewpoint of queer narratives included in this chapter, I wish to make four points of argument. First, whether in India or in South Asian communities elsewhere, queer narratives are confounded by the discourses of national cultural identity. Second, these issues become most starkly obvious in the questions of ancient national cultural traditions and the place of alternative sexual identities, especially homosexuality. Third, queer narratives are shaped and normalized by transnational cultural discourses of sexuality. Fourth, these narratives also negotiate these normalizing transnational discourses to articulate the possibilities of identities that are rooted in transnational alliances. It is in these respects that the queer narratives included in this chapter are both illuminating and instructive.

What is especially remarkable is how questions of national cultural and sexual identities are tightly linked across gay and lesbian narratives produced within India and in South Asian communities outside of the nation-state. If questions of nationalisms and sexualities are used to exclude and marginalize Indian and South Asian queers, then these gay, lesbian, bisexual, and transgendered narratives also rightfully demand a place within the national community. In these current contestations over nation and sexuality, the role of ancient national tradition becomes especially salient. As reflected in the quote by the state AIDS programme officer, an ancient and continuous national tradition is used to justify forms of homophobia. But, in queer narratives this national reality that "is untinged in its tradition of high morality," is not so easily settled. Exploring queer narratives helps indicate not only how questions of national history become tied to the contemporary politics of nationalisms and sexual identities but also how this ground of national affiliation may be effectively negotiated. As explored below, Giti Thadani's book, *Sakhiyani: Lesbian Desire in Ancient and Modern India*, proffers a particularly useful instance of challenging the premise of the Indian national cultural identity and its exclusion of lesbian identities.[13]

What is equally evident in these queer narratives, as reflected in the above excerpt quoted from Trikone's introductory pamphlet, is the impact of transnational processes. Within these queer narratives, terms such as "gay," "lesbian," and "bisexual" are shaped by transnational cultural dicourses of sexual identity. Widely used across diverse social contexts, these terms have putative connotations of sexual identity based in same-sex sexual desire, in Indian and South Asian narratives as well. Although gay, lesbian, bisexual, and transgendered Indian or South Asian identities are not the same as, for example, black gay representations in the United States, neither are they incomparable. Furthermore, as indicative of sexual identities, terms such as *gay, lesbian, bisexual, transgendered,* or *queer* help marshall an oppositional politics.

But though queer narratives make possible oppositional politics, they also constrain them at the same time. Put differently, certain narratives of identity and its politics are produced only as other identities and politics are suppressed. But, the queer narratives included in this chapter also raise visions of a politics that goes beyond identity politics. Produced at the intersection of nationalisms and transnational cultural discourses, these queer Indian and related South Asian narratives are only partly about sexual identities and the roots of these identities. As both queer and of Indian affiliation, but not reducible to either queerness or Indianness, these narratives also raise the possibilities of a different sort of cultural politics. What appears different about the politics reflected in these queer narratives is the attempt to transcend notions of self and identity to a more transformational set of practices based in transnational alliances.

To explore queer narratives within India and of South Asian origin, particularly in the United States, this chapter is divided into two broad sections. The first section focuses on the impact of the fraught discourses of post-colonial national cultural identity, looks at how, from the vantage point of contemporary politics of sexual identities and nationalisms, perceptions of ancient cultural tradition become highly contested. The second section considers the transnational context and its effects on queer narratives. In this section, I highlight how queer narratives are both shaped by transnational cultural discourses of sexual identity but also go beyond the limitations of a politics rooted in sexual identities. To this purpose, I explore the case of Trikone as the oldest continuous South Asian, and indeed Indian, gay and lesbian organization.

Narratives and National Traditions

Scholarly considerations of homosexuality among Indians are preoccupied with the role and meaning of alternative sexualities within Indian antiquity. The search is for a univocal, authentic Indian history against which a sexuality can be legitimated as culturally appropriate or proven to be inappropriate. The period of the "Classical Age" is central to this unitary, hegemonic notion of the past. But there appear to be two problems underlying attempts to link questions of homosexuality with ancient national tradition: first, the received wisdom on ancient Indian history itself; second, the dubiousness of undertaking social rather than political histories.

A part of the post-colonial legacy of history, notions of Indian antiquity are shaped by nineteenth-century collusions between sympathetic but racist Orientalists and anticolonial nationalists. As argued by Uma Chakravarti in her compelling essay on the politics of constructing a national past in the nineteenth century, Orientalists helped crystallize a national Indian identity by constructing a classic and golden age of Indian antiquity rooted in elitist Brahmanical scriptures of the Vedic and post-Vedic periods.[14] This Classical Age of Indian history, roughly the period between the third century B.C.E. and the seventh century C.E., is demarcated as the glorious period of Indian antiquity, which was already declining by the first few centuries of the Christian era. Although the outright romanticism of the Orientalists is not as influential on contemporary readings of ancient history, notions that this period and its scriptures hold vital clues about aspects of contemporary national (mostly Hindu) cultural traditions continue to prevail.[15] The scholarly literature on sexual identities is subject to the same influences.

But, as Dipesh Chakrabarty astutely notes, histories compiled at academic institutions in post-colonial nations—like in India or Kenya—are likely to be based on the sovereignty of Europe.[16] Put differently, these are the social histories that are shaped by the pernicious influence of colonialism and the colonial attempt to shape a European self-identity by projecting contradistinctive histories onto its colonies. If post-colonial national identity in the ex-colonies is shaped by the effects of colonialism, then uncritical social histories of the nation end up reinscribing the past as shaped by European colonization. In so doing, uncritical social scholarship on Indian antiquity also implicitly ends up reinforcing what are, more accurately, narratives about Europe.

In contrast to social histories of the kind, Shah explores the use of history as counternarrative—what I call *doing political history*. Acknowledging South Asian gay and lesbian history as refreshingly self-conscious, Shah notes that history is not about recovery but about the "politics of knowledge and the politics of position."[17] He suggests that the more compelling gay and lesbian histories of the past are those that reconstruct and revise the contentious master narratives that have sought to erase differences. But, Shah also cautions against overemphasizing history, for it may limit what is possible (and permissible) in the present.

In the following section, I would like to delineate these differences between social and political forms of history with respect to alternative sexualities, particularly homosexuality, and the ancient cultural past. In so doing, I would like to highlight the tensions of histories of alternative sexualities from these two positions. More broadly, I hope this discussion will bring to the forefront how, why, and to what effect questions of national identity plague the question of alternative sexualities, and conversely, how the question of (homo)sexuality complicates the question of national identity in contemporary, post-colonial India.

Social Histories and the Question of Alternative Sexualities

That scholarship on alternative sexualities is imbricated in the discourses of the post-colonial nation-state is evident from the scholarly preoccupation with the ancient past. As a result, this scholarship appears to be shaped by assumptions of a distant, classical past gradually undergoing decline. More specifically, notions of ancient Indian Hindu scriptures as being *sex-positive* (or looking at sexuality in a positive light) have shaped this scholarship, and, more significantly, narratives of the ancient past. In his book *Orientalism*, Edward Said writes that by the nineteenth century the notion of the Orient as a place for licentious sex was so firmly rooted among Orientalists that virtually no European traveler could travel to the Orient without considering matters of sexuality.[18] Richard Burton's preoccupations with overtly sexual Indian and Eastern texts were perhaps most responsible in crystallizing the perception that ancient Indian civilization (i.e., Hindu) was remarkably sex-positive; associated with the Indian Classical Age, the Kamasutra was held to be a case in point.

Since Burton's "discovery" of the Kamasutra, it has generated much curiosity among Europeans and, more recently, in India and countries such as the United States. Within post-colonial India, the Kamasutra is used as a particularly vivid instance of an ancient, tolerant, and sex-positive Indian society. A recent version of the Kamasutra by the well-known French Indologist Alain Danielou resonates with the stated need to demystify India and "[S]how that a period of great civilization, of high culture, is forcibly a period of great liberty."[19] Not surprisingly, the Kamasutra is also perhaps the artifact most frequently cited to support contentions that ancient India was tolerant of homosexuality and alternative sexualities. But such interpretations of the Kamasutra as exemplar of sexual liberty are also among the most eggregious representations of European meta-narratives under the guise of histories of ancient Indian civilization.[20] Fueled by perceptions of the Kamasutra, but by no means exclusive to it, notions of (classical) Hinduism as sex-positive continue to shape the search for the role and meaning of alternative sexual identities in Indian history.

Nowhere does the task of exploring ancient Indian notions of homosexuality collide more clearly with perceptions of sex-positive Hinduism than in an essay by Arvind Sharma, titled "Homosexuality and Hinduism."[21] Sharma is correctly cautious about extrapolating the term and meaning of homosexuality out of its contemporary context. But despite the many variants of Hinduism and various time periods that he might have considered, Sharma's explorations of the perception of homosexuality are primarily focused on the Brahmanical scriptures of the Classical Age. This implicitly reinforces the association of the national past with an elitist and temporal phase. Based on his considerations of Brahmanical scriptures, and to a lesser extent on Hindu Tantric literature, Sharma reaches the awkward conclusion that Hinduism is a sex-positive religion but that homosexuality is a matter of marginal concern and disapproval. This is how he summarizes his analyses.

> It appears from the foregoing account that, *save for the emphasis on renunciation*, Hinduism is a sex-positive religion in relation to all the three ends of human life—dharma, artha, kama—and even in relation to *moksa* in the context of Tantra. This should not be taken to mean, however, that it also views homosexuality within the general field of sex in a positive light. Dharma and Artha literature is somewhat opposed to it; Kama literature is not opposed to it but is not markedly supportive either. In any case, it is constrained by Dharma values. Moksa literature would have no sex at all, heterosexual sex as in some forms of Tantra, or only symbolic Hinduism in some forms of devotional Hinduism. That even some forms of Hinduism should be latently homosexual is indeed significant.[22]

Is it not questionable to claim in an exploration of homosexuality and Hinduism that although Hinduism views homosexuality mostly negatively, it is nonetheless sex-positive? To claim that classical Hindu scriptures were opposed to sexual variations that might fall within the range of the contemporary category of homosexuality suggests the normative regulation of sexuality. Where sexuality may be a matter of normative regulation, the meaning of the term "sex-positive" needs to be evaluated, not assumed. In light of the politics of homosexuality, but also heterosexuality, linked to national cultural identity, instead of reinforcing a complacency about a superior and sex-positive national past, which ironically seems to disapprove of anormative sexual variation, the problems with defining what is normal and what is anormal need to be challenged.

Though Michael Sweet and Leonard Zwilling's analysis on classical Indian medicine's understanding of sexual variations is less concerned with reinforcing notions of a sex-positive Hinduism, in their predictable focus on the Classical Age they are unable to avoid the influence altogether.[23] In their essay, Sweet and Zwilling turn to classical Indian medicine to compare non-Western and Western medicalizations of gender and sexual variations. Focusing on the terminologies and taxonomies in classical Indian medicine, they note that there appear to be numerous classifications of physical sexual anomalies and dysfunctions, atypical gender-role behaviors, and sexual variations of paraphilias. Sweet and Zwilling suggest that there are several similar terms within classical Indian medicine that overlap with these contemporary, Western categories of gender and sexual variations, but the writers caution against conflating culturally disparate categories. What is similar across these two sets of medical literatures, according to them, are that both systems view gender and sexual variation as congenital pathology, as deviations from gender normality, and that both systems stigmatize the individuals associated with these behaviors.

For Sweet and Zwilling the fundamental, and significant, point of difference between classical Indian medical literature, along with related Buddhist and nonmedical literature of that time period, and Western medical literature on gender and sexual variation lies in their contrasting attitudes toward sexual deviations. They argue that although sexual variations are perceived to be deviations from normative expectations of sexual anatomy, physiology, gender roles, and sexual behaviors in Indian medical literature, there is no impulse parallel to that of Western medicine to cure and normalize the deviations. For instance, noting that gender variations are ascribed to limitations in the ability or inclination to procreate, the authors argue that beyond the specification of etiology, systematic attempts to cure these sexual or gender variations in Indian classical medical or, for that matter, nonmedical literature, are absent. Curiously, Sweet and Zwilling impute this difference between the classical Indian and nineteenth-century Western medical literatures to the generally positive or neutral attitudes toward sex of Hinduism and Indian Buddhism versus the negative attitude of the Christian, nineteenth-century West. Unlike Sharma, at least Sweet and Zwilling explain what they mean by positive and neutral attitudes in an attached footnote.

What is less controvertible in the cross section of the literature on homosexuality and classical Hinduism is that homosexual behaviors were not positively regarded. There is consensus that homosexuality was considered an offense in the Arthashastra (300 B.C.E.) but that male homosexuality was regarded as more deviant than female homosexuality.[24] Another Dharmashastra (300–100 B.C.E.) is said to have considered homosexuality to be as heinous as killing a Brahmin, the embodiment of religious and social authority.[25] The later and more well-known Dharmashastra, Manusmriti (100 C.E.), is held to have regarded homosexuality as a source of ritual pollution to be expiated by Brahmin males through the relatively mild penance of ritual immersion.[26] The Manusmriti appears far less tolerant of female homosexuality.[27] Widely associated as a reflection of and catalyst in the decline of the status of women in ancient India, this text is also interpreted to treat female homosexuality more punitively. Nonetheless, with reference to the Manusmriti, Sweet and Zwilling suggest that penalties were relatively mild for homosexual behavior in Indian traditional law books and cite little evidence for these penalties being enforced.[28] With reference to the more populist epics, the Mahabharata and the Ramayana treat homosexuality with repugnance.[29]

In effect, plagued by the legacies of Indian antiquity, the awkwardness of extrapolating the contemporal category of homosexuality, the limited nature of the materials used, and the interpretations of the Hindu scriptures, homosexuality does not emerge resplendently from the archives of Indian history. In the otherwise "sex-positive" tradition of Hinduism, there appear enough points of discomfort with forms of homosexuality and alternative sexualities to not establish an effective platform of queer politics within contemporary India or among South Asian organizations elsewhere. A more equivocal image of alternative sexualities in the ancient past emerges. But then again, if feminist historiographies of the nineteenth century or of the Classical Age are any indication, such a possibility was already inherently limited.

Political Histories of Alternative Sexualities

Although not directly addressing issues of alternative sexual behaviors, feminist historian Romila Thappar highlights pervasive gender-, class-, and caste-based inequities through this time period.[30] According to Thappar, through the Classical period, social laws were encoded in scriptures to counter the shifting balance of power and secure the authority of the Brahmins. Instead of a society at the pinnacle of civilization, Thappar argues, this time period was one marked by pervasive inequalities, where power was being encoded to protect against threats to the established social hierarchy. This historiography not only disrupts any residual romanticism of sex-positive attitudes in a stratified state society, but also problematizes tolerance for sexually variant or deviant behavior in a society marked by the devaluation of women and the subordination of women and men by caste and class.[31] What is different about Thappar's reading of ancient Indian history is that it self-consciously avoids romanticizing the past as the repository of exemplary tradition, and by implication, a society marked by tolerance for alternative sexualities and notions of gender.

If readings of history are shaped by the politics of the present, then feminist historiographies on ancient India are also commentaries about contemporary, post-colonial India. Viewed through this lens, the problem with the scholarship of homosexuality and alternative sexualities in ancient or classical India is not that it ends up painting mostly unflattering images of the perceptions of these sexualities in the past. The deeper problem is that this scholarship does not challenge the marginalization of alternative sexualities and genders within ancient India. Since the search for homosexuality in national historical tradition is fueled by the emergence of contemporary sexual politics within India and in South Asian communities elsewhere, I would question why the past is not evaluated from a more critical perspective. Devoid of such a critique, the scholarship on alternative sexualities and genders ends up reinforcing notions of an historical, continuous, heterosexist national tradition.

Contrary to this scholarship on homosexuality and alternative sexualities, a particularly useful instance of feminist historiography on alternative sexual identities is Giti Thadani's book, *Sakhiyani: Lesbian Desire in Ancient and Modern India.* Where Thadani also attempts to explore the terrain of ancient India for lesbian expressions, unlike the scholarship cited above, it is done as a self-conscious act of challenging the dominant and recovering that which may have been suppressed. Like in other feminist historiographies, Thadani begins by problematizing the ways in which notions of "Indian" tradition have been invented, but also goes on to challenge how this tradition has been heterosexualized. This is where Thadani's history of lesbian desire in ancient India most radically departs from the previously cited histories.

Acknowledging the usual ambivalence regarding the category lesbian, Thadani unequivocally appropriates it as a political category. According to her, "[Lesbian] foregrounds erotic and sexual desire between women."[32] If lesbian is an act of political choice, then the driving force of the historiography only reinforces the viewpoint. Summarizing the objective of the project, Thadani says, "My aim is to excavate layers of erotic memories and thus recreate historical continuums from the location of the present context of lesbian invisibility."[33] It is perhaps this recognition that leads Thadani to also frame her exploration as a critique of normative patriarchal traditions. From this vantage point, Thadani challenges contemporary Hinduism's impulse to present itself as a unified religion and in the process ally itself with "androcentric, heterosexist and phallocentric traditions."[34] Thadani casts her historiography as an attempt to excavate languages of feminine sexuality, cosmogonies, and philosophies that have been obscured, appropriated, or silenced.

The differences between Thadani's historiography and the previously cited scholarly literature is perhaps most apparent in her treatment of the scriptures and lesbian sexuality. It is not that Thadani comes away with radically different interpretations of the scriptures, but that she casts it as the "control of lesbian sexuality." Equally important, Thadani challenges the Classical Age as the period associated with normative heterosexuality. Put differently, what is compelling about Thadani's historiography is that it implicates, rather than implicitly privileges, tradition, Hinduism, the Classical Age, heterosexism, in the suppression of lesbian desire. This is what defines Thadani's historiography of lesbian desire in ancient and modern India a political, not social, history; it challenges the politics of the contemporary nation-state and the present marginalizations of lesbian sexuality.

That questions of alternative sexualities are fused with the questions of nationhood is inarguable. From the perspective of gays and lesbians in India or people of Indian origin elsewhere, it is not surprising that a paramount strategy to counter forms of homophobia and heterosexism lies in claiming a history of homosexuality and alternative sexualities inherent to Indian-Hindu and to Islamic traditions. Intuitively, the act of reclaiming history also signals a break with that tradition. It is conceivable to claim that an exemplary tradition has degenerated into the marginalization of gay and lesbian women and men. But this also lays itself open to counterreactions that since homosexuality did not play a visible role in the Hindu scriptures, the fact that gay and lesbian women and men are staking a claim within the contemporary, post-colonial nation-state is the better indication of the degeneration of tradition. The claims and counterclaims are easily appropriated, divisive, and potentially endless. Rooted in some of the scholarly literature, these claims also reinscribe notions of history that are based in the binaries of the ancient versus the modern, the liberal past versus the repressive present, among others. In effect, another European version of history is troublingly ressurected.

But, regardless of the political positions taken toward claims by queers in India and of Indian origin elsewhere, these claims articulated on the basis of sexual identity are not easily ignored. As Shah summarizes it, "South Asian lesbians and gay men are present now. On that alone we demand acknowledgment and acceptance."[35] This is also the reason that Thadani's historiography is effective. These narratives about alternative sexualities and nationhood not only demand a legitimate space for gays and lesbians but, in effect, also unravel the heteronormative, heterosexist discourses of the contemporary nation-state. From this perspective, the link between contemporary national cultural identity and sexuality becomes quite clear. What is particularly questionable is the implicit heterosexualization of the nation at the cost of the repression of that which is considered anormative—alternative sexualities and genders.

To challenge dismissive and homophobic attitudes and seek a rightful place within contemporary Indian society, then, the recovery of a deep historical cultural tradition that avowed homosexuality is an effective political strategy. Queer narratives seek to appropriate the ground of Indian history and identity. Where others have noted the urgency of the past in the questions of present nationalism, within Indian gay and lesbian narratives these interminglings gain new political meanings.[36] It is thereby possible to claim that queerness is integral, and not external, to Indian and especially Hindu cultural traditions. Careful examinations of a timeless, ancient cultural history may indicate that homosexual behavior was not only tolerated but accepted. To that end, the report *Less Than Gay* emphasizes the importance of recovering the "rich national heritage." In the section on culture and heritage the authors say, "In fact we do not need an Alfred Kinsey to discover the rich possibilities of same-sex eroticism and to appropriate these in the form of modern gay sexuality. It's all there in our art, culture, religion, philosophy, and sculpture."[37] Citing extensive evidence from ancient Hindu texts, such as the Kamasutra, the report *Less Than Gay* attempts to reveal histories of homosexuality and an ancient, tolerant national cultural tradition.

If in the contemporary nation-state homosexuality and alternative sexual identities are discounted as the degeneration of ancient national cultural tradition, then the recovery of tradition by gay and lesbian groups has the potential of making effective counterarguments. It might become possible to suggest that a more just and accepting national cultural tradition has degenerated into one in which people are subjected to severe persecution and discrimination based on their sexual identities. It also becomes possible to allege, as does the report *Less Than Gay*, that not only is homosexuality not a Western phenomenon, but the *phobias* about homosexuality are Western importations—introduced via medical theories, the penal code, and bourgeois morality. By exploring the histories of homosexuality and national cultural traditions, the arguments against homosexuality or alternative sexual identities are turned on their proverbial head.

Outside of India, queer organizations are also becoming increasingly visible in nation-states such as the United States, England, and Canada.[38] As reflected in a groundbreaking collection based on the experiences of South Asian gays and lesbians within the United States, *Lotus of Another Color*, these groups face issues that are both different from and similar to those based primarily in the larger cities within India.[39] In the introduction to the collection, the editor, Rakesh Ratti, highlights the role of South Asian gay and lesbian organizations in mitigating the universal isolation of South Asian queers not only against the homophobia of the larger South Asian communities, but also against the racist and exclusionary Western gay and lesbian organizations.[40] Speaking of the discomfort of South Asian communities on sexualities, Ratti challenges the marginalizations of gay and lesbian South Asians rooted in beliefs that these sexual identities are the products of foreign or Western influences. At the same time, the cultural differences between gay and lesbian South Asians and their Western counterparts intensify their marginalization in a different way. Describing a mushrooming of such groups in numerous cities in the United States, Canada, England, and India, Ratti emphasizes the importance of South Asian gay and lesbian communities in establishing a distinct self-identity while gaining greater visibility among South Asian communities and Western gay and lesbian cultural groups.

What is curious is how the question of cultural tradition and homosexuality assumes parallel importance within the context of South Asian orgnaizations as well. To place gay and lesbian South Asian identities within a deep

historical and continuous cultural tradition is one effective strategy for forging a sense of self-identity and countering the homophobia within South
Asian communities. In their desire to imagine the nation, these queer South
Asian organizations are no different from other diasporic organizations.
Speaking of the consequence of questions of nation among diasporic communities, Homi Bhabha details how the nation helps fill the void left in the
uprooting, and turns loss into a language of metaphor as the mundaneness of
daily life in exile must be recast within the framework of a national culture.[41]
But Bhabha suggests that the process of "performing" the nation is never the
same as the received wisdom of what the nation is. For queer South Asians,
then, sketching a South Asian tradition is especially complicated, although
no more or less imaginative than notions of Indian cultural identity reflected
in the narratives of gays and lesbians within India.

Since the term *South Asia* is an umbrella for a number of culturally distinct
groups, cultural tradition is invented through collages of multiple religious
traditions, most notably Hinduism and Islam. For instance, the first article in
the collection *Lotus of Another Color* primarily explores alternative sexualities in
forms of early Hindusim, and briefly, in Islam. In this attempt to recover "an
unbroken line [of cultural heritage] 4,000 years old," the cultural and political history of India becomes especially important.[42] In effect, for gay and lesbian groups within India, and curiously, for South Asian groups elsewhere,
the question of Indian cultural history is of strategic and political importance.
By appropriating histories of alternative sexualities through Hinduism, and to
a lesser extent, Islam, Buddhism, and Christianity, it is conceivable to counter
homophobic attitudes and forms of sexual discrimination within India and
among South Asian communities in countries such the United States. Briefly
put, despite the differences between gay and lesbian narratives produced
within India and South Asian narratives in countries such as the United States
and Canada, striking similarities appear in the concerns with and approaches
to ancient Indian historical traditions.

Theorizing the Transnational

If queer narratives in India and those of South Asian affiliation in countries
such as the United States are shaped by discourses of post-colonial Indian
national identity, then they are also constituted within a transnational arena.
Part of the purpose in bringing these narratives into the same analytical focus
is to highlight the ways in which the contentious legacies of the post-colonial
state pervade the transnational arena. Even though there are differences
between the issues pertinent to South Asian queers and those within the geo-

graphic boundaries of the nation-state, questions of national tradition and its past persist. The politics of self-representation of Indian and South Asian queers are shaped by the need to resurrect a past national tradition in order to defend the visibility in the present. But, there are more profound similarities across national boundaries that foreground how queer narratives are being constituted within a transnational cultural arena—shaped by, but not limited to, the politics of sexual identities.

Perhaps the transnational, globalizing cultural context of sexualities is most vividly expressed in the terms *gay, lesbian, bisexual, transgender, transsexual,* and *queer,* among others. To say that these terms and constructs are not bounded within the circumference of the imagined political community is to state the obvious. Even though terms such as *gay* and *lesbian* are associated with industrial capitalist cultures, they have gained wide currency in diverse cultural contexts.[43] Shaped by what are termed *identity politics,* the terms *gay* and *lesbian* are recognizable as politicized forms of identity, rooted in the choice of sexual partners. Where identity is articulated as essential and pre-social in some cases, it is shaped by the model of social construction, in other cases.[44]

For example, in the report *Less Than Gay,* the authors see the term *gay* as a self-descriptor to encompass the area of same-sex eroticism. While the terms *gay* and *homosexual* are used interchangeably elsewhere in the report, the authors make explicit that they see "gay" as a politicized self-identity that challenges the regulation of homosexuality.

> When we employ the word "gay" we do not mean to reduce these rich and varied exotic spaces into a medical model of "heterosexual," "homosexual" and "bisexual" behavior. We use it consciously both as a description of people who see themselves as gay and as a sensibility encompassing the entire area of same-sex eroticism. We feel that "gay" should be used as a politically desirable intervention in a context of state (legal and medical) regulation of homo/sexuality.[45]

What these authors explore, without making their positions explicit, are prevalent essentialist versus social constructionist notions—that homosexuality is an innate, fixed aspect of self-identity or the result of social factors and political choices.

Exploring similar themes, the South Asian collection *Lotus of Another Color* is premised on the importance of self-empowerment as South Asian gays and lesbians. Foregrounding the politics of self-identity, the introduction links empowerment to self-definition as gay and lesbian South Asians.

> Until now, the mainstream world has defined us, as it does with any subgroup, within its parameters. The pages of this book offer us an opportuni-

ty to define ourselves. The power of self-definition is awesome because words are tremendously effective tools for reconstruction. When people who were labeled as faggots and dykes chose to refer to themselves as gays and lesbians, when those who were called niggers chose to call themselves black or African-American, they began to claim for themselves the power of self-definition and thus cut through the world's stereotypes of who they were. While it is true that some of these stereotypes continue to exist, they are but mere shadows of what they were once.[46]

Within this framework, terms such as *gay*, *lesbian*, and *bisexual* clearly shift the focus from possibilities of sexual behaviors to forms of self-representation that seek inclusion by dismantling the hegemony of heterosexual and heterosexist norms.

But, despite the currency of these terms, they cannot and do not represent a singular or unified politics of sexual identity. Especially the writings of lesbian and bisexual women of color in the United States have raised awareness of understanding identities in complex and multiple ways. At first the collection *Home Girls*, and soon thereafter, the equally important book *This Bridge Called My Back*, foregrounded the importance of understanding and analyzing the cultural and historical differences that shape the politics of identity in the United States.[47] Collections such as these, and numerous others since, make it impossible to assert that simply because queer narratives included in this chapter are shaped within a transnational cultural context, they are necessarily homogenous.[48]

Partially reflecting the particularities of an emergent gay and lesbian movement, the report *Less Than Gay* addresses the importance of understanding what is culturally specific about being gay or lesbian within the context of contemporary India by understanding the history of cultural traditions as well as the legal and medical discourses of colonialism and post-colonialisms. The collection *Lotus of Another Color* self-consciously sets itself apart from the more dominant and exclusionary Western gay and lesbian subcultures. The importance of charting the particularities of gay and lesbian identities within India or as South Asians shapes the tone and direction of each of these volumes. From the viewpoint of Indian or South Asian gays and lesbians, what is inarguable is the emergence of a cultural politics rooted in sexual identity and, in turn, the choices of one's sexual partner in a transnational context. But, it is also clear that it would be a mistake to assume direct parallels for terms and concepts that resonate within a transnational arena. Put bluntly, as argued in Chapter Five, that which is globalizing is not necessarily homogenizing.[49]

The narratives of Indian and South Asian queers are both shaped by notions of sexual identity that cut across national boundaries, and normalized through them. For example, in his review of the politics of sexuality, identity, and history, Shah astutely notes the emphasis on "coming out" in these narratives.[50] These narratives achieve two effects—to explain the process of developing a queer identity as well as how desire develops out of politics, according to Shah. Shah argues that while the process of developing a queer identity in the narratives is tied to objects of sexual desire, a second set of narratives, limited to women, also seeks to explain lesbian identity as political choice. Recounted as making a transition from silence to voice, from isolation to community, and from repression to resistance, these narratives represent radical possibilities even as they constrain others.

Whether in the collections *Lotus of Another Color*, *Our Feet Walk the Sky*, or the report *Less Than Gay*, what is incontrovertible is the ways in which these sexual identities become the basis for a politics of resistance and social change.[51] Shah describes the ways in which a queer South Asian identity has enabled a struggle against silence and invisibility. South Asian queer identity has also had to fashion appropriate language for itself in order to name the self and to challenge heterosexist oppression, according to Shah. Forging self-identities is crucial to establishing supportive and safe communities that provide respite from a preponderant sense of isolation articulated in gay and lesbian narratives. Indeed, as reflected in the collection *Lotus of Another Color* identifying terms such as gay and lesbian can often help crystallize a sense of one self as well as being part of a wider, if dispersed, community.

But gay and lesbian identities are also limiting. In his essay on identity and politics in the "postmodern" gay culture within the United States, Steven Seidman articulates the limits of sexual identities.[52] Citing poststructuralist discontent with identity-based politics, Seidman notes that if "heterosexuality" and "homosexuality" are mutually determining, hierarchical terms, then positing identity necessarily reproduces the relationship of normality and exclusion. However open to multiple differences, by definition gay identity produces exclusion, represses some kinds of difference, and normalizes what it means to be gay. Seidman summarizes the inherent contradictions of producing gay identities in these words,

> Furthermore, gay identity constructions reinforce the dominant hetero/homo sexual code with its heteronormativity. If homosexuality and heterosexuality are a coupling in which each pre-supposes the other, each being present in the invocation of the other, and in which this coupling assumes hierarchical forms, then the epistemic and political project of identifying a gay subject reinforces and reproduces this hierarchical figure.[53]

Expressing her discomfort with the territorial and commodifying ramifications of the term "lesbian," Robyn Weigman notes that it is by no means an innocent category.[54] Citing Judith Butler, Weigman expands on the ways in which that which was potentially liberatory about lesbian identity becomes a way to contain, regulate, and commodify sexuality. Weigman suggests that it is disturbing that commodified notions of lesbian identity often pass within and outside lesbian communities as signs of political progress. In Weigman's reading, what is of immediate concern is how the category *lesbian* circumscribes and contains the more radical possibilities. By definition, identities, however multiple, ackowledge what it can and should mean to be a lesbian. Thereby, identities that help marshall a cultural politics also limit the possibilities of envisioning social change.

The queer narratives recounted within the pages of *Less Than Gay* or the collection *Lotus of Another Color* bespeak a kind of normalization about what it means to be homosexual, gay, or lesbian that is not limited to putative notions of being Indian or of Indian origin. These narratives gain a certain amount of coherence as other narratives remain inarticulated or sidelined. In this legitimate concern about identity politics, what gets confounded is the impact of a transnational, globalizing cultural context on shaping but not determining notions of identity and desire. In the collection, *Scattered Hegemonies*, the editors Grewal and Kaplan explore the nuances of transnationalism in terms of structural, hegemonic constraints but also the possibilities for transnational feminist alliances and practices (see Chapter One). By theorizing the transnational with respect to feminist politics, the authors note the transnational mobility of capital and patterns of accumulation, as well as the transnationalization of cultural forms; this Grewal calls "scattered hegemonies."

But Grewal and Kaplan also emphasize the political necessity of envisioning feminist practices and transnational alliances within this framework of "scattered hegemonies." Analogously, by locating the politics of queer Indian and South Asian identities within a transnational framework, we can consider how these narratives reveal the possibilities of sexual identities cast amid prevailing discourses linked to the transnationalization of cultures and "scattered hegemonies." If the framework for queer narratives included here is no less than transnational and globalizing, then it is more useful to consider these gay and lesbian narratives as reflections of political strategies in the face of wide-ranging and transnational structural hegemonies. What distinguishes these narratives from the more narrowly conceived politics of identity is that these narratives self-consciously attempt to transcend the limitations of identity based in either Indianness or sexuality.

Reading Queer Narratives: Trikone

As the oldest surviving gay and lesbian South Asian organization, Trikone offers a useful starting point to consider the tensions as well as the possibilities of sexualities, nationalisms, and transnational cultural processes. I choose to focus on this organization not only because of its duration but also because Trikone has influenced gay and lesbian organizations in India.[55] Although consistently representing itself as South Asian, Trikone is marked by the need to establish queer identities primarily within the framework of Indian nationalism. Yet, it draws on more than one history to establish the premise of queer identities. Not only are these histories not directly shaped by Indian nationalism, but they also challenge the ways in which the Indian nation-state marginalizes or oppresses gays and lesbians, among others. In her essay in the collection *Our Feet Walk the Sky*, Grewal remarks on the transnational nature of the constitution of South Asian and South Asian American politics of location to suggest that it is shaped by linkages between nationalist politics of contemporary India, colonial discourses, and new affiliations demanded by immigrant contexts.[56] I would argue that Trikone also reflects transnational linkages and alliances in at least three ways to subvert any narrowly conceived notions of self-identity while forging a politics based in transnational communities.

Trikone was founded in 1985 by Arvind Kumar, a first-generation Indian immigrant. In January 1996, Trikone published its first newsletter also called *Trikone*. Since April 1993 *Trikone* has been published as a quarterly magazine. Kumar says that he founded the organization and its newsletter in order to provide safety, empathy, and community to members who would relate to being South Asian and gay or lesbian. Trikone seeks to increase queer visibility while eradicating the reactionary violence and sexual discrimination in South Asian communities. Reflecting these dual concerns, in its mission statement, Trikone articulates its task as fourfold.[57] First, to address the specific needs of lesbian and gay people of South Asian descent and mitigate their sense of isolation. Second, to make connections across national boundaries and thereby increase queer visibility within diverse communities. Third, to understand and challenge the links between sexism and homophobia in order to oppose sexual discrimination. Finally, Trikone seeks to demolish preconceptions that homosexuality is a Western import by recovering ancient Hindu and Moghal texts as evidence otherwise. On the one hand, as reflected in this mission statement, Trikone raises issues of sexual and national identity. At the same time, Trikone clearly sees itself as culturally apart from other gay or lesbians organizations; it seeks to meet the needs of gays and lesbian specifically in their capacities as South Asians.

The other important vector of identity that is reflected in the mission statement is nation-based. Even though Trikone is shaped by the presence of second-generation queers of Indian origin, first- and second-generation queers of Pakistani, Bangladeshi, and Sri Lankan descent, among others, the connections with Indian nationhood are constantly maintained. But the persistent link between nationalisms and sexualities is offset by invoking more than one history of gay and lesbian identities. The term *Trikone*, which means triangle in Sanskrit, a language associated with Indian antiquity, is also historically associated with the repudiation of the persecution of homosexuals by Nazis in Germany.

Reprinted in the 10th anniversary special edition of the magazine *Trikone*, the first editorial identifies "tri-kon" as a sign "embraced by gay men and women not only as a reminder of injustices of the past, but also as a symbol of gay pride." In her examination of how nation is reimagined and romanticized within middle-class Indian diasporic communities, Sandhya Shukla notes how reconstructed notions of identity are both national and transnational at the same time.[58] In much the same way, albeit from a much more consciously oppositional location, Trikone evinces the melding of multiple historical narratives in order to establish its legitimacy. Though recovering the ancient Hindu and Moghal traditions is important to Trikone, so is not forgetting the transnational and transhistorical persecutions of homosexuals and alternative sexualities. These multiple histories allow Trikone to forge a more complex self-identity even as histories of nationalisms and sexualities are partially reinscribed.

Yet, the other two aspects of the mission statement—establishing connections across national boundaries and challenging the links between sexism and homophobia—lend added measures of complexities to the mission and politics of the organization. As encapsulated in this mission statement, Trikone evinces the possibilities of a politics not as easily reduced to nationalist and sexual categories of identity. Trikone raises such possibilities in not two but three ways: by locating the organization as South Asian, by opposing sexism and other kinds of discrimination, and by emphasizing and sustaining transnational alliances.

In the organization, South Asia is specified, in alphabetical order, as Afghanistan, Bangladesh, Bhutan, Burma, India, Maldives, Nepal, Pakistan, Sri Lanka, and Tibet. Reflecting on conceptualizations of South Asia in the context of the United States, Amarpal K. Dhaliwal correctly notes how South Asia is "overdetermined by 'India'" to produce homogenized, static, singular constructions of the term.[59] Sampling a cross section of *Trikone* issues, the magazine does not appear to have resolved this contradiction. However, by consistently presenting Trikone and the magazine as South

Asian, the organization is striving toward what Kamala Visweswaran identifies as coalitional identities.[60] Also speaking of terms such as "Asian-American," "South Asian," and "Women of Color," Visweswaran argues that these are deliberately constructed coalitional solidarities which attempt to distance themselves from the logic of nation-states. Despite the contradictions, it is politically inclusive and strategic for Trikone to locate itself as a South Asian organization through the editorial statement in the first newsletter printed in January 1986. More recently, describing the impetus for establishing itself as a South Asian, instead of possibly Indian, organization, founder Arvind Kumar says that it never made cultural or political sense for Trikone to be only Indian; it was more important to "draw strength from each other."[61]

Despite its contradictory "overdetermined Indianness," to borrow Dhaliwal's phrase, what I find more persuasive about Trikone, compared to other South Asian narratives, is that it never sought to "include" others from the vantage point of Indianness. According to Kumar, at first the term "Indian subcontinent" was considered to represent Trikone but quickly discarded in favor of "South Asia" as a disavowal of Indian nationalism. This is what does not easily reduce Trikone's narrative of self-representation to the politics of liberal discourse. Kumar recounts how the reality of this South Asian representation changed over the years, with the presence of self-acknowledged South Asians from a variety of backgrounds, but adds that the positioning of Trikone as South Asian was never challenged in a way that the issue of gender parity has been a matter of struggle for the organization.

On the matter of challenging the links between sexism and homophobia, the editorial statement in the first *Trikone* reads as much like a disclaimer as an apology on gender exclusions within the organization. In the words of the coeditors of this issue,

> Because we are both men, you will find us lapsing into the masculine gender third person in our writings, but we hope that our female readers will bear with us. These lapses are unintentional and by no means meant to exclude them from this group. Rather, we welcome the participation of men and women alike in our activities. We are all in this together, and we have to start by working with each other.[62]

That gender exclusions persisted within the organization despite this commitment is a matter of the organization's historical record. In 1990, Trikone published an open letter from a South Asian lesbian confronting the "Trikone men" with their rhetoric on the underrepresentation of women, and charging them with the task, "Make the ending of sexism one of Trikone's reasons for being."[63] In the next issue of *Trikone*, the organizational mission was changed to end sexism and discrimination against women in all forms.

More recently, Dipti Ghosh, a queer woman cochair of the magazine, addressed Trikone's organizational commitments with respect to queer women— including not inviting any more men to serve on the organization's board until gender parity is achieved, and also emphasized the importance of the continued involvement of women at all levels of decision making.[64] What makes Trikone's stance on gender meaningful is not only its internal organizational struggles but the ways in which it links homophobia and sexism. The organization seeks to challenge not only the invisibility of lesbians because of the cultural primacy of women's identities as wives and mothers, but also the links between the social marginalization of women and the contempt directed toward homosexual men rooted in perceptions of their "effeminacy."

That Trikone perceives the issue of gender and sexism within a larger framework is apparent from the organizational commitment to networking as widely as possible. According to Kumar, the impetus for establishing alliances transnationally and expansively is a political response to the sense of personal isolation that is characteristic of being a South Asian queer.[65] He says that from its inception, Trikone set a worldwide framework for itself with little indication about its success. Besides distributing the magazine as widely as possible, Trikone is mailed free of charge to readers in South Asia. Summarizing the need to establish widely constituted transnational alliances, Kumar says that networking is a matter of survival and establishing mutual relationships. But, what appears to distinguish these alliances from affiliations conceived solely on the basis of identity—South Asian and queer—is that these alliances are sought on the basis of histories of marginality, or what Chandra Talpade Mohanty has elsewhere called a common context of struggle.[66]

The 10th anniversary issue of *Trikone* includes an excerpt from Urvashi Vaid that effectively supports the organizational narratives of Trikone while extending them in important directions toward this "common context of stuggle." Expressing her concerns with identity-based politics, Vaid articulates how it is nonetheless essential to the visibility of gay and lesbian South Asians as well as in promoting self-acceptance. But she also cautions that politics that are bounded by identity-based interests will not result in strong, politically progressive movements. In her words,

> Identity-based organizing ought not be seen as an end in iitself, but as a means to a larger objective that involves the transformation and end of systems of racism, sexism, homophobia, and economic exploitation.
>
> Our discovery of our South Asian Queer identities is an essential part of becoming whole and healthy human beings. But our creation of a progres-

sive, multi-racial, multi-issue movement for social justice is the political component which I believe we must commit to in order for us to realize our objectives of being free to be gay, lesbian, bisexual, or transsexual people.[67]

In so many words, Vaid not only expresses the narratives of intent of Trikone but also challenges it toward a vision of social justice that is grounded in a struggle against homophobia, sexism, but also racism and class-based exploitations.

Conclusion

Amid prevailing tensions and contradictions of sexualities, nationalisms, and transnational effects, queer narratives provide useful starting points about why these matter at all. Although reflected in middle-class women's narratives on heterosexuality, queer narratives are far more explicitly imbricated in discourses of nationalisms. To explore narratives on queer identity, then, is to raise questions about how Indian sexuality is normalized as heterosexuality but also contested from the margins of sexual identity. While the questions of nationalisms and sexualities continue to be important in the political context of the late twentieth century, queer narratives are instructive about the ways in which these politics might be better negotiated. In the example provided by Thadani's exploration of the history of lesbian sexualities, the postcolonial nation-state and notions of cultural nationalism are indicted instead of being bolstered as historically "sex-positive."

Especially as reflected in the narratives of the South Asian gay and lesbian organization Trikone, it is amply clear how these queer narratives are also shaped by transnational cultural discourses. Understanding these queer narratives against the grain of transnational cultural discourses helps clarify how alternative sexualities are normalized as gay, lesbian, bisexual, and transgendered identities. But, in its capacity as the oldest continuous South Asian or Indian gay and lesbian organization, Trikone provides another instructive example—about how matters of sexual identities and national, and transnational cultural discourses may be unsettled by attempting to challenge multiple forms of inequality and to forge and sustain transnational alliances among diverse communities.

Yet, as a case study, Trikone does not lend itself to romanticism. Although as an organization Trikone is more self-conscious about the effects of racism experienced at the hands of "Western" gay and lesbian organizations, unlike issues of sexism, what is less well articulated is its complicity in reproducing hierarchies of race either within the United States or in other parts of the world. Similarly, the hierarchies of social class remain relatively unacknowledged within the organizational narratives. Thus Vaid's account serves to support Trikone's political commitments while encouraging a wider vision of social justice and social transformation. Taken together, this is what makes these queer narratives illuminating and instructive—for writing counternarratives not only to normative sexuality but also to nationalisms and transnational cultural discourses.

Chapter Eight

Conclusion: Considering New Courses or Stoking Fire

I started this book with the conviction that hegemonic codes not only shape middle-class women's narratives and queer narratives on gender and sexuality, but also help sustain the seemingly self-evident nature of these categories. I identified nation-state-based and transnational cultural discourses as crucial to understanding the contours of these narratives. Each of the chapters in this book sketches the connections between these hegemonic codes and what women have to say about five aspects related to sex, gender, and sexuality—menarche and early menstruation, sexual aggression, erotic sexuality, marriage, and motherhood—and lastly, how queer narratives are also shaped by the constraints of these discourses. But, it should be apparent by now that to challenge the effects of nationalist and transnational discourses on these narratives of gender and sexuality also dismantles putative notions of "Indianness" or national identity.

What is clear in the narratives of middle-class women is that insofar as they reproduce these hegemonic codes, they also reconstitute their nationally based gender, class, and racial categories and heterosexual normativity. This process has been obscured by a scholarship that does not question the effects of these modernist categories in women's lives. Although the scholarship has been largely directed at challenging the constraints in women's lives, this has been at the cost of obscuring how categories of nationalisms, womanhood, sexuality, race, and class are mutually constitutive and reproduced in lived practice. These narratives help shed light on the ways in which lived practices help sustain the coherence of these categories. To that extent, these narratives also fill in the gaps in critical feminist scholarship that is focused on literary and abstract textual analyses. The narratives highlight aspects of womanhood related to sexed bodies, heterosexuality, and gender roles—marriage and motherhood. These narratives establish the importance of not understanding gender as merely the cultural overlay upon the biological, dual-sexed body. On the contrary, the sexed body presents a fundamental means through which these women are subjected to hegemonic codes at crucial points in their lives. The seemingly unquestionable naturalness of the sexed body helps normalize and reinforce social mandates related to heterosexuality and womanhood. Instead of the use of force, this subjection relies on their consent and cooperation. But, women's narratives also provide crucial insights into how these discourses may be disrupted. The mundane acts related to menstruation, sexual aggression, heterosexuality, marriage, and motherhood become political battlegrounds. Not only do these lived practices present ways of challenging the effects of normalization and regulation in women's lives, but of undermining the stability of categories of womanhood, nationalism, race, sexuality, and class.

The post-colonial Indian nation-state is neither a singular entity nor a mirror image of its emergence under colonialism. But it is fraught with hegemonies of gender, sexuality, class, ethnicity, and caste that are barely masked by the rhetoric of "we Indians." At the same time, these persistent but altering hegemonies are imbricated in transnational, globalizing cultural discourses. Whether in the codes of personal hygiene and menstruation or in how the language of sexuality appears to shape the narratives of these women, transnational cultural discourses cannot be isolated out of the analytic framework of the contemporary, post-colonial nation-state. Although I have annalytically separated nationalist and transnational discourses, the lines are less than distinct—for example, the fusion of modernity and personal hygiene, or the links between sexual respectability and romantic love. But I use the term *transnational* to identify those hegemonic codes that proliferate within national boundaries and cut across them in complex ways. These are the hegemonies and effects that are played out on middle-class, urban women's narratives to constitute, normalize, and regulate their sexed bodies, genders, and sexualities.

The connections between hegemonic, normalizing codes and women's narratives become clear especially in Chapters Three, Four, Five, and Six. Narratives on menarche and early menstruation provide important insights into the ways in which the female body is constituted and made to appear the natural basis of womanhood. Sexual aggression is hardly represented as a normal or desirable aspect of these women's socialization. Nonetheless, it is striking how its threat and violence constitute and naturalize the parameters of the sexed body by engendering fear and concern related to womanhood.

Narratives on desire and sexual pleasure serve only to reinforce the heterosexual normativity of the sexed body and adult womanhood. What is realized through aspects such as menstruation, sexual aggression, and erotic sexuality is further crystallized through the social mandates of marriage and motherhood.

Viewed in this way, the narratives in these chapters raise crucial questions about the mechanisms and strategies through which womanhood is enforced. Menarche and early menstruation may not initiate gendered and sexualized forms of social control in these women's lives, but their narratives do suggest how these concerns are intensified since then. Women's narratives on menarche and menstruation say much about the regulation of women's bodies and sexualities through mechanisms of self-surveillance and self-control. These narratives suggest how the contradiction between the social importance of the changing female body and the internalization of control by these middle-class women may be shaped by nationalist discourses of tradition and modernity, but may equally have transnational parallels. For example, the transnational discourse of personal hygiene—buffered through tampons and deodorants—surely exacerbates the nature of social regulation of women's bodies early on in their lifecycle. Identifying the effects of these discourses helps decode the nuances of women's narratives on menarche and menstruation every as they both reproduce and disrupt them.

That the narratives on sexual aggression directed toward the women also erupt from the contradiction of internalized social control is apparent. These narratives on sexual aggression pose a different sort of analytical challenge from the accounts of menarche and menstruation because sexual aggression is not represented as a normal aspect of gender and sexual development. But what is evident is that the narratives on sexual aggression are shaped by class-, gender, and nation-based concerns with sexual respectability—how women describe themselves and the male sexual perpetrators. Even though sexual aggression may not be culturally represented as normal, women's narratives reveal how the concerns with sexual respectability are pervasive and in effect act as instruments of social regulation in their lives. Sexual aggression may not be normal, but sexual respectability seems to be normalized.

Nowhere are nationalisms and womanhood more clearly linked than in the narratives on heterosexuality and womanhood. What is striking is how these middle-class women see premarital sexual activity as a matter of sexual respectability. In their narratives, some women refuse to engage in premarital sexual intercourse because of their respectability as Indian women, but others are able to participate in sexual intercourse because of romantic love. These women's narratives also suggest ways in which they negotiate the constraints of sexuality before and after marriage. In these cases, they appear to deploy a transnational cultural discourse of romantic love to justify premarital sexual activity. But, in either case, it is notable how both premarital and marital sexual activity are cast within a romanticized framework. What is especially striking about these middle-class women's narratives on sexuality is the effect of spoken English. For this group of women, alongside the language of romantic love, English, albeit in its specific form, becomes a primary language through which to represent sex.

Indications of how women counter the social regulations of their genders and sexualities glimmer through the accounts on menarche and menstruation, sexual aggression, and the realm of erotic sexuality, and are crystallized in their narratives on marriage and motherhood. With respect to the most clearly prescribed, normative social statuses, in their accounts these middle-class women suggest how they negotiate aspects of marriage and motherhood so as to mitigate their vulnerabilities. The language of understanding husbands and marital intimacy helps consolidate their positions in conjugal families, and motherhood offers far more opportunities in which their positions may be further enhanced. What is also evident is that the narratives on marriage, husbands, and marital intimacy are not easily categorized within the cultural boundaries of the contemporary nation-state. The language on marriage and its aspects reasonates more broadly within a transnational cultural context.

What is most compelling across these narratives is that if women see themselves at the receiving end of social injustice as women, then they also see themselves as agents of social change. There appears to be no single, dominant narrative about how they may be constrained as women, and there is no single narrative about the direction of social change. What some women see as limitation, others see as a test of fortitude. These differences were perhaps best captured in the juxtaposition of Venita's, Vani's, and Rati's accounts at the end of Chapter Six. Especially visible in the narratives on marriage and motherhood, but by no means limited to these accounts, middle-class women appear to find ways in which they can negotiate and challenge their social marginalizations. At the same time, it makes them less likely to question their privileges as middle-class women or see themselves as part of cross-class coalitions among women that might bring social change. It also makes them less likely to question their roles in the normalization of heterosexuality.

In contrast, queer narratives help identify and challenge heteronormative mandates but also the uneven effects of nationalisms and transnationalisms. By examining queer narratives produced within the boundaries of India or the narratives generated amid South Asian groups in countries such as the United States, the powerful link between heteronormativity and nationalism becomes more naked. In either case, queer narratives appear to contend with questions of sexual identity and belonging within a received national cultural tradition. Thadani's work on lesbian desire perhaps best exemplifies how this tradition may be implicated and reworked. What is additionally apparent in queer narratives, both within India and amid South Asian communities, is how they are normalized within the broader transnational cultural context through notions of sexual identities. But concerns that these narratives may be effectively limited by prescriptions of gay, lesbian, bisexual, or transgendered identities are offset by the possibilities of a transnational politics. These narratives compellingly raise the possibilities of challenging multiple forms of inequalities and establishing and sustaining transnational alliances.

Finally, viewing these narratives on gender and sexuality through a feminist, postcolonial lens problematizes the ways in which contemporary nationhood is gendered, sexualized, and racialized. Highlighting the mutual constitution and inseparability of discourses of nationalisms, gender, and sexuality in women's narratives and queer narratives also raises questions about how the nation-state is unevenly articulated in gendered and sexualized terms. For example, in Chapter Two, analyzing the state-sponsored sex education materials makes the androcentric nature of medical discourses and the heterosexualization of normality starkly visible. At the same time, binaries that are reflected in these materials such as India/East and West, morality and sexual promiscuity also sustain racialized expressions of nationality and national identity. But identifying the role of transnational hegemonic codes helps attenuate the importance of the nation-state and, instead, turn attention to the possibilities of class- and race-based parallels in the regulation of women in diverse social locations.

So what do the narratives on gender and sexuality tell us? The narratives of middle-class women on matters of gender and sexuality point toward the class-based social regulation of women not through overt coercion but through the process of normalization. Social control in this form is far more insidious. Women may challenge the social constraints imposed upon them after menarche, but are less likely to question how their female bodies are made to seem natural partly as a result of this event. They express anger against the male perpetrators of sexual aggression but are less able to be reflexive about how their narratives might be shaped by internalized concerns of sexual respectability. Furthermore, in their narratives on erotic sexuality they challenge and negotiate what may be sexually respectable behavior but do not repudiate the premise of sexual respectability altogether. Yet, when these women speak about the social norms of marriage and motherhood, they are far more expressive about the constraints and how to effectively negotiate them.

What these narratives by middle-class women also make clearly obvious is the importance of attending to the similarities and differences in the ways that gender and sexuality are normatively regulated among various groups of women. These narratives help us problematize the centrality of middle-class, mostly Hindu women to the construct and articulations of the post-colonial nation-state. But these narratives also raise questions about middle-class women's collusion with the hegemonic nation-state in asserting control over, for example, poor urban and rural women. Furthermore, the narratives make us sensitive to how transnational processes, "scattered hegemonies," may indeed shape middle-class, urban Indian women's lives, and to the importance of further uncovering class- and race-based effects of transnational discourses in women's lives.

Through this approach to middle-class women's narratives on gender and sexuality it is possible to move away from putative and invidious binaries between "tradition" and "westernization" or "modernization," between "Third" and "First" worlds, between "Indian" and "Western" women. These binaries only obscure and stereotype the significant material differences in women's lives. When these differences are applied within the boundaries of the nation-state, the notion of tradition confounds how tradition is invented and naturalized, and the construct of westernization blurs the pervasive, if dynamic, effects of transnational processes that are not limited to elite women within the nation-state. At the very least, these binaries blind us to the material, instead of superficial, differences in women's lives within the boundaries of the nation-state; worse, they deflect attention from the hegemonic nation-state.

Similarly, assuming differences between "Third World" women or "First World" or "Western" women further blurs the invidiousness of transnational hegemonies. Especially when these assumptions remain implicit, they tend to reinforce questionable notions of national differences and obscure the prevalence of complex cultural and globalizing discourses that cut across national boundaries. Scholarship that is ostensibly cross-cultural may identify the effects of transnational cultural patterns only to isolate these patterns from their interaction with nationalisms. More often than not these kinds of approaches end up reinforcing essentialist distinctions under the guise of cultural relativism.

So where do we go from here? If this question is implicit in the foregoing discussion, then so are possible directions to be pursued. It is important to further investigate aspects of gender and sexuality, in particular, and related aspects of women's lives, within and across post-colonial nation-states. Within the parameters of the nation-state, it would be useful to consider how aspects of gender and sexuality explored in this book are normalized and contested in the lives of women belonging to various social classes and ethnic groups, paying special attention to the historical impact of nationalisms and transnational processes. It would be helpful to consider how differently constituted women are implicated in the tensions of the nation-state but also resistant to them. Scratching further beneath the cultural discourses of transnationalism within a globalizing context would be useful to think through the uneven effects of transnational processes on gender and sexuality for women across social classes within the boundaries of the nation-state.

It would be equally important to consider class-based similarities across national boundaries. These parallels will help not only implicate the multifarious, contradictory effects of the nation-state in the lives of women within national parameters, but also demystify the parallels and the differences across the national boundaries. To identify the parallels between the ways that transnational processes affect women constituted by intersecting social vectors of class, sexuality, age, race, ethnicity, would help challenge their expansions. But identifying these transnational hegemonies would also help attune us to the contradictory effects of transnational gobal discourses for women in disparate national settings.

Finally, implicating the normative links between the constructs of gender and sexuality and the post-colonial nation-state riven by transnational processes from the viewpoint of women, would also help identify the possibilities of transnational alliances. Grewal and Kaplan acknowledge that identifying feminist oppositional practices that are not isolated under the brunt of the transnational economic and cultural hegemonies is contingent on understanding how these hegemonies are taking new globalizing and contradictory forms. Extending Grewal and Kaplan's argument, I would suggest that this approach is imperative not only to envisioning more connected feminist political practices but also seeking new ways of challenging the nexus between post-colonial nationalist and transnational discourses. Drawing strength from the oppositional practices of women in disparate social locations would help challenge the materiality of hegemonies while reshaping categories such as feminist, gender, sexuality, woman, and resistance.

It is to this purpose that I would like to end this book with one example—the recent film *Fire*. Based on the lives of two middle-class women in New Delhi in their mid-20s to mid-30s, this film presents a useful parallel to middle-class women's and queer narratives included in this book. This film offers an example of how constructs of gender and sexuality may be challenged within the context of the contemporary nation-state from the viewpoint of middle-class women in urban India. But what is especially compelling about this film is that it marshalls an oppositional politics that is not easily categorized as feminist or lesbian, and therefore, not as easily contained, despite persuasive readings to the contrary. Taking my lead from the opening frames of the film—a recurrent dream sequence in which young Radha's mother tells her that if she wants to see the ocean amid the field of yellow flowers, then she must look just so—I would like to see the film in a way that allows us to imagine new possibilities.

Stoking "Fire"

Written and directed by the Canada-based Indian immigrant Deepa Mehta, this film has generated much speculation. *Fire* documents a burgeoning intimacy between two women, the wives of two brothers, that culminates in their shared departure from the conjugal family and husbands. While exploring the seemingly ordinary setting of married, middle-class, conjugal family life, this film documents the characteristic hypocracies, tensions, and inadequacies from the viewpoint of these two women. As married women, Radha and Sita's compliance to this middle-class, heterosexual, but discordant arrangement comes at a high personal cost. Where Radha has apparently coped with the exigencies of the situation, the newlywed younger woman, Sita, is far less patient. In this setting, their intimacy, initiated by Sita but quickly a matter of mutual pleasure, blossoms into a sexual relationship.

Although there is some question whether *Fire* can be cast as a lesbian film, its transnational conditions of production, language, and themes make it easily appropriated to categories of lesbian sexuality, feminism, and national identity.[1] Very much a transnational production, the film was first distributed in countries such as Canada and the United States.[2] In the United States, for example, there is some speculation whether this is a lesbian film. Nonetheless, there is a tendency to cast *Fire* as a lesbian film,[3] this despite the director's disavowal. In her interviews, Mehta suggests that this is a film about choices, not about immanent lesbian identities.[4] More recently, the film has been distributed in India and served as a flash point of contention between a small but violent right-wing faction, English-speaking audiences, and left intellectuals.[5] In India, as well, *Fire* is mainly described as a lesbian film. What appears to reinforce this characterization is that the film is shot in a culturally specific version of English. This may make the film accessible to a wider, transnational audience, but it speaks to a more limited audience in India. Where dubbing can only simulate meanings, spoken English helps provide a more literal framework for a transnational language on intimacy, marital relations, expressions of sexuality, and opposition. It helps normalize categories such as lesbian. In

India, the film's language reinforces the perception that matters of sexuality can be more easily articulated through spoken English, especially what are, for the most part, unspeakable issues such as lesbian sexuality. Such characterizations make the director's readings of her film moot. Conversely, if *Fire* seeks to distance itself from the emergent politics of gay and lesbian identities within India, then Mehta's thesis that this is a film about choices is suspect.

The film is framed by the perversions of cultural traditions and modernity. Mehta unrelentingly contests the notions of tradition and compliance to it. Tradition provides the contours to the film, especially through the characters of Biji, the mother-in-law, and Ashok, the older brother. In her mute, but omniscient presence, Biji symbolizes cultural tradition and its ubiquitous moral force. Her inability to speak suggests the paralysis of tradition when confronted by pervasive, deviant sexual behaviors in the context of modernization and westernization. But contentious cultural traditions take on a much more Hindu, nationalist cast in Biji and Ashok's religious preoccupations. Biji is presented as the would-be consumer of the televised Hindu epic Ramayana, albeit mostly thwarted by the sexual depravations of the male servant, Mundu. As a TV serial, Ramayana also represents the turning point of Hindu nationalism's dissemination into popular discourse through technology.

On the other hand, her son Ashok is obsessed with erasing sexual desire by leading an ostensibly pure and ascetic life under the guidance of a swami and Hindu traditions and religious beliefs. In a manner reminiscent of M. K. Gandhi, Ashok also tests his sexual control by asking Radha to lie next to him. His sexuality (abstinence) is constituted through the perception of Radha's sexuality as passive. As a middle-class, Hindu man, his sexual urges must be primarily directed toward procreation, whereas her sexuality is passively expressed in terms of an urge to marry and have children. In the narrative of the film, Radha's physical inability to bear children provokes Ashok to tightly leash his sexual urges and lead a religiously guided life. As a respectful daughter-in-law and dutiful wife, Radha initially represents compliance with these cultural and religious traditions.

As newlyweds, Jatin and Sita mark the break with tradition. In contrast to his brother, Jatin represents the modern, Nehruvian younger brother. Until the end of the film, he disparages religion and his brother's devotion to the swami. Jatin runs a video store that supplies contraband pornographic films to adults and children. He also has a Chinese mistress (disappointingly, a stereotyped character) whom he wanted to marry out of love but was unable to because of her unwillingness. Jatin agrees to the marriage to Sita because of the pressure from Ashok and Biji. As Sita experiences and learns the source of Jatin's indifference, she is neither accepting nor much affected by it. Mehta seems to impute Sita's intolerance for Jatin's infidelity to her self-assurance as a young, modern woman. But Sita's relative disregard of Jatin is also linked to her desire for Radha.

The relationship that blossoms between Radha and Sita is intimate, passionate, and sexual but difficult to categorize. As the older sister-in-law, Radha acts in a sisterly manner to nurture and help Sita in her adjustment to a new husband and a new family. But, early on, when Radha attempts to console a distraught Sita, she expresses her desire for Radha. The relationship then quickly assumes a more passionate and sexual form of intimacy without supplanting the more conventional one. At one point, Radha adorns Sita with glass bangles, not atypical between two women in the household. But, the visible eroticism makes the exchange more meaningful as well. By questioning Radha's compliance as a daughter-in-law and wife, Sita also invokes a modernistic critique of tradition. As Sita captures the sentiment, "This tradition thing is overrated."

Nonetheless, tradition as lived within the heterosexual, hierarchical, conjugal family unit is the standard to which all of the main characters must comply. The male servant, Mundu, or Jatin's mistress, Julie, may be less bound by these conventions, but they also remain marginal to the center of the familial unit. On the other hand, as married women, Radha and Sita are unequivocally marked by and confined within the dictates of cultural tradition. Mehta uses fire as the most recognizable and eggregious motif of national cultural tradition that is metaphorically and literally played out on women's bodies. The scene from the ancient epic Ramayana, in which Sita must prove her chastity to her husband by walking unscathed through fire, is repeatedly invoked in the film through the television which Biji watches and through the enactment of the episode at the swami's ashram. But fire also has a more literal and deathly meaning in the lives of primarily lower-middle-class women in northern India, where women are set afire by husbands and in-laws or driven to self-immolation by dowry-related harassment. In the discourses of Sati, fire has an equally ominous connotation for women. In a twist to the auspicious and ominous meaning of fire in national cultural tradition, fire threatens Radha's life at the end of the film. But, after a few suspenseful minutes, in their reunion (notably in a Muslim, not Hindu, place of worship), Radha and Sita's mutual, passionate, intimate, and sexual relationship also successfully challenges fire as a test of women's purity. Mehta also reinterprets fire as a test of women's resilience, their resistance, and their fight for life through mutual desire. At one point, when Sita says that life is not worth living without desire, she crystallizes the premise of the film.

What makes this film compelling is that aside from the women, their fight for life and life with one another, little else emerges unscathed. If tradition is indicted through representations of Biji and Ashok, then so, through Jatin, is modernity. Aside from the mutual passion and intimacy, all other forms of sexuality are unequivocally deviant. Ashok's vow of celibacy is suspect as a form of cruelty toward his wife. The swami, who is also presumably celibate, suffers from enlarged, painful testicles. Jatin is not only involved in an illicitous relationship but without much substance, it lacks credibility. His perfunctory sex act with Sita is not only devoid of meaning but implicitly violent. Mundu's sexual transgressions while watching pornographic videos in sight of the mute Biji, are deviant although not harshly treated in the film. Mundu invokes the characterization of lower-class men, who without appropriate outlets, cannot be expected to control their sexual urges. As the sexual temptress, driven by the "hunt" rather than commitment, Julie caricatures the "westernized" mistress. The film demolishes the normative and marginal forms of sexuality to open up possibilities for women's resistance and passions for life and each other, instead of a politics marked by, or easily contained by, feminist or lesbian categories.

If the conjugal, heterosexual family unit provides conditions for promoting deviant sexual relations between women, then it can also serve to manage and contain such behaviors as long as they remain unspeakable. The social mandate of heterosexuality remains intact. But, once these sexual relations became visible, as the film suggests, the threat to heterosexuality can not be easily ignored. The visibility of Radha and Sita's intimate, sexual relationship and their subsequent escape from the hypocracies and tyrannies of middle-class, married, heterosexual lives confirms the film's oppositional stance. The ending may be rather utopian considering the complexities of their situation as middle-class women, but no less radical for it. What this film unravels effectively is the normative social regulation of middle-class women's sexuality. What it does not do is prescribe a clearly marked set of oppositional politics. By avoiding this prescriptive politics, I would suggest that the strength of the film lies in how it wittingly or unwittingly opens up possibilities of transnational categories that are frequently normalized and thereby contained— such as lesbian and feminist. Precisely because *Fire* seems to sidestep these categories, it necessitates that we reconsider feminist political practices that implicate notions of national and transnational hegemonies in ways that are not easily appropriated.

Notes

Chapter One

1. I will cite and explore this literature in fuller detail in Chapters Three to Seven. However, I do wish to note here some of the more helpful exceptions that I draw upon. Feminist literature that explores aspects of gender and sexuality from a more critical viewpoint that destabilizes constructs of gender, sexuality, and nationality, include, for example, Rajeswari Sunder Rajan, *Real and Imagined Women: Gender, Culture and Postcolonialism* (New York: Routledge, 1993), and Kamala Visweswaran, *Fictions of Feminist Ethnography* (Minneapolis and London: University of Minnesota Press, 1994). The title of this chapter was inspired by Visweswaran's book. See also, Kumkum Sangari and Sudesh Vaid, eds., *Recasting Women: Essays in Colonial History* (New Delhi: Kali for Women, 1989); Patricia Uberoi, ed., *Social Reform, Sexuality, and the State* (New Delhi: Sage Publications, 1996); and Mrinalini Sinha, *Colonial Masculinity: The "Manly Englishman" and the "Effeminate Bengali" in the Late Nineteenth Century* (Manchester and New York: Manchester University Press, 1995). Also see, Zoya Hassan, ed., *Forging Identities: Gender, Communities and the State* (New Delhi: Kali for Women, 1994); Uma Narayan, *Dislocating Cultures: Identities, Traditions, and the Third World Feminism* (New York and London: Routledge, 1997).

   More recently, the book Mary E. John and Tanaki Nair, eds., *A Question of Silence: The Sexual Economics of Modern India* (New Delhi: Kali for Women, 1998), has come to my attention. This book contains a particularly useful set of essays on sexuality, which I would have like to consider in succesive chapters.

2. Here I draw on feminist historiographies of colonial India that suggest how racialized, class-based notions of womanhood were inextricably linked to elitist, anticolonial forms of Indian nationalisms. These hegemonic nationalisms shaped the formation of the independent nation-state in 1947. For example, see Sangari and Vaid's collection *Recasting Women* (cited above). Especially see the Introduction and the essays by Uma Chakravarti and Partha Chatterjee. Also see Partha Chatterjee's *The Nation and Its Fragments: Colonial and Postcolonial Histories* (Princeton, NJ: Princeton University Press, 1993).

3. I refer to the work of theorists such as Judith Butler, Biddy Martin, Eve Sedgwick, among others who have questioned these definitions of sex and gender. See citations below.

4. These definitions are fairly standard across introductory texts. For a couple of examples, see Anthony Giddens, *Introduction to Sociology* (New York and London: W. W. Norton & Company, 1996), and Joan Ferrante, *Sociology: A Global Perspective* (Wadsworth Publishing Company, 1995).

5. For example, see texts such as Bernice Lott, *Women's Lives: Themes and Variations in Gender Learning* (California: Brooks/Cole Publishing Company, 1994), Margaret Anderson, *Thinking About Women: Sociological Perspectives on Sex and Gender* (New York: Macmillan Publishing Company, 1993). Also see Michael S. Kimmel and Michael A. Messner, *Men's Lives* (New York: Macmillan Publishing Company, 1992), and Claire M. Renzetti and Daniel J. Curran, *Women, Men, and Society* (Boston: Allyn and Bacon, 1992). For a useful exception see Judith Lorber, *Paradoxes of Gender* (New Haven and London: Yale University Press, 1994).

6. For example see the work of Ruth Hubbard, *The Politics of Women's Biology* (New Brunswick, NJ: Rutgers University Press, 1990), and Thomas Laqueur, "Orgasm, Generation, and the Politics of Reproductive Biology" in Catherine Gallagher and Thomas Laqueur, eds., *The Making of the Modern Body: Sexuality and Society in the Nineteenth Century* (Berkeley: University of California Press, 1987), and Emily Martin, *The Woman in the Body: A Cultural Analysis of Reproduction* (Boston: Beacon Press, 1987).

7. Judith Butler, *Gender Trouble: Feminism and the Subversion of Identity* (New York and London: Routledge, 1990), p. 7. In fact, as feminist scholarship has consistently emphasized, it is important to not conflate these two constructs. If the dual categories of sex and gender as conceptualized in this sociological framework are inadequate, then it is clear that neither correspond to one another.

8. Ibid., p. 8.

9. For useful and critical discussions on these points see Butler, *Gender Trouble*, Butler, *Bodies That Matter: On the Discursive Limits of "Sex"* (New York and London: Routledge, 1993), and Butler, "Against Proper Objects," *differences* 6, nos. 2–3 (1994), Biddy Martin, *Femininity Played Straight: The Significance of Being Lesbian* (New York and London: Routledge, 1996), Rosalind C. Morris, "All Made Up: Performance Theory and the New Anthropology of Sex and Gender," *American Review of Anthropology* 24 (1995), and Eve Sedgwick, *Epistemology of the Closet* (Berkeley and Los Angeles: University of California Press, 1990).

10. Especially see Butler, *Bodies That Matter*, and Martin, *Femininity Played Straight*.

11. Morris, "All Made Up," pp. 568–569.

12. There is a rich and substantive body of feminist theorizing on the importance of understanding the category of "woman" in more complex ways. At the forefront have been feminists such as Barbara Smith, Gloria Anzaldua, bell hooks, Cherrie Moraga, and Chandra T. Mohanty.

13. Sedgwick, *Epistemology of the Closet*, as quoted in Martin, *Femininity Played Straight*, p. 72. See Martin's discussion on this point in Chapter Three.

14. Butler, *Gender Trouble*.

15. Morris, "All Made Up," p. 569.

16. Butler, *Gender Trouble*.

17. In many ways the distinctions between postmodernism and identity politics are simplified. While not rehearsing the debates here, it seems to me that feminists theorizing "identity politics" do not see identity as an essentialist category. Nor do "post-modern" feminists suggest that the inadequacy of the category of woman as the political basis for feminism means that it can simply be politically discarded.

18. See Martin, *Femininity Played Straight*, p. 48, on this point. Martin suggests that to destabilize gender categories is not to undo them, but to make them less controlling.

19. Gayle Rubin, "Thinking Sex: Notes for a Radical Theory of the Politics of Sexuality," in Carole S. Vance, ed., *Pleasure and Danger: Exploring Female Sexuality* (Pandora Press, 1989). For useful reflections on the use of this essay in queer theorizing see Butler, "Against Proper Objects," and Martin, *Femininity Played Straight*, Chapter Three.

20. See Butler, *Bodies That Matter.*

21. In the introduction to the collection, Michael Warner, ed., *Fear of a Queer Planet: Queer Politics and Social Theory* (Minneapolis and London: University of Minnesota Press, 1993), uses the concept of heteronormativity to question the understanding of heterosexuality as an elemental form of human association, as the model of intergender relations, as the indivisible basis for community, and as the means of reproduction without which society would not exist (p. 21). For a particularly useful consideration of non-heteronormative sexualities among South Asians, see Gayatri Gopinath, "Nostalgia, Desire, Diaspora: South Asian Sexualities in Motion," *Positions* 5, 2 (Fall 1997).

22. Michel Foucault, *History of Sexuality v. 1* (New York and London: Vintage Books, 1990).

23. Ibid.

24. For an excellent analysis of Foucault's *History of Sexuality* and the omission of considerations of race, see Ann L. Stoler, *Race and the Education of Desire: Foucault's History of Sexuality and the Colonial Order of Things* (Durham, NC, and London: Duke University Press, 1995).

25. Chandra T. Mohanty, "Cartographies of Struggle: Third World Women and the Politics of Feminism," in Chandra T. Mohanty, Ann Russo, and Lourdes Torres, eds., *Third World Women and the Politics of Feminism* (Bloomington and Indianapolis: Indiana University Press, 1991).

26. Inderpal Grewal and Caren Kaplan, eds., *Scattered Hegemonies: Postmodernity and Transnational Feminist Practices* (Minneapolis and London: University of Minnesota Press, 1994).

27. Nira Yuval-Davis and Floya Anthias, eds., *Woman-Nation-State* (New York: St. Martin's Press, 1989).

28. Benedict Anderson, *Imagined Communities: Reflections on the Origin and Spread of Nationalism* (London: Verso, 1983).

29. See Yuval-Davis and Anthias, *Woman-Nation-State;* Kumari Jayawardena, *Feminism and Nationalism in the Third World* (New Delhi: Kali for Women, 1986); Denise Kandayoti, *Women, Islam and the State* (Philadelphia: Temple University Press, 1991). For additional work on gender and Islamic state societies, see Valentine Moghadam, *Modernizing Women: Gender and Social Change in the Middle East* (Boulder, CO, and London: Lynne Rienner Publishers, 1993).

30. Yuval-Davis and Anthias, *Woman-Nation-State,* and Floya Anthias and Nira Yuval-Davis, *Racialized Boundaries: Race, Nation, Gender, Colour, and Class and the Anti-Racist Struggle* (New York and London: Routledge, 1992).

31. Andrew Parker, Mary Russo, Doris Summer, and Patricia Yaeger, eds., *Nationalisms and Sexualities* (New York: Routledge, 1991).

32. Mohanty, "Cartographies of Struggle."

33. See the collections, Anthony D. King, *Culture, Globalization, and the World-System: Contemporary Conditions for the Representation of Identity* (Binghamton: State University of New York, 1991); Michael Featherstone, ed., *Global Culture: Nationalism, Globalization and Modernity* (Sage Publications, 1990).

34. Janet Wolff, "The Global and the Specific," in *Culture, Globalization, and the World-System* (see note 33).

35. Fredrick Cooper and Ann Stoler, eds., *Tensions of Empire: Colonial Cultures in a Bourgeois World* (Berkeley, Los Angeles, London: University of California Press, 1997). For another useful discussion of discourses of gender and sexuality across metropole and colony, see Kumkum Sangari, "Relating Histories," in Svati Joshi, ed., *Rethinking English: Essays in Literature, Language and History* (Bombay, Calcutta, Madras: Oxford University Press, 1994).

36. Grewal and Kaplan, *Scattered Hegemonies*.
37. M. Jacqui Alexander and Chandra Talpade Mohanty, eds., *Feminist Genealogies, Colonial Legacies, Democratic Futures* (New York: Routledge, 1997).
38. See the collections, Patrick Williams and Laura Chrisman, eds., *Colonial Discourse and Post-Colonial Theory: A Reader* (New York: Columbia University Press, 1994); Bill Ashcroft, Gareth Griffiths, and Helen Tiffin, eds., *Post-colonial Studies Reader* (New York: Routledge, 1995); Deepika Bahri and Mary Vasudeva, eds., *Between the Lines: South Asians and Postcoloniality* (Philadelphia: Temple University Press, 1996). These collections include useful reflections and concerns about the meaning and ramifications of the term post(-)colonialism.
39. Gayle Rubin, "Sexual Traffic." Interview with Judith Butler, *differences* 6, nos. 2-3 (1994), p. 93.

Chapter Two

1. For example, see Patricia Uberoi, ed., *Social Reform, Sexuality, and the State*. In this collection, the essays interrogate the multiple, uneven, and somewhat contradictory ways in which the state regulates aspects of sexuality and gender. Especially see the Introduction to the collection and articles by Uma Chakravarti, Ravi S. Vasudevan, Meera Kosambi, Kalpana Ram, and Patricia Uberoi.
2. Louisa Schein, "The Other Goes to Market: The State, the Nation, and Unruliness in Contemporary China," *Identities* 2, 3 (1996). This article is part of a special issue of the journal *Identities*. Especially see the introductory article by David Beriss and the commentary by Virginia R. Dominguez, "Engendering the Sexualized State of the Nation?"
3. Although I have briefly cited some of this literature in the previous chapter, I refer to the vast body of literature that helps problematize the links between specific definitions of womanhood and an anticolonial, elitist nationalism. For additional references see Malavika Karlekar, *Voices From Within: Early Personal Narratives of Bengali Women* (New Delhi: Oxford University Press, 1991); Bharati Ray, ed., *From the Seams of History: Essays on Indian Women* (New Delhi: Oxford University Press, 1995); J. Krishnamurthy, ed., *Women in Colonial India: Essays on Survival, Work and the State* (New Delhi: Oxford University Press, 1989); Meredith Borthwick, *The Changing Role of Women in Bengal 1849–1905* (Princeton, N.J.: Princeton University Press, 1984).
4. For example, see the recent collection, Tanika Sarkar and Urvashi Butalia, *Women and Right-Wing Movements* (London and New Jersey: Zed Books 1995) for useful discussions on the links between women and Hindu nationalisms.
5. Michel Foucault, *History of Sexuality, Discipline and Punish*, trans. By Alan Sheridan (New York: Pantheon Books, 1977); Colin Gordon, ed., *Power/Knowledge* (New York: Pantheon Books, 1980).
6. *Discipline and Punish*, p. 152.
7. *Discipline and Punish*, p. 155.
8. On this point especially see Karlekar, *Voices from Within*, Sonal Shukla, "Cultivating Minds: 19th Century Gujarati Women's Journals," *Economic and Political Weekly* (October 26, 1991); Tanika Sarkar, "Hindu Conjugality and Nationalisms," in *Indian Women: Myth and Reality*, ed. Jasodhara Bagchi (Hyderabad: Sangam Books, 1995); Himani Bannerji, "Attired in Virtue: The Discourse on Shame (lajja) and Clothing of the Bhadramahila in Colonial Bengal," in *Seams of History*; and Himani Bannerji, "Mothers and Teachers: Gender and Class in Educational Proposals for and by Women in Colonial Bengal," *Journal of Historical Sociology* 5, 1 (March 1992).

For parallel discussions on conduct books that historically shaped notions of womanhood, feminine proprieties, and domesticity among the English middle classes, see Nancy Armstrong, *Desire and Domestic Fiction: A Political History of the Novel* (New York and Oxford: Oxford University Press, 1987). For a useful discussion on discourses of sexuality in American marital education literature, see Michael Gordon, "From an Unfortunate Necessity to a Cult of Mutual Orgasm: Sex in American Marital Education Literature 1830–1940", in *Studies in the Sociology of Sex*, ed. James M. Henslin (New York: Meredith Corporation, 1971), and Michael Gordon and Penelope J. Shankweiler, "Different Equals Less: Female Sexuality in Recent Marriage Manuals," *Journal of Marriage and Family* (August 1971).

9. Family Planning Association of India, Annual Report (Mumbai, 1995); Informational leaflet on SECRT.

10. For an overview of the history and role of FPAI, see Mrs. Avabai B. Wadia, *The Family Planning Programme in India: The Non-governmental Sector* (Mumbai: FPAI, 1984).

11. My point is not that FPAI is merely an instrument of the state. While FPAI has found itself opposing state policies in some instances, nonetheless it has worked closely with the state since 1953. As an institutionalized voluntary organization, it plays such an integral mediating role between state bureaucracies and smaller NGOs that the ideological lines are often blurry. As one social researcher on NGOs said in a personal communication, because of its history and role, FPAI is considered more or less synonymous with the state.

12. Personal interview with an official of FPAI, Mumbai.

13. *Sex Education: What Why How & Who* (Family Planning Association of India).

14. Ibid.

15. Curiously this booklet also contains a brief section titled, "Love Amongst the Peer Group." Although this section appears to implicitly acknowledge the possibility of homoerotic desires, the content of the section and its characterization of love as "attraction towards the opposite sex" belie such intent.

16. *Problems of Adolescent Sexuality*, pp. 9–10.

17. *Teenagers Ask, The Doctor Answers* (Bombay: Family Planning Association of India, 1990), pp. 32–33.

18. *Teenagers Ask, The Doctor Answers*, p. 33–34.

19. For example, Steven Seidman, *Romantic Longings: Love in America, 1830–1980* (New York: Routledge, 1991).

20. I am aware of the need for caution against assuming cultural globalization/homogenization. In this case, I raise the issue of globalization to bring attention to the proliferation in transnational cultural discourses that might be parallel, but perhaps not the same, in diverse social locations.

21. *Preparing for Marriage* (Mumbai: Family Planning Association of India).

22. On this point, see Claude Alvares, "Science, Colonialism and Violence: A Luddite View," in *Science, Hegemony and Violence*, ed. Ashis Nandy (New Delhi: Oxford University Press, 1988).

23. There are numerous feminist critiques on science and the medical discourse. But for especially useful discussions, see Emily Martin, *The Woman in the Body*; Sandra Harding, ed., *The Racial Economy of Science: Toward a Democratic Future* (Bloomington: Indiana University Press, 1993); and Sandra Harding, *The Science Question in Feminism* (Ithaca, NY: Cornell University Press, 1986).

24. *Sharir Ki Jankari* (New Delhi: Kali for Women, 1989).

Chapter Three

1. M. K. Indira, *Phaniyamma: A Novel* (New Delhi: Kali For Women, 1989).
2. Ibid, p. 109.
3. Leela Dube, "On the Construction of Gender: Hindu Girls in Patrilineal India" in Karuna Channana, ed., *Socialization, Education, and Women: Explorations in Gender Identity* (New Delhi: Nehru Memorial Library, 1988).
4. This chapter is based on the narratives of 52 women. Two of the 54 women interviewed for this book were not asked about issues related to menarche and menstruation.
5. Susan Bordo, *Unbearable Weight: Feminism, Western Culture and the Body* (Berkeley: University of California Press, 1993).
6. See *Discipline and Punish*, p. 136.
7. Bordo, *Unbearable Weight*, p. 166.
8. Emily Martin, *The Woman in the Body*.
9. Other studies, such as Asha Bhende, "A Study of Sexuality of Adolescent Girls and Boys in Underprivileged Groups in Bombay," in *Readings on Sexuality and Reproductive Health*, and Anjali Monteiro, "On the Making of Kahani Nanachi" (Bombay: ASTHA-Xavier Institute of Communications, 1982), although based on working-class women, also suggest traumatic responses to menarche.
10. Thomas Buckley and Alma Gottlieb, "A Critical Appraisal of Theories of Menstrual Symbolism" in Thomas Buckley and Alma Gottlieb, eds., *Blood Magic* (Berkeley: University of California Press, 1988), p. 26.
11. It is likely that menstruating at earlier ages with greater frequency for longer spans in women's lifetimes may well be an historical aberration. See Buckley and Gottlieb, *Blood Magic*, on this point, pp. 44–45.
12. Veena Das, "Femininity and the Orientation to the Female Body," in *Socialization, Education, and Women: Explorations in Gender Identity*.
13. Ibid., p. 197.
14. Catherine Thompson, "The Power to Pollute and the Power to Preserve: Perceptions of Female Power in a Hindu Village," *Social Science and Medicine* 21, 6 (1985).
15. *Problems of Adolescent Sexuality*, p. 7.
16. *Teenagers Ask, The Doctor Answers*, pp. 20–21.
17. Martin, *The Woman in the Body*, especially see Section Two.
18. Vanaja Dhruvarajan, *Hindu Women and the Power of Ideology* (Granby, MA: Bergin and Garvey Publishers, 1989).
19. Robert Snowden and Barbara Christian, *Patterns and Perceptions of Menstruation: A World Health Organization International Collective* (New York: St. Martin's Press, 1983).
20. Jocelyn Krygier, "Caste and Female Pollution," in Michael Allen and S. N. Mukherjee, eds., *Women in India and Nepal* (Sterling Publishers Private Limited, 1990).
21. Mary Douglas, *Purity and Danger* (London: Routledge and Kegan Paul, 1966).
22. Rama Mehta, *The Western Educated Hindu Woman* (New York: Asia Publishing House, 1970).
23. *Teenagers Ask, The Doctor Answers*, pp. 22–24.
24. Snowden and Christian, *Patterns and Perceptions of Menstruation*, pp. 50–52.
25. Dube, "On the Construction of Gender," p. 174.
26. Curiously, these middle-class women's narratives of menarche and menstruation are remarkably consistent with recent research done in countries such as the United States. For example, the book by Janet Lee and Jennifer Sasser-Loen, *Blood Stories:*

Menarche and the Politics of the Female Body in Contemporary U.S. Society (New York: Routledge, 1996) documents menarche, menstruation, and menopause based on surveys of a diverse group of women in the United States. Except for the narratives on menopause, the content and the language of women's narratives in *Blood Stories* closely approximate those of the women in this study.

Chapter Four

1. John Berger, *Ways of Seeing* (Penguin, 1972).
2. In feminist scholarship, the issue of violence against women covers issues ranging from sexual physical assaults to dowry deaths, sati, and female feticide. For example, the recent collection by Kumari Jayawardena and Malathi de Alwis, *Embodied Violence: Communalising Women's Sexuality in South Asia* (New Delhi: Kali for Women, 1996), draws important connections between communal violence, rape, nationalisms, and state-sanctioned forms of violence. For another useful overview of the range and theories of violence, see Gail Omvedt, *Violence Against Women: New Movements and New Theories in India* (New Delhi: Kali for Women, 1990).
3. For a particularly useful overview of feminist agitation against various forms of rape, see Radha Kumar, *The History of Doing: An Illustrated Account of Movements for Women's Rights and Feminism in India, 1800–1990* (London and New York: Verso, 1993).
4. For an example of materials that address these problems for individual women or for grassroots organizations, see Lawyer's Collective, *Domestic Violence: Legal Aid Handbook* (New Delhi: Kali for Women, 1992).
5. Shobha A. Menon and Suresh Kannekar, "Attitudes Toward Sexual Harassment of Women in India," and Suresh Kannekar and Vidyut Lata Dhir, "Sex-Related Differences in Perceptions of Sexual Harassment of Women in India," *Journal of Psychology* 133, 1 (1992).
6. Menon and Kannekar, "Attitudes Toward Sexual Harassment" p. 1941, and Kannekar and Dhir, "Sex-Related Differences," p. 119.
7. "Schools Take Initiative," *Times of India* (November 19, 1997) and another article in *Sunday* (June 1–7, 1997).
8. "Every Lane a Terror for Eves," *Pioneer* (September 19, 1997).
9. *Teenagers Ask, The Doctor Answers*, p. 37.
10. He was singing the chorus verse of a sexist, and therefore controversial, popular Hindi film song.
11. A man who may be described as *cheap* in this context is someone who is sexually offensive—for example, he may deliberately press himself to a woman in a bus or may scratch his genitals while in a public space. This descriptive term is usually applied to men of lower socioeconomic classes.

Chapter Five

1. Two women referred to the possibilities of lesbian desire. In the first case, Sheetal referred to a close friendship with a woman friend. Sheetal said that although others have raised the possibility that they were lesbians, that was not the case. Sheetal characterized the friendship as intense but different from lesbian desire. In the other instance, Rati talked about her discomfort with watching pornography with "lesbian scenes." She said that though she has "nothing against them," she does not like sexually explicit scenes of this kind.

2. Javed Anand, "Sexuality: Now That Shame Is Dead," *Sunday Observer* (August 25–31, 1991).

3. For example, see "No Sex Please but We're not Prudish," *Telegraph* (April 29, 1993). Also, "Madras: Promiscuity behind Prudery," *Pioneer* (December 29, 1993).

4. A number of journalistic writings on the changing face of sexuality in India stress how women's roles and expectations on sexuality help indicate the depth of the changes.

5. For example see Javed Anand, "Sexuality: Now That Shame Is Dead."

6. See Uberoi, "Introduction," in *Social Reform, Sexuality and the State.*

7. Sudhir Kakar, *Intimate Relations: Exploring Indian Sexuality* (Chicago: University of Chicago Press, 1990). In her article titled "Sex, Sacrament and Contract in Hindu Marriage," Uberoi suggests that although the normative expectation of premarital virginity is linked to a "patriarchal" concern to control women's sexuality in order to ensure caste purity, and where applicable, legitimate heirs to the family estate, within legal discourse it has psychological and moral implications as well. See Uberoi, "When Is a Marriage Not a Marriage? Sex, Sacrament and Contract in Hindu Marriage," in Patricia Uberoi, ed., *Social Reform, Sexuality and the State,* p. 343.

8. For example, see Lillian Rubin, *Erotic Wars: What Happened to the Sexual Revolution?* (New York: Farrar, Straus and Giroux, 1990).

9. *Teenagers Ask, The Doctor Answers,* p. 27.

10. I borrow this phrase from Steven Seidman, *Romantic Longings.*

11. Dhruvarajan, *Hindu Women and the Power of Ideology.*

12. Das, "Femininity and the Orientation to the Female Body."

13. See Kakar, *Intimate Relations.* For another article that explores middle-class women's sexualities, albeit from the perspective of sexual oppression, see Meenakshi Thappan, "Images of the Body and Sexuality in Women's Narratives on Oppression in the Home," *Economic and Political Weekly* (October 28, 1995).

14. In her essay on Tamil cultural nationalism, Christian priests, and the projects of reforming gender and sexuality, Kalpana Ram unravels similar assumptions of the links between sex and the quality of marital relationships that undergird Christian reformist literature. Analyzing two texts written by Tamil Christian priests aimed at reforming sex by reintegrating it within the more general ambit of social life and reformed relationships between women and men, Ram notes that the project reasserts the institutions of marriage and family. Any respectable discourse of sex outside of marital love and monogamy is completely rejected, according to Ram. Moreover, grounded in oppositions between sex with love and sex without love, sex is privileged upon the basis of a companionate, gender egalitarian model marriage. See Kalpana Ram, "Rationalism, Cultural Nationalism and the Reform of Body Politics: Minority Intellectuals of the Tamil Catholic Community," in *Social Reform, Sexuality and the State.*

15. Over the last few years, independent cable operators provide services to cities such as Mumbai and New Delhi. Some of them also broadcast blue films later in the night.

16. The lines between "soft porn" and "hard-core" pornography appear to overlap with the distinctions between films and videos that are rated from single x to triple x. From the narratives it also appears that the formalistic differences are rather superficial. The chief difference suggested in the narratives between the various kinds of pornographic film and video is that in the soft porn films/videos there is some kind of narrative context for the sexual explicitness whereas in the latter case, not only are the videos/films more sexually explicit but they do not have the semblance of a narrative context.

17. Most of the single women, when asked about blue films, said that they have watched such films mostly out of curiosity in the company of their friends.

18. Preeta is referring to a system whereby she can call a video store and have a film delivered to her home.
19. The other three women casually indicated that they did not particularly enjoy blue films but did not expand on their reasons.
20. See Seidman, *Romantic Longings*.
21. In "Sex, Sacrament and Contract in Hindu Marriage," Uberoi also suggests challenges to the normative links between sex and marital relations. In her analysis of judicial discourses on marital sexuality, Uberoi suggests that a woman's surrender of virginity to her husband upon marriage is expected to bond the wife in unity and loyalty to the husband and ensure his responsibility to her support and maintenance so long as she remains chaste.
22. Kakar, *Intimate Relations*.
23. Ibid., p. 20.
24. Alastair Pennycook, *The Cultural Politics of English as an International Language* (New York and London: Longman, 1994).
25. Ibid., p. 28.
26. See Stuart Hall, "The Local and the Global: Globalization and Ethnicity," and the Introduction by Anthony D. King, in *Culture, Globalization, and the World-System*. Also see B. B. Kachru, "The Alchemy of English," in *Post-colonial Studies Reader*.
27. Hall, "The Local and the Global," p. 28.

Chapter Six

1. For discussions on the exigencies of married life for women, see Sudhir Kakar, *The Inner World: A Psycho-Analytic Study of Childhood and Society in India* (Delhi: Oxford University Press, 1981), Karin Kapadia, *Siva and Her Sisters: Gender, Caste and Class in Rural South India* (Boulder, San Francisco, Oxford: Westview Press, 1995), and Dhruvarajan, *Hindu Women and the Power of Ideology*. In an introduction to the section on marriage, alliance, and affinal transactions in the book Patricia Uberoi, ed., *Family, Kinship and Marriage in India* (Delhi: Oxford University Press, 1994). Uberoi suggests that there are two broad types of writings on marriage in India: descriptive anthropology in which various marriage practices are interpreted and explained; and those writings that are directly or indirectly influenced by Claude Levi-Strauss which focus in the structural outcomes of different types of marriage "alliances." Of greater relevance to this study, the first category of literature is useful but inadequate. What was said in the previous chapter about the construct of sexuality is paralleled here—that the descriptive literature unfailingly stresses the role and significance of marriage for women but does not theorize the meaning of marriage and, furthermore, there is a dearth of literature from the viewpoint of middle-class, urban women.
2. In her book *Siva and Her Sisters*, Karin Kapadia documents the changing context of marriage in Aruloor, a large village in southern India, and the intensifying subordination of women. Exploring aspects of marriage such as gender preference, dowry, and social mobility through marriage and dowry, Kapadia suggests that women's subordination is intensifying through marriage. Marriage practices that reflected and exacerbated the inequality of women and were peculiar to the Brahmin castes are extending to the non-Brahmin castes as well, according to Kapadia.

   Dhruvarajan also reports comparable cross-caste concerns with women and marriage in her study of a village in south-central India. She suggests that in all cases, parents seek early marriages for their daughters to ensure their purity and chastity. Within the context of marriage, Dhruvarajan reports that women tend to be highly deferent toward their husbands; normatively, there is an emphasis on deference and obedience from wives rather than expectations of love and affection. Indeed, women describe their first few years of marriage, until the birth of a son, as living hell, she says.

Also see Johanna Liddle and Rama Joshi, *Daughters of Independence: Gender, Caste and Class in India* (New Brunswick, N.J.: Rutgers University Press, 1986). In this study of educated, professional women, Liddle and Joshi stress both the centrality of marriage in the lives of these women as well as the ways in which they struggle to strike a balance between work-related demands and their roles as wives, mothers, and daughters-in-law. While they paint an informative picture of the issues and the problems—the dual burden, the joint family arrangements—the authors do not investigate the meaning of marriage or wifehood from the viewpoint of the 120 women in their study.

3. Sudhir Kakar, *The Inner World*, Chapter Three. Kakar suggests that marriage marks a transition from girlhood to womanhood and the patrilocal arrangement of marriage makes the first few years of married life rather uncertain for women. Kakar suggests that as outsiders wives constitute a threat to the unity of the extended family. Therefore, mothers-in-law and sisters-in-law may attempt to hinder the development of intimacy between wives and husbands.

4. Patricia Caplan, *Class and Gender in India: Women and Their Organizations in a South Indian City* (London and New York: Tavistock Publications, 1985), pp. 41–55. Dismissing notions of intimacy between wives and husbands, Caplan suggests that middle-class women are ready to fall in love with their husbands arranged by their parents but unable to spend much time with their husbands due to the segregation of the sexes. Ideals of marriage are not based on expectations of companionship between wives and husbands, according to Caplan. In Caplan's analysis the important aspects of marriage are reduced to the more exotic cultural differences such as girl-viewing and dowry. Such descriptions serve to reinforce rather than question the prevailing wisdom of the nature of marriage in India.

5. For instance, see Pramod Kumar and Sushma Trivedi, "Generational Study of Marital Adjustment," *Indian Journal of Social Work* 51 (1990). In their article on generational comparison of marital adjustment within contemporary India, Pramod Kumar and Sushma Trivedi note a more egalitarian husband-wife role relationship among the younger generation due to higher education of women and greater exposure to Western lifestyles. They suggest that this contemporary model of marriage is distinct from the "traditional" model of the husband-wife relationship in that it is marked by a woman's ability to more freely express her views, pursue her interests, share in the decision-making process, and have a more expressive and satisfying sexual relationship. On the other hand, the "traditional" husband-wife role relationship is hierarchical, rigid, based on the physical and sexual needs of the husband, and deeply frustrating for women, according to this study. Also see S. S. Nathwat and Asha Mathur, "Marital Adjustment and Subjective Well-being in Indian-educated Housewives and Working Women," *Journal of Psychology* 127 (1993). S. S. Nathwat and Asha Mathur also frame their article as a shift from the agrarian, traditional society to one shaped by the inexorable modern effects of urbanization and industrialization.

6. See Seidman, *Romantic Longings,* for a discussion on the meaning and significance of companionate marriage. Also see discussions by Meredith Borthwick, *The Changing Role of Women* and Tanikar Sarkar, "Hindu Conjugality and Nationalism," in Jasodhara Bagchi, ed., *Indian Women: Myth and Reality* (Hyderabad: Sangam Books, 1995) for discussions on the relevance of companionate marriage for Bengali women in colonial India. Also see, Malavika Karlekar, *Voices from Within.* These authors explore the chang-

ing face of conjugality against the backdrop of an elitist anticolonial nationalism and colonialism, *not* modernization and westernization. Curiously, these insights on the shifts in the ideals of marriage and marital relations are ignored in the literature on marriage in contemporary India; no attempt is made to historically contextualize contemporary research on marriage.

As regards contemporary India, the discourse of companionate marriage shapes women's English-language newsmagazines, such as *Femina*. Notions of marriage as based on mutual love and partnership are fundamental to the hugely popular romance novels avidly read by young, middle-class women. It is believed that India is the largest consumer of Harlequin Romance novels written in Canada and England. For further discussion on this point, see Jyoti Puri, "Reading Romances in Postcolonial India," *Gender & Society* 11, 4 (August 1997).

Furthermore, widely popular Hindi films (India is the largest producer of films in the world) also reinforce ideas of mutual affection, romance, and partnership in marriage. In the films, while romantic relationships are consistent across genres, love stories are a genre in their own right. Although these stories are urban- and class-biased, they are popular across social classes and settings.

7. Neetu is the exception in this study who said that she is unable to bear children due to physical reasons. After repeated confirmations that she cannot bear children, Neetu says that although she did want to have children in the past, having children is no longer important in her life.

8. Leela Dube, "On the Construction of Gender."

9. For example, see Elisabeth Bumiller, *May You Be the Mother of a Hundred Sons: A Journey Among the Women of India* (New York: Random House, 1990).

10. For a useful exception to the literature on womanhood and marriage in contemporary India, see Gloria Goodwin Raheja and Ann Grodzins Gold, *Listen to the Heron's Words Reimagining Gender and Kinship in Northern India* (Berkeley: University of California Press, 1994), especially Chapter Four. With respect to women in rural northern India, Raheja examines women's songs and oral traditions among the nonliterate Gujars. Raheja also paints a complex picture of women's perceptions of conjugality. Analyzing their subversive connotations, Raheja notes that these songs emphasize the importance of establishing conjugal intimacy in their transition from their natal to their conjugal homes.

11. As suggested in Chapter Two, the educational texts from FPAI and SECRT reflect similar notions of marriage and marital relationships but merely present them as liberal choices.

12. See Caplan, *Class and Gender in India*; Das, "Masks and Faces" in *Family, Kinship and Marriage in India*; and Dhruvarajan, *Hindu Women and the Power of Ideology*.

13. Rajeswari Sunder Rajan, *Real and Imagined Women: Gender, Culture and Postcolonialism* (New York: Routledge, 1993), Chapter Four.

14. Caplan, *Class and Gender in India*; Kakar, *The Inner World*.

15. For example, see discussions of the meaning of marriage and gender roles in contemporary United States in Francesca Cancian, *Love in America: Gender and Self-Development* (Cambridge University Press, 1987). Also see the discussion on sex and intimacy in Steven Seidman's *Romantic Longings*.

16. *Teenagers Ask, The Doctor Answers*, pp. 48–49.

17. Das, "Masks and Faces."

18. Kakar, *The Inner World*.

19. Caplan, *Class and Gender in India*.

20. Kakar, *The Inner World*.

21. Caplan, *Class and Gender in India*.
22. Kakar, *The Inner World*.
23. Caplan, *Class and Gender in India*.
24. Dhruvarajan, *Hindu Women and the Power of Ideology*.
25. One of the aspects that remains obscure in these middle-class women's narratives is the use of amniocentesis in sex selection and sex selective abortions in order to have male children. Feminists have noted that the use of amniocentesis is primarily a middle-class phenomenon. Two of the currently married women indicated that they underwent "fertility treatment." In the first case, gender preference does not appear to have been the issue, since she had twin daughters as a result of medical intervention. In the other case, gender preference was clearly the issue, but the woman seemed to evade questions of sex selective abortions in the process. In another account, a currently married woman indicated that she had undergone an abortion but stated that it was due to the ill timing of her pregnancy.
26. Das, "Masks and Faces" in *Family, Kinship and Marriage in India*.

Chapter Seven

1. Quote attributed to Dr. K. Abhayambika, professor of medicine and state AIDS programme officer, Medical College, Trivandrum, Kerala, in *Less Than Gay: A Citizen's Report on the Status of Homosexuality in India* (New Delhi: AIDS Bhedbhav Virodhi Andolan, 1991), p. 48.
2. *Teenagers Ask, The Doctor Answers*, pp. 37–38.
3. This quote is taken from an introductory pamphlet of the San Francisco–based lesbian and gay South Asian organization, Trikone's.
4. Anuja Gupta, "A Testimony," in *Trikone*, Decadence: A Tenth Anniversary Special 11, 1 (January 1996), p. 33.
5. Also see Thadani, *Sakhiyani* (note 13 below), for additional examples of homophobia by people in positions of authority.
6. *Less Than Gay*, p. 23.
7. Ibid., p. 48.
8. Other than passing references to homosexuality with respect to AIDS, this is the only reference to homosexual desire in all the available materials put out by FPAI/SECRT.
9. Jonathan Katz, "The Invention of Heterosexuality," *Socialist Review* 20, 1 (1990).
10. In this chapter I use the terms *gay*, *lesbian*, *bisexual*, and *transgendered* interchangeably with the term *queer*.
11. In the collection, Rakesh Ratti, ed., *Lotus of Another Color: An Unfolding of the South Asian Gay and Lesbian Experience* (Boston: Alyson Publications, Inc., 1993), as well as *Trikone*, Decadence: A Tenth Anniversary Special, it is noted how authors of gay and lesbian writings frequently rely on pen names to protect their identities.
12. Nayan Shah, "Sexuality, Identity, and the Uses of History," in *Lotus of Another Color*, p. 126.
13. Giti Thadani, *Sakhiyani: Lesbian Desire in Ancient and Modern India* (London and New York: Cassell, 1996).
14. Chakravarti, "What Happened to the Vedic Dasi?" in *Recasting Women: Essays in Colonial History*.
15. The Manusmriti is perhaps the most frequently used scripture to either explain historical origins of the subordinate status of women in contemporary India or to mark the declining of women's status historically.

16. Dipesh Chakrabarty, "Postcoloniality and the Artifice of History: Who Speaks for 'Indian' Pasts?," *Representations* 37 (1992).
17. Shah, "Sexuality, Identity, and the Uses of History," p. 121.
18. Edward Said, *Orientalism* (New York: Vintage Books, 1978), p. 190.
19. Alain Danielou, *The Complete Kamasutra: The First Unabridged Modern Translation of the Classic Indian Text* (Rochester, VT: Park St. Press, 1994), Foreword.
20. On this point see Jyoti Puri, "What's Wrong with the Kamasutra?" unpublished paper.
21. Arvind Sharma, "Homosexuality and Hinduism," in Arlene Swidler, ed., *Homosexuality and World Religions* (Valley Forge, PA: Trinity Press International, 1993).
22. Ibid., p. 68.
23. Michael Sweet and Leonard Zwilling, "The First Medicalization:The Taxonomy of Queerness in Classical Indian Medicine," *Journal of the History of Sexuality* 3, 4 (1993).
24. See Sharma, "Homosexuality and Hinduism," and David Greenberg, *The Construction of Homosexuality* (Chicago: The University of Chicago Press, 1988).
25. David Greenberg, *The Construction of Homosexuality*, p. 100.
26. See Sharma, "Homosexuality and Hinduism," and Greenberg, *The Construction of Homosexuality*.
27. Ibid.
28. Sweet and Zwilling, "The First Medicalization."
29. Sharma, "Homosexuality and Hinduism," p. 55.
30. Romila Thappar, *A History of India: Volume One* (Penguin Books, 1966).
31. The work of feminist anthropologists on stratified state societies negates the possibility of gender equity between women and men across social class groups. This body of literature also suggests that gender hierarchy always coincides with other social hierarchies such as race and class. Especially see Christine W. Gailey, "Evolutionary Perspectives on Gender Hierarchy," in Beth B. Hess and Myra M. Ferree, eds., *Analyzing Gender* (Newbury Park, LA: Sage, 1987). I argue that in the context of stratification, it is unlikely that the realm of sexuality is insulated from these social inequalities. Put differently, state societies are likely to be characterized by notions of sexual normality and deviance. Also see Greenberg, *The Construction of Homosexuality*, on this point. These approaches make the idea of "sex-positive" orientations within the highly unequal stratified context of ancient India highly dubious.
32. Thadani, *Sakhiyani*, p. 9.
33. Ibid., p. 10.
34. Ibid., p. 12.
35. Shah, "Sexuality, Identity, and the Uses of History," p. 123.
36. See Anthony Appiah, "Is the Post- in Postmodernism and the Post- in Postcolonial?," *Critical Inquiry* 17, as cited in Sandhya Shukla, "Building Diaspora and Nation: The 1991 'Cultural Festival of India,'" *Cultural Studies* 11, 2 (1997).
37. *Less Than Gay*, p. 48.
38. For example, organizations Khush in Toronto, Canada, and Masala in Boston, United States, among numerous others.
39. Some of the gay and lesbian groups in India include the Humsafar Trust and its magazine, *Bombay Dost*, based in Mumbai; Sakhi, a lesbian organization based in New Delhi, among others.
40. *Lotus of Another Color*, p. 14. For a useful discussion on non-heteronomatic sexualities and the South Asian diaspora, see Gopinath, "Nostalgia, Desire, Diaspora."
41. Homi Bhabha, "Dissemination: Time, Narrative and the Margins of the Modern Nation," in Homi Bhabha, ed., *Nation and Narration* (New York: Routledge, 1990).
42. *Lotus of Another Color*, p. 11.

43. For example, see Arlene Stein, *Sisters, Sexperts, Queers: Beyond the Lesbian Nation* (New York: Plume, 1993).

44. For a useful discussion of the politics and limitations of sexual identities see Steven Seidman, "Identity and Politics in a 'Postmodern' Gay Culture: Some Historical and Conceptual Notes," in Michael Warner, ed., *Fear of a Queer Planet.*

45. *Less Than Gay*, p. 5.

46. *Lotus of Another Color*, p. 16.

47. See Barbara Smith, ed., *Home Girls: A Black Feminist Anthology* (New York: Kitchen Table—Women of Color Press, 1983); Cherrie Moraga and Gloria Anzaldua, eds., *This Bridge Called My Back: Writings of Radical Women of Color* (New York: Kitchen Table—Women of Color Press, 1983).

48. See Emmanuel S. Nelson, ed., *Critical Essays: Gay and Lesbian Writers of Color* (New York: Howarth Press, 1993).

49. Stuart Hall, "The Local and the Global."

50. Shah, "Sexuality, Identity, and the Uses of History."

51. The Women of South Asian Descent Collective, eds., *Our Feet Walk the Sky: Women of the South Asian Diaspora* (San Francisco: Aunt Lute Books, 1993).

52. Seidman, "Identity and Politics in a 'Postmodern' Gay Culture."

53. Ibid., p. 130.

54. Robyn Weigman, "Introduction: Mapping the Lesbian Postmodern," in Laura Doan, ed., *The Lesbian Postmodern* (New York: Columbia University Press, 1994).

55. For example, I refer to the organization that publishes *Bombay Dost* in Mumbai. Issues of *Bombay Dost* and *Trikone* acknowledge the links. This was also confirmed by Arvind Kumar in a personal communication. While the multitude of gay and lesbian organizations in India would be equally useful to explore, I focus this analysis on Trikone because, as the oldest, continuous running organization, it has generated numerous newsletters, magazines, pamphlets, and statements of mission that provide a useful and rich site for analysis.

56. Inderpal Grewal, "Reading and Writing the South Asian Diaspora: Feminism and Nationalism in North America," in *Our Feet Walk the Sky*, p. 231.

57. See Trikone's introductory pamphlet.

58. Shukla, "Building Diaspora and Nation."

59. Amarpal K. Dhaliwal, "Introduction. The Traveling Nation: India and Its Diaspora," *Socialist Review* 4 (1994), p. 5.

60. Kamala Visweswaran, "Predicaments of the Hyphen," in *Our Feet Walk the Sky*, p. 305.

61. Personal communication.

62. As reprinted in the 10th-anniversary special issue of *Trikone*, p. 10.

63. Shah, "Sexuality, Identity, and the Uses of History," p. 126.

64. See Dipti Ghosh's editorial statement in the 10th-anniversary special issue of *Trikone*, p. 4.

65. See Arvind Kumar, "In the Beginning . . ." Interview with Sandip Roy in the 10th anniversary special issue of *Trikone*, pp. 8–9; also personal communication.

66. Mohanty, "Introduction: Cartographies of Struggle."

67. Urvashi Vaid, "Building Bridges: Thoughts on Identity and South Asian G/L/B/T Organizing," in *Trikone*, Decadence: A Tenth Anniversary Special, pp. 64–65.

Chapter Eight

1. For a parallel discussion and analysis on *Fire*, see Gopinath, "Nostalgia, Desire, Diaspora".

2. Perhaps because Deepa Mehta is a resident of Canada, the film is enabled by a multi-national crew, producers, and sponsors. The film is categorized as Canadian and Indian. It was shown at the International Film Festival in India and then, more recently, released in the larger cities.

3. See the numerous reviews of the film available over the Internet, among them: Edwin Jaheil *www.prairienet.org/ejaheil/fire.htm*; Joe Baltake, The Online Movie Club, Fire, HYPERLINK *www.sacbee.com/leisure/themovieclub/reviews/archies/97fire/*; Fire: Denver.Sidewalk; *denver.sidewalk.com/link/15392*.

4. Interview with Deepa Mehta on Rediff On the Net, Movies: An Interview With Deepa Mehta; Suparn Verma; *www.redifindia.com/entair/oct/24.htm*.

5. Over the past few weeks, there have been numerous reports in newspapers and news-magazines about the instances of violence spearheaded by the right-wing *Shiv Sena* to prevent the film from running, particularly in larger cities. Until these incidents, the film was running to packed audiences. This right-wing terrorism, which has been endorsed by some prominent politicians, has sparked much public discussions regarding lesbian sexualities, but also about censorship. A number of feminists, well-known film celebrities, and left intellectuals have been vocal in decrying the ways in which this film has been appropriated to further a right-wing agenda.

Index